Moreton Morrell Site

CONSUMERS
AND SERVICES

CONSUMERS AND SERVICES

Mark Gabbott
Monash University

and

Gillian Hogg
University of Stirling

JOHN WILEY & SONS

Chichester · New York · Weinheim · Brisbane · Singapore · Toronto

Reprinted January 1999

Other Wiley Editorial Offices

John Wiley & Sons, Inc., 605 Third Avenue,
New York, NY 10158-0012, USA

WILEY-VCH Verlag GmbH, Pappelallee 3,
D-69469 Weinheim, Germany

Jacaranda Wiley Ltd, 33 Park Road, Milton,
Queensland 4064, Australia

John Wiley & Sons (Asia) Pte Ltd, 2 Clementi Loop #02-01
Jin Xing Distripark, Singapore 129809

John Wiley & Sons (Canada) Ltd, 22 Worcester Road,
Rexdale, Ontario M9W 1L1, Canada

Library of Congress Cataloging-in-Publication Data

Gabbott, Mark.
    Consumers and services / by Mark Gabbott, Gillian Hogg.
        p.   cm.
    Includes bibliographical references and index.
    ISBN 0-471-95797-6 (hb : alk. paper). – ISBN 0-471-96269-4 (pbk. alk. paper)
    1. Customer relations.   2. Relations marketing.   3. Service industries—marketing.
4. Professions—Marketing.   5. Consumer behavior.   6. Customer relations—Case studies.
I. Hogg, Gillian.   II. Title.
HF5415.5.G33   1998
658.8'12—dc21
97–45612
CIP

British Library Cataloguing in Publication Data

A catalogue record for this book is available from the British Library

ISBN 0-471-95797-6 (cased)
ISBN 0-471-96269-4 (paperback)

Typeset in 12/14pt Bembo by Mayhew Typesetting, Rhayader, Powys
Printed and bound by Antony Rowe Ltd, Eastbourne

This book is printed on acid-free paper responsibly manufactured from sustainable forestry, in which at least two trees are planted for each one used for paper production.

CONTENTS

CONTRIBUTORS

Christine Ennew is Professor of Marketing in the School of Management and Finance at the University of Nottingham. She received her PhD from the University of Nottingham in 1985 and spent two years working at the University of Newcastle upon Tyne before returning to Nottingham in 1987. She was appointed Reader in Marketing in 1993 and Professor of Marketing in 1995. Her research interests lie primarily in the area of services marketing with a particular interest in the marketing of financial services, although she has also been active in research relating to the financing of small business and agricultural and food marketing.

She is editor of the *International Journal of Bank Marketing* and is author of a range of academic and non-academic books and articles on the subject of marketing. Recent publications have appeared in the *European Journal of Marketing, Journal of Business Research, Journal of Business Ethics* and the *British Journal of Management*. She has worked closely with a variety of organisations in the financial services sector including providing marketing training for Bank of Scotland and TSB and consultancy work for Lloyds Bank, TSB, AIB Bank, Yorkshire Bank, Royal Bank of Scotland and Co-operative Bank. In addition she has been involved with the Bank of England's Advisory Committee on the Financing of Small Firms where she has provided an input relating to issues arising from the nature of the banking relationship.

Mark Gabbott is Professor of Electronic Marketing at Monash University, Melbourne, Australia. Mark graduated from the University of Essex with a BA(Hons) in Economics followed by an MSc in Technology Management from Imperial College, University of London. After working in government for 6 years in consumer policy and protection, he joined the University of Stirling to complete a PhD in Marketing. He was Lecturer and then Senior Lecturer at Stirling researching and teaching in the areas of electronic and direct marketing, marketing services, consumer behaviour and consumer policy. He joined Monash University in 1997 as Professor of Electronic Marketing.

He has published research in a variety of academic journals including the *Journal of Public Policy and Marketing, European Journal of Marketing, Journal of Marketing Management* and *Journal of Healthcare Marketing*. He sits on the editorial boards of three international journals and has been joint guest editor this year of the *Journal of Business Research* and the *Service Industries Journal*. Consultancy activities have included a range of projects for both private and public sector clients including a variety of consumer and market research agencies, the European Commission, the Scottish Office, the National Health Service, IBM, Forth Group, UK Consumers Association, and the UK Government's National Consumer Council.

Monica Hanefors is a social anthropologist and has a position as Senior Lecturer with the Institute of Tourism and Travel Research at Dalarna University in Borlänge, Sweden. She also has practical experience from work in the tourism industry. Her research interests include tourist behaviour, tourism encounter and impacts, and imagery. She is the author of two books on tourism and a vast number of articles on the same topic.

Sally Hibbert is a lecturer in the Department of Marketing at the University of Strathclyde. Her main area of conceptual research is in the field of consumer behaviour and she is a member of the Department's Centre for Consumer Behaviour Research. The areas of applied research in which she specialises are donor behaviour (charity fundraising) and shopping behaviour (retailing). Her published work on donor behaviour focuses on donor decision making. In addition, she has addressed issues such as the competitive positioning of charities and the adoption of relationship and database marketing by fundraisers. Her PhD research is on 'mood and motivation in shopping behaviour' and a number of publications have been developed from this work.

Among the journals in which Sally has published are the *European Journal of Marketing*, the *Journal of Consumer Marketing*, the *Journal of Non-profit and Voluntary Sector Marketing* and the *International Journal of Retail and Distribution Management*.

Gillian Hogg is a lecturer in the Department of Marketing, University of Stirling. She has a degree in English from the University of Dundee and a PhD in Marketing from the University of Stirling. After spending 5 years as a manager in the NHS, Gillian joined the University of Stirling as a researcher in the area of service quality and has numerous publications in the services area. She is currently co-ordinator of the UK Academy of Marketing Special Interest Group in Services Marketing and organises the annual Services Marketing Workshop at the University of Stirling. In addition, she has recently co-edited two special editions of journals on services marketing and two readers in the area.

Suzanne Horne lectures in Marketing at the University of Stirling. Her primary teaching interest is in social and non-profit marketing and her research specialises in the issues surrounding the marketing of, and fundraising for, non-profit organisations. She has published extensively on aspects relating to charity fundraising, including charity trading, box collection schemes, affinity credit cards and donor behaviour. Her present research is focused on the marketing of religious organisations and specific donor behaviour. Much of the research is driven from practical experience as a governor of a children's charity, and an assessor for a grant-making body.

Joby John is currently Associate Professor of Marketing, Bentley College in Waltham, Massachusetts, USA. He holds a BS in Pharmacy, MBA and PhD (Marketing) and was formerly employed as a marketing officer with Pfizer Limited (India). His PhD dissertation topic was on 'patient perceptions of quality' and his research on health care has appeared in such publications as *European Journal of Marketing, Health Care Management Review, Health Marketing Quarterly, Journal of Health Care Marketing, Journal of Hospital Marketing*. He has also presented research at national, and international conferences on health care and patient satisfaction. Has been a member of the editorial review board of the *Journal of Health Care Marketing*, and has held local and national offices in the American Marketing Association. His primary teaching interest is in services marketing, and research interest is in service quality and cross-cultural issues. In addition he has conducted several patient satisfaction studies and customer service training for hospitals and nursing homes.

Kitty Koelemeijer is Research Fellow at the Centre for Supply Chain Management at Nijenrode University, the Netherlands. In addition to services marketing, her research interests include retail assortments, marketing channels, consumer satisfaction/dissatisfaction, and quantitative methods in marketing. She has published in a variety of journals, including the *International Journal of Service Industry Management*, the *International Journal of Logistics Management*, and the *Journal of Business and Industrial Marketing*.

Sally McKechnie is Lecturer in Marketing in the School of Management and Finance at the University of Nottingham. After holding a research post at the University of Strathclyde, she gained several years' practical marketing experience in the area of exhibitions and direct marketing. Since returning to academia, she has conducted research evaluating the effectiveness of television advertising. Her main research interests lie in the area of services marketing, with a particular interest in buyer behaviour.

Lena Larsson Mossberg has a position as Senior Lecturer with the School of Economics, Göteborg University in Sweden. She holds a

PhD in Business Administration and has interests in tourist behaviour, service encounter evaluation and service loyalty. She has published several books and a number of articles – most of them focusing tourism marketing. She has been involved in international tourism and marketing programs, for example as a tourism management expert for the United Nations.

Marco Vriens is Client Service Director Management Sciences at Research International USA Inc. Prior to joining Research International, he served on the faculties of Tilburg University and the University of Groningen in the Netherlands. He holds a Master's degree in Psychology and a PhD in Economics. His interests lie in the development and implementation of realistic marketing models and he has published articles in the *Journal of Marketing Research*, the *International Journal of Research in Marketing*, *Marketing Letters*, the *Journal of Marketing Management*, the *Journal of Direct Marketing*, the *European Journal of Marketing*, and the *Journal of the Market Research Society*.

Acknowledgements

The writing of this book has been a long and sometimes arduous task, partly because the material has been difficult to synthesise, but also due to the number of events that have overtaken us during the time. We realised early on that walking the tight rope between consumer behaviour and services marketing was not going to be easy. The final product is in no small part due to the tenacity of Steve Hardman from Wiley who has always kept his cool despite being stretched to the limit and to whom we are very grateful. We would like to thank our contributing authors for providing us with the material for the context chapters, without whom this book would be lacking in scope and also in its depth. Equally we would like to thank the ranks of anonymous reviewers for their time and for providing us with the necessary objective comment which we both found useful and challenging. Finally we would like to thank the many colleagues, members of our respective families and friends who have encouraged, supported and put us with us during the process: this book is dedicated to them.

Mark Gabbott
Gillian Hogg

PART I

THE SERVICE CONSUMER

Introduction to Part I

Despite the myriad of evidence to suggest that services are becoming critical to economic growth in most developed economies, thus requiring some fairly substantial reflection from both business and government, marketing and its related disciplines seem remarkably insulated from this trend. We teach and we research in an area which has become the repository for specialist knowledge, building our own structures and relying upon our own endeavours to pursue an understanding of the services phenomena. In teaching, most courses are delivered as Services Marketing and if we look to our colleagues, very little services material appears in introductory marketing courses, or in buyer behaviour courses often seen as the core of our discipline's teaching. In research we have created an innovative, and enthusiastic community, but often too parochial in our dissemination. At some point, to adopt the Darwinian metaphor, we not only need to walk erect, but more importantly take this knowledge beyond our cave, our micro-discipline. This book is an attempt to break out in one direction toward the buyer behaviour literature, to take some services knowledge and deliver it in a form useable by students, teachers and researchers and encourage consideration of service products within a fundamental teaching and research discipline. At the same time we hope to codify some of the main tennets of buyer behaviour for use within services and to stimulate some re-examination of some accepted truths. You will notice that this book doesn't fit squarely into a particular subject; it is our intention that this work will appear on the reading lists of many subjects.

The emerging importance of services comes as little surprise and perhaps we should be self-congratulatory about our foresight in developing an area of study which such urgent appeal. However, it is our belief that one of the major challenges currently facing services marketers is the market place itself. Experience in delivering services to non-services audiences including other academics, has suggested that there is considerable reservation about whether services really are that different or distinct in marketing terms, and perhaps more importantly, whether consumers treat them any differently.

Are the benefits from services really more difficult to evaluate than those of physical goods? Is the process of product development and planning different? What about x service? Are all services the same? All common questions in that early exposure phase and all valid. Perhaps the most fundamental, however, is whether consumers react differently, for if not, we are doing no more than filling in a small undulation in the knowledge landscape. If they do react differently, then how differently, and when and what changes do we need to make to our knowledge set and those of business practitioners to facilitate more robust services marketing activity?

This book is predicated on the latter view and we have presented the material in order to concentrate upon answering two questions. First to establish that consumers do indeed react differently to service-based products and second that there are some glaring inconsistencies when we try to import consumer behaviour literature into services marketing, or indeed export service products across this permeable boundary. We include a preliminary framework in chapter 1 and a review of the available literature pointing out where inconsistencies appear and where there is essentially no evidence of a product perspective on behaviour. In chapters 2, 3, and 4 we explore the process of consumption from a service perspective considering the pre, during and post consumption time frames. However, by necessity we also have treated services as one 'block' of products and this brings us to the second question we have attempted to answer. Can services can be treated as whole (as many consumer behaviour textbooks treat physical goods) or do particular services represent variant forms of consumer reaction? In the second part of the book we present a selection of chapters to explore this theme.

CHAPTER 1

CONSUMERS AND SERVICES

INTRODUCTION

With the developing interest in services and services marketing, it might be expected that the consumer behaviour literature would include references to the evaluation and consumption of intangibles. There are, however, very few examples of published works which refer explicitly to the consumption characteristics of services. There would appear to be an assumption, consistent with the interchangeability of terminology, that consumer behaviour related to goods is the same for all products, i.e. the difference between goods and services is not significant to the consumer. In the case of products where the 'good' element is dominant this may be a valid assumption, but for products where the dominant characteristic is service intangibility this assumption denies the significant impact of the characteristics of services upon consumption behaviour. This impact could be characterised as a series of problems or challenges to consumers which are additional to those presented by tangible goods.

The idea of services as problematic for marketers is a theme which has been developed across a broad range of literature over the last 25 years, see for instance, Levitt (1972), Berry (1980), Lovelock (1996) and Rust, Zahorik and Keningham (1996) to name but a few. Most authors propose responses which will tackle some of the fundamental characteristics of services. These include making services appear less intangible by focusing upon physical dimensions, or less heterogeneous through standardised delivery, or by recognising the importance of word of mouth information sources using such techniques as personal endorsement. However, rather than reiterate the managerial implications of service characteristics which form the basis of a substantial part of the services literature, in this text we endeavour to concentrate upon consumer behaviour, specifically the demands placed upon consumers by service products and the consumer's behavioural response. The aim of this book is to consider the current understanding of consumer purchase behaviour in the services context.

Consumption is universal and a large part of marketing research is concentrated on attempting to understand and predict how consumers make purchase decisions. However, most of this work assumes that 'product' is generic and that in attempting to understand behaviour the product is less relevant than the individual and the context of the purchase. Whilst the interpretivist school of consumer research has moved away from a simple attempt to isolate cause and effect into the broader context of life experiences, there is an inherent assumption in all research in this area that consumption can be generalised across product categories. This text challenges that view by drawing attention to the nature of services and the characteristics of services upon our understanding of consumer behaviour. The structure of this book is inherently positivist in that it adopts a cognitive, reductionist approach. However, whilst this provides a convenient framework for consideration of the issues, it does not imply that the cognitive perspective provides the best context for understanding the service consumer. Rather, the decision process model provides a convenient way of understanding what Statt (1997) refers to as 'the life of the consumer in all its messy complexity'.

THE NOTION OF EXCHANGE

All market economies operate, both theoretically and practically, upon exchange and this approach to business has dominated marketing thought for the last 30 years. Essentially the economy functions by providing an environment in which parties enter into an agreement with each other to transact values. Simply, both parties must desire something that the other possessés in order that both sides of the exchange can gain something of value to them, otherwise the motivation for such behaviour is lost. In the case of a business transaction, for instance, the business desires the revenue provided by the consumer and the consumer desires the goods or services provided by the business. While this clearly motivates all business activity at a basic level, other considerations such as reputation, brand equity and product awareness are equally important as mechanisms for the achievement of this basic goal. What is less clear, and of central importance, is why consumers desire the goods and services on offer and what is the nature of the value that they place on, or receive from them. The answers to these questions are bound up with the products themselves, the individual who buys and the situation or context in which the purchase takes place; each is notoriously difficult to study and cannot be considered in isolation. The one common element in the context of a purchase is the buyer and it is this aspect of their behaviour (namely, 'purchase') which is of interest to business.

As a business discipline concerned with the creation, communication and delivery of values, modern marketing has long recognised the importance of understanding how and why consumers buy, since only by understanding how value is achieved can goods and services be designed and presented in such a way as to attract customers. Clearly every business has the same aim, therefore competitive advantage is firmly based on understanding customers better than the competitors and being able to deliver the products that the customer wants, ahead of the market. The problem for business is in understanding buyers who are notoriously unpredictable, irrational and complex and where the actual transaction is but one element in their consumption behaviour.

The core of the business/customer relationship is the exchange of values and if nothing is to be gained from the exchange or more can be gained elsewhere there is no need to repeat the exchange. The motivation for exchange for the business is the generation of revenue through sales and the motivation for the customer is considered to be the anticipation of the use of the product. This simplistic view of the exchange process is based upon a particular view of the world which is populated by rational objective consumers, who make purchases from

7

businesses who in turn are only concerned with minimising cost and maximising profit. In reality both businesses and consumers are motivated by a complex range of considerations which affect their actual behaviour. For the business, considerations related to brand image or customer loyalty may mean that minimising cost is not the most efficient way of maximising profit. For the consumer, they are interested in much more than the utilitarian aspects of exchange—as Levy (1959) points out, people buy things not only for what they can do but also for what they mean (p. 118). Bagozzi (1975) suggested that mankind's behaviour is much more than the outward response to stimuli; it is purposeful, intentional and motivated. Any exchange, therefore, is more than just a transfer—it has both social and psychological significance. As a result, the first activity of marketing is understanding the customer and the way that they view competing products and the values associated with them.

The overt aim of this book is to integrate two relatively new areas of study; consumer behaviour and services marketing. However, the very idea of integration presents a number of interesting questions. First, and perhaps most important, is whether or not the consumption of services is sufficiently distinct from the consumption of other products to merit special consideration. Allied to this is the old 'chestnut' of whether services themselves are a distinct product category. If the answer to these questions is 'no' this book is based, at best, on an artificial construction and at worst is just plain wrong. We hope that on reading this book and considering the case studies in different areas of services research you will be convinced that the answers to both are in the affirmative. The aim of this book is to provide evidence that service marketing and consumer behaviour theorists can learn a great deal from each other in understanding consumer behaviour.

This first chapter is an introduction and as such covers a large range of material. In an attempt to make this as manageable as possible we concentrate upon two key tasks. The first is to introduce some background in consumer behaviour theory, which is applicable regardless of product, in order to explain how consumer behaviour is currently conceptualised. The second task is to introduce the distinctive characteristics of services which affect the way that the consumer perceives the purchase. However, it is not the intention of this book to tread the well-worn path in establishing the evolution of services marketing and the place of services in westernised economies. Readers who wish to pursue this theme should consult one of the many comprehensive texts on the subject, for example, Lovelock (1996), Bateson (1996), Zeithaml and Bitner (1996). This chapter is concerned with consumers and the demands placed upon them by services; it does not offer a re-examination of the 4 Ps in a service context, but rather focuses upon understanding consumption and the nature of services in general. The remaining chapters then consider the implications of these in specific service industries.

Defining Consumer Behaviour

It is traditional to start any analysis by defining terms, therefore it is appropriate at this point to consider the meaning of the term *consumer behaviour* and to investigate some of the aspects of behaviour which are likely to be important in understanding the consumption of services. Any survey of the marketing literature will produce a variety of terms and definitions which relate to understanding consumers, but fundamentally we can think of consumers as undertaking a variety of different roles. Consumers are often referred to as customers, but in general the term 'customer' is typically used to describe someone who purchases a product from a business. This is a very narrow view since it treats consumer behaviour as consisting of only a discrete transaction, i.e. the customer is only of interest in terms of what they buy from the business. While this is obviously of concern to the individual business (and 'market' as opposed to 'marketing' researchers), it is clearly a valid perspective only in as much as it describes a small part of a complex set of behaviours. What is lacking in this perspective is how the single purchase relates to other purchases which comprise the individual's consumption behaviour. There is also a construction on the term 'customer' which implies a simple economic relationship between a business and a buyer, i.e., that the relationship is based upon monetary exchange.

This view has been broadened over the years to recognise that it is not necessary to engage in any direct financial relationship to consume. For instance, we consume political ideas without any direct financial exchange, we consume the countryside and fresh air. Therefore the term 'customer' to characterise consumption is unsatisfactory and other distinctions need to be drawn. What is of interest primarily to the marketer is the person who makes or influences a consumption decision and this may or may not be the buyer. In a typical household the person who buys the food may not be the same person who consumes it and similarly the decision of precisely what to buy may be taken in consultation with several members of a household. This is particularly true when we consider the purchase in a business-to-business context. In this case a business decision of what to purchase and from where, may be taken by a specialist group, but initiated by other members of the organisation. As a result the term buyer is equally unsatisfactory in describing the full range of consumption behaviour.

The common way of addressing these ambiguities is to present a definition which encompasses all possible roles played during the consumption process. These include the initiating or authorising role where the person may determine that some need or want is not being met—the influencing or information-generating role of someone who, while not necessarily party to the decision, has a bearing upon the outcome; the buyer who will actually conduct the transaction; and finally the user who is involved in the consumption of the product. Whether all these roles are adopted by a single person or many individuals, single companies or industries, these are all facets of consumer behaviour and are, therefore, relevant when we consider the consumption of a particular class of products. The term consumer is of a higher order and encompasses a number of relationships including the specific cases of the customer and buyer. As a consequence: 'consumer behaviour defines a wide range of activities and behaviours, the processes involved when individuals or groups select, purchase, use or dispose of products, services, ideas or experiences'. All of the activities have implications for purchase and re-purchase behaviour and can be affected by marketing activity to different degrees. By understanding these different facets of consumer behaviour we can tailor product offerings in such a way as to maximise customer value and thereby encourage repeat purchase behaviour.

Having provided a definition, of sorts, it is worth considering the background to consumer behaviour and to the discipline before presenting some general variations in perspectives on consumption which will impact upon the material presented later in this book.

BACKGROUND TO THE DISCIPLINE OF CONSUMER BEHAVIOUR

The academic discipline of consumer behaviour is firmly rooted in marketing, yet its development has drawn upon a number of other disciplines. In the early phase of development the dominant way of looking at consumer behaviour was that presented by economists such as Bentham (1907). This view was based upon an assumption of rationality among individuals, who make decisions about what to purchase based upon objective measurable criteria. The consumer was considered capable of handling large amounts of price and product information and engaging in a complex mathematical algebra in order to estimate and then maximise utility. While the analysis was tenable at a simple level, in an increasingly complex economy it was clear that there were limitations to this explanation of behaviour; in particular the shortcomings of price as the dominant motivating factor of choice, the increasing availability of information, and questions about the capacity of consumers to process large amounts of information. More fundamentally, however, the assumption of rationality ignored the symbolic aspects of exchange.

Individual Phase

A response to these criticisms of the economic model of behaviour was to consider consumption as going beyond just satisfaction through purchase. This approach treated consumption as multi- rather than uni-motivational. In considering a wider range of behaviours the link between consumption behaviour and other areas of academic study became evident and researchers started to look towards psychological explanations of behaviour. They began to consider that consumption behaviour could be explained in the same terms as other forms of behaviour using constructs such as cognition, attitudes, personality and culture. This moved the study of consumer behaviour away from simple descriptions of exchange in attempting to understand why consumers behave as they do. These studies were almost exclusively focused upon the individual and while they laid down the basis of the discipline there was a natural limit to how far behaviour could be explained without reference to the wider social context in which the behaviour took place.

Group Phase

The next development in the field of consumer behaviour research was the recognition that consumers operate in a complex network of groups. Much, if not most, of our consumption of goods and services is affected by groups of one kind or another and is subject to encouragement and sanction. Behaviours adopted by individuals are formed as a function of the society in which we live and the roles allocated to us by other people, e.g., student, parent, employee, family member, friend and so on. All of us play different roles in our lives depending upon immediate circumstances and, therefore, these must also be included in any attempt to understand and predict behaviour related to consumption. Other social constructs such as lifecycle, sub-culture and diffusion had particular attraction to early consumer behaviourists and the next stage in the development of the discipline was an attempt to construct comprehensive explanatory models of behaviour.

Modelling Phase

By the late 1960s these various strands of the discipline were combined into so-called 'comprehensive models' of consumer behaviour which were used by researchers and marketing practitioners to explain and predict behaviour. Three models proved to be the most influential; those presented by Nicosia (1966), Howard and Sheth (1969) and Engel, Kollatt and Blackwell (1968). For some, these models epitomised the ultimate achievement of study: the explanation of behaviour. For many more they merely provided a framework to draw together the various disparate strands of a new and growing discipline, but were inherently flawed in their combination because they had little explanatory power and were generally untestable. It was in terms of the latter that the models became best known and most influential; as organising frameworks which allowed for the incorporation of both individual, situational and social influences upon purchase outcome.

A current review of the discipline would identify three broad strands of research allied very closely to the root disciplines of economics, psychology and anthropology. These can be summarised as the information processing perspective (the cognitive consumer), the behavioural perspective (the learning consumer) and the postmodern/experiential perspective (the feeling consumer).

- *The Cognitive Consumer.* The fundamental assumption is that the individual consumer, when faced with a 'buy' task will, adopt a structured and logical approach to solving the question of 'what to buy?'. The approach is dominated by the view that consumers will use information to establish, assess and evaluate the potential benefits associated with the alternatives available and then make a rational and conscious decision.
- *The Learning Consumer.* This approach is based upon a view that consumer behaviour is determined by an individual's response to different stimuli, in particular the responses characterised by approach/avoidance. Consumers are able to learn rewarding and punishing behaviour through the experience of consequences. It is based on the assumption that there is a systematic relationship between experience and subsequent behaviour. From this perspective rewarding behaviour is repeated and preferences are thereby established. It is notable that the stimuli can be sourced in both

product and environment and this approach implicitly recognises the importance of the individuals' reaction to their environment.

- *The Feeling Consumer.* Those who subscribe to the idea of a feeling consumer reject any form of structure to the consumption experience. From this perspective a consumer's behaviour is beyond explanation and cannot be predicted. The constructs of choice and decision and learning are inherently modern and are rejected in favour of consumption motivated by fantasy, pleasure, hedonism and symbolism. From this postmodern perspective consumer research is best directed toward the analysis of transitory experience where style becomes more important than utility.

There is no single explanation of consumer behaviour and intuitively we can recognise elements of all of these approaches in our own behaviour. However, it is not possible to pursue each of these approaches in this book, rather it is necessary to adopt a structured approach to the analysis of consumer behaviour and services and this tends to favour the information processing perspective—'the thinking consumer'. That is not to say that the others are either invalid or inappropriate to the consideration of services; rather, that the information processing approach offers a clear framework to structure the discussion. This choice can also be defended on the basis that it is the dominant paradigm and as such is both accessible and well documented. Where appropriate we will refer to the other approaches, but the framework for this book is taken from the perspective of a cognitive consumer.

THE COGNITIVE CONSUMER

Whilst recognising that there are a number of influences on behaviour, the idea of a cognitive consumer is based upon a fundamental agreement that the actual purchase process is a sequence of tasks characterised as a problem-solving exercise. The problem is formulated as a desired outcome where the consumer must evaluate the components of the environment in order to construct a solution or course of action

Figure 1.1
Stages in Problem Solving

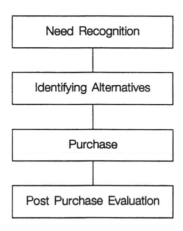

to achieve the desired outcome. This problem-solving behaviour comprises a number of distinct stages (see Figure 1.1).

Like most models, these stages are a simplification of reality, but its strength is in providing a format within which to consider not only individual and group behaviour, but also marketing and business response. The first stage is the growing recognition of a need or want that can be satisfied through some form of consumption. This stage in the process is characterised in mechanistic terms by a sense of tension experienced as the consumers ponder their current 'state' in comparison with an 'ideal state'. Where the difference is large a need will be recognised. Alternative constructions talk of motivational states which reflect deeply held drives, or hierarchies of needs. In addition to these internally derived cognitions, consumers may respond to external things like the smell of food, the sight of a product or a particular situation. For the marketer there is an opportunity here in the presentation of new or revised products as new 'ideal states' and in the comparison of the ideal with the current. Similarly appeals to basic drives or beliefs may also provide a route to the triggering or arousing of consumption activity. An important distinction here is in the recognition that not all needs will be translated in to goal-orientated behaviour, e.g. we may recognise a desire to eat at a particular restaurant, but not be motivated to do anything about it. Alternatively we may have a desire to pass an exam or achieve some goal, but not be able to achieve it. In business-to-business markets the need may be signalled much more clearly in the form of a decision to acquire a particular product, the need to replenish stocks or as part of a long-term investment programme.

The second stage in this simplistic model is the identification of alternatives which may satisfy our need, and their detailed evaluation. This process is sometimes divided into an information search phase (where consumers collect information about alternatives from memory or advertisements, other people, trade magazines or company databases), followed by an evaluation stage where the consumer engages in some sort of attribute algebra to arrive at a ranking of the identified product alternatives. During this stage of the process communication is especially important. Providers of goods or services will be concerned to communicate product attributes or benefits via advertising or direct means which closely match those sought by the consumer. Similarly the consumer is assumed to be using a wide range of sources and types of information, some of which may contradict or conflict with experience or other messages. For instance, a friend or another manufacturer may have something detrimental to say about a product which is presented as the best. This process of evaluation continues right up to the purchase of the product and can be upset if new information is presented such as a reduced price, special offer or the unexpected attributes of a previously dismissed alternative. For marketers the pre-purchase activity is possibly the most important phase of the decision in terms of the opportunity to influence and shape behaviour.

The culmination of the pre-purchase stages of consumption is the purchase itself. The inclusion of this behavioural activity as a separate stage has come under some criticism since it is difficult to extract it from the previous stage. Nevertheless it focuses attention on the physical acquisition of products, the payment method, delivery, the shop format and role of staff and other people, as well as the time taken and the human interaction that takes place. When considering goods acquisition this is a minor stage in the process. However, in relation to services this a major consumption stage and is discussed in detail in Chapter 3.

Once the purchase is complete we move to the final stage and one which is becoming increasingly important: post-purchase assessment. Traditionally this final phase of the decision process was only concerned with satisfaction and disposition of the product. The positive evaluation of the purchase, i.e. meeting or exceeding expectations, would lead to satisfaction, and vice versa would lead to dissatisfaction. The former would be associated with a higher probability of repeat purchase. Disposition or disposal is important in terms of second-hand markets, recycling behaviour (of both product and experience) and retention or renewal behaviour. Increasingly this phase of the decision process is seen as an opportunity to build and create longer term relationships, for the removal of post-decision regrets, and the retention of positive attitudes toward product and supplier which outlive the product's life. From a business point of view this phase of consumption includes consideration of possession rituals such as cleaning and care, improvements, upgrades, customisation etc. which provide avenues of further consumption opportunities. Because this phase is associated with satisfaction and evaluation and is based upon first-hand experience by the consumer it is particularly associated with word of mouth referral behaviour. The satisfied consumer is credible and beneficial to the organisation by spreading positive word of mouth information, but the unsatisfied consumer is credible and highly detrimental, and is likely to tell ten times the number of people than will the satisfied consumer.

This simplified process orientation allows complex behaviour to be broken down into meaningful 'chunks' and allows for the accommodation of individual/product and market variation in the analysis. One important variation is the observation that different purchases seem to require different degrees of mental effort on behalf of the consumer, depending upon the type of purchase. This leads to the second important consideration. It is apparent from observation and from our own consumption that individuals have a variety of consumption behaviours. We know, for instance, that some products or services mean that we will spend a great deal of time and effort evaluating alternatives and coming to a decision. Conversely there are also occasions when it really doesn't matter what product we buy or from whom as long as we obtain it. These variations in consumption behaviour are dependent upon a number of factors but we can identify three main decision formats from the existing consumer behaviour literature.

New/Big Consumption

Situations where we are presented with a completely new purchase situation are in fact very rare. There are always some elements of the purchase which are familiar, for instance, although we may not know anything about computers we do know about other products which comprise a 'box' and a 'screen', e.g. television. We also have some idea of the attributes and facilities available and those we are looking for; we know how shops operate and our expected role as a customer, and we probably know about different payment options. However, the description 'new task' is usually applied to purchases which we make infrequently and usually without the benefit of recent experience, either because the product is different in some way, or we believe that things have changed since the previous purchase occasion. This type of purchase is generally referred to as *high involvement*. In these circumstances the consumer is likely to spend a great deal of time and effort on their purchase looking for a number of different suppliers and comparing brands and prices.

This behaviour can also be observed in purchases described as 'big task', for instance life-threatening decisions, decisions which involve lots of money or which will change the person's life in some way, as well as decisions which involve the physical person. If we consider the service product, which by definition is heterogeneous, the logical conclusion is that each service consumption decision is a new decision. However, while the service itself may differ from encounter to encounter, aspects of the service product will remain constant. For instance, although hairdressing services differ from those of beauticians, for example, the place of delivery remains fairly comparable in terms

18

of its tangible components, the presence of a person to deliver a service remains constant and the process of delivery also remains fairly comparable. If we accept that these aspects of the service delivery are part of the service product, despite the claim of heterogeneity in services, this certainly suggests that service purchases are not uniquely new task.

Repeat Consumption

There are many situations in which consumers buy something fairly frequently and this kind of behaviour can be informed by previous experience, in the knowledge that the last occasion is recent and the information relevant to the current task. For instance many food purchases are repeat task—we know which products we want and we know where to find them and, therefore, all we need to do is go and physically pick them up. Equally for service products, there are some service-dominated products we consume on a regular basis, for example fast-food. In these circumstances there will be little in the way of conscious evaluation of alternatives available, prices or aspects of the purchase and the habitual or repeat purchase actually requires very little cognitive effort on the part of the consumer. The ease of the repeat task is dependent upon an implicit assumption that 'things are the same'. By this we mean that the circumstances of purchase are similar to each other. If things are different, i.e. if the product has changed in appearance or is not available, the consumer may decide that this is now a new task and will resort to a more complex and time extended decision.

Involuntary Consumption

Most consumption is undertaken on the basis of free choice, so called 'voluntary consumption', which describes the majority of the situations of interest to marketers. However, there are situations where consumption has to take place. For instance, if you have to present audited accounts then you need to use a chartered accountant, or if you want a university degree then you must consume the educational services of a university. More usual, though, is the consumption of some related product. If you own a computer you will need to purchase software, a house—electricity and water, a car—petrol. Consumption of this type is involuntary and may attract less effort on behalf of the consumer than even repeat consumption, since repeat consumption can become new consumption where a new product or an attractive alternative is recognised. In the involuntary consumption scenario this opportunity is rarely available. Although the consumer has the ability to decide which brand or supplier to use, the fact that the choice is frequently limited, or trivial in that there are few perceived differences between alternatives, means that involuntary consumption does not result in extended decision making.

The usual approach to the understanding of behaviour is predicated upon the assumption that individuals are fully aware of their actions and act in a rational manner. The decision formats identified are all predicated on the assumption that products are inherently similar in terms of the decision process. In reality products are not similar and make different demands upon the consumer. They may be intrinsically different, presented in different environments and evaluated on different bases. Therefore, in any consideration of buyer behaviour it is necessary to look at both the context in which the consumption takes place and at the nature of the product.

THE NATURE OF PRODUCTS

A central component in the exchange process, other than the parties involved, is some conceptualisation of a product. This has been defined as 'any bundle or combination of qualities, processes and capabilities (goods, services and ideas) that a buyer believes will deliver satisfaction' (Enis and Reoring (1981) p. 17). It is clear from this definition that product is multi-dimensional and dependent upon how the buyer responds to different facets of the offering. Levitt (1986) describes a product as a complex cluster of value satisfactions and identified five levels of product in terms of customer perceptions. The central part of the product is the *core benefit*, defined as the fundamental benefit or service that the customer is buying. Around the core are four additional product levels: the *generic product*, the *expected product*, the *augmented product* and the *potential product*. Each of these describes a different dimension of the product with the capacity to differentiate the offering on the basis of consumer response. Therefore, in reality we are dealing with a relationship between the business and the customer through the medium of product. In this text only one product class is under consideration—services.

SERVICES

Literature on the subject of service management and marketing has been driven in recent years by an acknowledgement that service products are distinctive and that service-based industry is an increasingly important part of developed economies (see for example Lovelock 1996, Berry 1980, Rust and Oliver 1994). While academics are notoriously cautious about recognising a new subject discipline, services marketing and management is already aspiring to be recognised as credible. However, in the process of maturity the roots of the subject in physical goods marketing and product management are becoming increasingly strained. As the services tree flourishes, with branches extending into financial services, not-for-profit services, retailing, leisure and tourism, the full scope of the service product becomes apparent. Considerable effort has been expended by academics over the last 20 years in establishing that services are different to other products (see for instance Berry 1980; Shostack 1977, Bateson 1995) and that these differences present special challenges to the service consumer. Berry (1980) suggests that services marketing has been a stepchild to goods marketing, in the sense that it has developed from it, but is not directly related to it. While there are clear parallels and differences due to context, the relationship between goods and services marketing is still the subject of debate. As already stated, the purpose of this book is to consider services from the consumers'

21

perspective and to investigate the distinctive nature of services consumption. Although some aspects of the debate are worth rehearsing, the main focus of this book is that services present particular challenges to consumers and that these challenges themselves provide opportunities for service marketers and academics to extend the services discipline still further.

Previous research in the services marketing and management area has pursued three distinct schools of thought concerning the relationship between goods and services marketing. The first, presented by Lovelock in 1981, argues that service marketing is a special case and that most normal marketing practices are not applicable. As a consequence service marketing must develop its own theoretical approaches, not in isolation but in parallel to goods marketing (Lovelock 1981). The second school of thought reflects the view that most marketing is situation specific and therefore only limited generalisation is possible within common situational boundaries (Rushton and Carson 1989). The third, and most persuasive, argument is that services marketing is an application of basic marketing principles, not a distinct discipline in its own right. This implies that there are concepts and techniques which can be applied regardless of product type, but that there are also a number of distinct product and/or context characteristics which require that these concepts be modified or adapted (see Rust and Oliver 1994).

The essence of the debate is whether or not general marketing approaches and theories can be usefully abstracted to the services context. This argument has been presented in terms of levels of abstraction in marketing theory, described by Blois (1974) and Rushton and Carson (1989). These authors present variations on a schematic representation of the relationships between general marketing principles and their applications. This suggests that the relationship between marketing and marketing in specific contexts, is one of levels of abstraction where higher order concepts of marketing are established through a process of abstraction from situation specific contexts (see Figure 1.2).

The basis of the argument in this book is that the consideration of buyer behaviour in services has been at too high a level of abstraction

22

Figure 1.2
Conceptual Framework

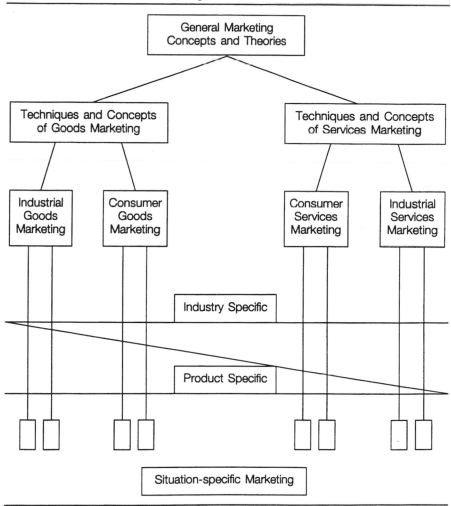

General Marketing
Concepts and Theories

Techniques and Concepts
of Goods Marketing

Techniques and Concepts
of Services Marketing

Industrial
Goods
Marketing

Consumer
Goods
Marketing

Consumer
Services
Marketing

Industrial
Services
Marketing

Industry Specific

Product Specific

Situation-specific Marketing

Adapted from Blois (1974), Rushton and Carson (1989)

that has not taken into consideration the specific characteristics of services and their affect upon consumers. Howard and Sheth (1969) for example, suggest that their theory of buyer behaviour is not limited to a product class or given type of product but encompasses the description of all types of buying behaviour. This approach has been adopted too readily by both consumer behaviourists and service marketers. In fact specific applications and adaptations of consumer behaviour in services are warranted, to reflect the special purchase and product context, although these must be cognisant of the generalisable services context.

SERVICES AS PRODUCTS

It has been already suggested that marketing theory has been dominated by concepts and terminology derived from the marketing of tangible goods. Inasmuch as products have been defined as 'bundles of benefits', it could be argued that the domination of a goods-orientated terminology is inconsequential, since it is merely semantic. However, in tracking the advance of the discipline of services marketing Fisk et al. (1993) identify an evolutionary process whereby services emerge from general marketing theory to be regarded as a separate phenomenon, which can be considered as a product class. Thus from an early defensive position, services marketing is now regarded as an established discipline with its own conferences, journals and research institutes. This has led to what Fisk et al. (1993) call the 'explosive' growth in marketing research and literature which has concentrated on the specific problems of service industries. Before discussing the way that consumers respond to the service product, it is necessary to rehearse these arguments and establish the key characteristics of services that affect consumer behaviour.

The first problem with discussing service products, rather than goods, lies in defining what a service is. There is no single universally accepted definition. Gronroos (1990) lists a selection of 11 definitions of the term dating from 1960 before arriving—reluctantly—at a definition which he describes as a 'blend' of those suggested by Lehtinen (1991), Kotler and Bloom (1984) and Gummesson (1987):

A service is an activity or series of activities of more or less intangible nature that normally, but not necessarily, take place in interactions between the customer and the service employee and/or physical resources or goods and or systems of the service provider, which are provided as solutions to customer problems.

Gronroos (1990) p. 27

The complexity and rather convoluted nature of this definition illustrates the problem in succinctly defining services. Gummesson (1987), referring to an unidentified source, suggests an alternative definition that is more of a criticism of attempts to find an acceptable definition:

Services are something which can be bought and sold but which you can not drop on your foot.

Gummesson (1987) p. 22

There is not even agreement amongst academics as to whether the differences between goods and services are significant enough to justify the distinction. Levitt (1976) states that there are no such things as service industries, only industries where the service components are greater or less than those in other industries. Shostack (1977) argues that there are very few 'pure' goods or services and describes a product continuum from tangible dominant goods to intangible dominant services. Kotler (1991) provides structure to the continuum by identifying four distinct categories of offering: purely tangible goods, tangible goods with accompanying services, a major service with accompanying goods and services, and pure services. The distinction is, therefore, between products where the core of what is being offered is a service and products that are dominantly physical goods. Similarly Wilson (1972) suggests that the classification should rest on the services relationship to tangible goods and describes three levels of services: services that make available a tangible, for example retail outlets; services providing added value to a tangible, for example dry cleaning, and services that provide pure intangibles, for example auctioneering. Whilst it is possible to argue with some of the examples that Wilson gives within each of his service categories, it is a useful way of considering the service end of the goods-service continuum. The distinction is between products where the core of what is being sold is a service and products where the core is a physical good with service used as an augmentation for competitive advantage.

An alternative way of regarding this definition problem in service products is presented by Rust and Oliver (1994) who conceptualise all business transactions as services, which may or may not involve a physical product. This argument is based on the idea that all products deliver some form of service, for example, a washing machine washes clothes, the washing machine is bought to deliver that service; along with the physical product the buyer also receives the service delivery, i.e. the experience of buying the washing machine, the service environment (the shop in which it is bought) and the service product which they define as the specifications of the offering. All products are, therefore, made up of these elements centred around the physical product which is present in goods and absent in pure services. The case for considering consumer behaviour in relation to services as distinct is based on the belief that there are a number of common characteristics of service products which distinguish them from goods. It is also apparent that these fundamental characteristics provide a rationale for considering the consumption of services as distinctive from the consumption of goods. Whatever the academic argument concerning the differences between these product forms, it is apparent that they demand a different managerial approach and that they elicit a different response from consumers. While the management of services has been recognised as a distinctive activity, the consumption of services has never been disentangled from the goods literature.

DISTINGUISHING CHARACTERISTICS OF SERVICES

Although a conceptualisation of the term 'service product' is difficult to arrive at, all products have characteristics, or attributes, that define the nature of the offering. For services these can be identified as intangibility, heterogeneity, inseparability, perishability and the concept of ownership (see Sasser et al. 1978; Lovelock 1981 and Gronroos 1978).

Intangibility. Intangibility (i.e. without a physical dimension) is one of the most important characteristics of service products. Often services are described using tangible nouns but this obscures the fundamental nature of the service which remains intangible. Shostack (1977) for instance points out that 'airline' means air transportation, 'hotel' means lodging rental. Berry (1980) describes a good as 'an object, a device, a thing', in contrast to a service which is 'a deed, a performance, an effort'. He argues that even though the performance of most services is supported by tangibles, the essence of what is purchased is a performance, therefore as McLuhan (1964) points out, it is the process of delivering a service which comprises the product. The implication of this argument is that consumers can not see, touch, hear, taste or smell a service; they can only experience the performance of it (Carman and Uhl 1973 and Sasser et al. 1978). This makes the perception of a service highly subjective and an abstract concept for the consumer. The inability to inspect or touch services means that in any pre-purchase situation the product remains abstract until it has been consumed. While services often are accompanied by 'physical evidence' which in some situations the consumer can utilise in order to make the product less abstract and more tangible, there will always be an intangible element to the service product.

Inseparability. The inseparability of the production and consumption aspects of the service transaction refers to the fact that the service is a performance, in real time, in which the purchaser cooperates with the provider (Bell 1981). According to Thomas (1978) the degree of this involvement between the transacting parties is dependent upon the extent to which the service is 'equipment based' or 'people based'. Equipment-based services (such as telephones and vending machines) deliver the same service to whoever consumes them. This can be contrasted with people-based services where the involvement of a human service provider inevitably means that individual consumers will experience variation in the service delivery. The implication of this distinction is that people-based services tend to be less standardised than equipment-based services or goods-producing activities. Goods are produced, sold and then consumed, whereas services are sold and then produced and consumed simultaneously (Regan 1963 and Cowell 1984). The inseparability of the role of service provider and consumer leads to a lack of standardisation since both the purchaser and the individual delivering the service can alter both the way in which the service is delivered, as well as what is delivered and this has important implications for the process of evaluation.

Heterogeneity. The characteristic of services referred as heterogeneity is also a function of human involvement in the delivery and consumption process. It refers to the fact that services are delivered by individuals and therefore each service encounter will be different by virtue of the participants, the time of performance or the circumstances. As a consequence each purchaser is likely to receive a different service experience. Whereas in the case of goods it is possible to standardise the product and guarantee replication of the same product over time this is not possible in services. This has implications for service management as well as for consumers. A great deal of the services literature has been concerned with mechanisms for achieving a degree of uniformity in service delivery, for instance, Levitt (1972, 1976) who considers the industrialisation of services, and to an extent the services quality literature, is also based upon some standardisation in delivery. However, it should also be noted that where individuals and interpersonal exchange is involved there may well be attractions in having personalisation and customisation.

Perishability. The perishability of services describes the real time nature of the product. Unlike goods, the consumer cannot store services and the absence of the ability to build and maintain stocks of the product means that sudden demand can not be accommodated in the same way as goods, i.e. the consumer cannot stockpile services against a possible need in the future. In certain circumstances the consumer may decide to delay consumption but not to consume more in advance of requirements. For the purchaser of services the time at which he/she chooses to use the service may be critical to its performance and therefore to the consumer's experience. For example, the experience of using public transport is different in the rush hour from other times of day. Kelley, Donnelly and Skinner (1990) make the observation that consumption is inextricably linked to the presence of other consumers and their presence can influence the service outcome.

Ownership. In addition to these characteristics of services, Judd (1964), Wyckham et al. (1975) and Kotler (1982) have identified the concept of ownership as a distinguishing feature of services. With the sale of a good the purchaser generally obtains ownership of it. By contrast in the case of a service the purchaser only has temporary access to or use of it. What is owned is the benefit of the service, not the service itself, e.g. in terms of a holiday the purchaser has the benefit of the flight, hotel and beach but does not own them. The absence of ownership stresses the finite nature of services for purchasers—there is no enduring involvement in the product, only in the benefit.

PROCESS AND OUTCOME

There is an important distinction to be drawn between the two principle components of the service product, the outcome i.e. what the service is designed to achieve, and the process of delivery i.e. how the service is delivered. It is frequently more difficult for a supplier to differentiate the outcome, for example an accounting audit must achieve certain criteria; the outcome—audited accounts—is not easily differentiated. The purchaser requires reliability of the outcome, differentiation takes place at the process dimension, how the accounts are audited. In many services this outcome is difficult for the purchaser to evaluate, even after the service has been delivered. It is possible for the purchaser to know, for example, that the accounts have been delivered but difficult to assess whether they have been audited in the most efficient or cost-effective way. In these circumstances the way the audit takes place, i.e. the process of auditing, is used to assess the competence of the auditors. Financial competence is implied from the manner in which the audit is conducted. Where the reliability of the outcome is essential—the service supplier must deliver the core service—much of the industry competition takes place at the process level.

Other models have been presented which have similar bases, despite different terminology, all of which describe a process and outcome form. For instance, Gronroos (1991) refers to technical v. functional aspects; Zeithaml (1988) uses an intrinsic v. extrinsic distinction; Lawson (1986) a motivation v. hygiene model, Iacobucci et al. (1994) describe 'core' and 'peripheral' aspects of the service. The word 'pairs' is not exactly interchangeable but there are strong conceptual parallels. The key factor is that in service products it is important to make a distinction between what is delivered and how it is delivered. The relationship between these two aspects is considered in more detail when considering service evaluation when the asymmetric relationship between these aspects is important. This theme is developed further in Chapter 3.

CONCLUSION

The argument presented so far is that service products have been recognised as a distinctive product category and that, as consumer behaviour is affected by product, the consumption of services merits consideration in its own right. There are considerable problems with trying to apply a service process driven approach to the consumption of services since a number of the 'stages' in the decision model occur simultaneously or in reverse when dealing with a service product. For instance, physical goods are evaluated, purchased and then consumed, whereas services are evaluated, purchased and consumed at the same time. As a consequence, in the following chapters, while a sequential process is implied, in reality the nature of service consumption is such that they should not be considered as independent or sequential stages.

REFERENCES

Bagozzi, R. (1975) 'Marketing as Exchange', *Journal of Marketing*, 39 (October), pp. 32–39.

Bateson, J. (1995) *Managing Services Marketing*, 3rd edn, (Fort Worth: Dryden).

Bell (1981) 'Tactical Service Marketing and the Process of Remixing', pp. 163–167 in Donnelly, J. and George, W. (eds) *Marketing of Services*, (Chicago: AMA).

Bentham, J. (1907) *An Introduction to the Principles of Morals v Legislation*, (London: Clarendon Press).

Berry, L. (1980) 'Services Marketing is Different', *Business*, 30 (May–June), pp. 24–29.

Berry, L. (1981) 'The Employee as Customer', *Journal of Retail Banking*, 3 (March), pp. 33–40.

Blois, K.J. (1974) 'The Marketing of Services: An Approach', *European Journal of Marketing*, 8 (Summer), pp. 137–145.

Carman, J. and Uhl, K. (1973) *Marketing: Principles and Methods*, (Homewood, Ill: Irwin).

Cowell, D. (1984) 'The Marketing of Services', (London: Heinemann).

Engel, J., Kollatt, D. and Blackwell, P. (1968) *Consumer Behaviour*, 2nd ed. (New York: Dryden).

Enis, B.M. and Roering, K.J. (1981) 'Services Marketing: Different Products, Similar Strategy', in Donnelly, J. and George, W. (eds) *Marketing of Services*, (Chicago: AMA).

Fisk, R., Brown, S. and Bitner, M.J. (1993) 'Tracking the Evolution of Services Marketing Literature', *Journal of Retailing*, 69, 1, pp. 61–103.

Gronroos, C. (1990) *Service Management and Marketing: Managing the Moments of Truth in Service Competition*, (MA: Lexington).

Gronroos, C. (1991) 'The Marketing Strategy Continuums: A Market Concept for the 1990s', *Management Decision*, 1, pp. 7–13.

Gummesson, E. (1987) 'The New Marketing: Developing Long-Term Interactive Relationships', *Long Range Planning*, 20, 4, pp. 10–20.

Howard, J. and Sheth, J. (1969) *The Theory of Buyer Behaviour*, (New York: John Wiley).

Iacobucci, D., Grayson, K. and Ostrom, A. (1994) 'The Calculus of Service Quality and Customer Satisfaction: Theoretical and Empirical Differentiation and Integration', in *Advances in Services Marketing and Management*, 3, pp. 1–67.

Judd (1964) 'The Case for Redefining Services', *Journal of Marketing*, 28 (Jan), pp. 58–59.

Kelly, S.W., Donnelly, J.H. and Skinner, S.J. (1990) 'Customer Participation in Service Production and Delivery', *Journal of Retailing*, 66, 3, pp. 315–335.

Kotler, P. (1982) *Principles of Marketing*, (New Jersey: Prentice Hall).

Kotler, P. (1991) *Marketing Management*, (New Jersey: Prentice Hall).

Kotler, P. and Bloom, P. (1984) *Marketing Professional Services*, (Englewood Cliffs NJ: Prentice Hall).

Lawson, R. (1986) 'Consumer Satisfaction: Motivation Factors and Hygiene Factors Marketing', Discussion Paper, (NZ: University of Otago).

Lehtinen, U. and Lehtinen, J.R. (1991) 'Two Approaches To Service Quality Dimensions', *Service Industries Journal*, 11, 3, pp. 287–303.

Levitt, T. (1972) 'Product-line Approach to Service', *Harvard Business Review* (Sept–Oct), p. 43.

Levitt, T. (1981) 'Marketing Intangible Products and Product Intangibles', *Harvard Business Review*, 59, pp. 94–102.

Levitt, J. (1976) 'The Industrialisation of Services', *Harvard Business Review* (September–October), pp. 63–74.

Levy, S.J. (1959) 'Symbols For Sale', *Harvard Business Review*, 37 (July/Aug), pp. 117–119.

Lovelock, C. (1981) 'Why Marketing Management Needs to Be Different', in Donnelly, J. and George, W. (eds) *Marketing of Services*, (Chicago: AMA).

Lovelock, C. (1996) *Services Marketing*, 3rd edn, (NJ: Prentice Hall).

McLuhan, M. (1964) *Understanding Media*, (New York: McGraw-Hill).

Nicosia, F. (1966) *Consumer Decision Processes: Marketing and Advertising Implications*, (New Jersey: Prentice Hall).

Regan, W. (1963) 'The Service Revolution', *Journal of Marketing*, 27 (July), pp. 57–62.

Rushton, A.M. and Carson, D.J. (1989) 'The Marketing of Services: Managing The Intangibles', *European Journal of Marketing*, 23, 8, pp. 23–44.

Rust, R.T. and Oliver, R.L. (1994) *Service Quality: New Directions in Theory and Practice*, (London: Sage), pp. 1–21.

Rust, R., Zahonik, A. and Keningham, T. (1996) *Service Marketing*, (New York: Harper Collins).

Sasser, W., Olson, R. and Wyckoff, D. (1978) *Management of Service Operations*, (Boston MA: Allyn & Bacon).

Shostack, L. (1977) 'Breaking Free from Product Marketing', *Journal of Marketing*, 41 (Apr), pp. 73–80.

Statt, D. (1997) *Understanding the Consumer*, (Basingstoke: Macmillan Press).

Thomas, D. (1978) 'Strategy is Different in Service Businesses', *Harvard Business Review*, (July), pp. 158–165.

Wilson, A. (1972) *The Marketing of Professional Services*, (Maidenhead: McGraw-Hill).

Wyckham, R., Fitzroy, P. and Mandy, G. (1975) 'Marketing of Services: An Evaluation of the Theory', *European Journal of Marketing*, 1, 1, p. 61.

Zeithaml, V. (1988) 'Consumer Perceptions of Price, Quality and Value: A Means End Model and Synthesis', *Journal of Marketing*, 52 (July), pp. 2–22.

Zeithaml, V. and Bitner, M. (1996) *Services Management*, (New York: McGraw Hill).

CHAPTER 2

PRE-CONSUMPTION OF SERVICES

INTRODUCTION

In the previous chapter the point was made that the stages of consumption familiar in relation to physical goods are not sequential when considering the consumption of services. However, there are clearly elements of the stages that can be identified in both situations. The focus of this chapter is upon those elements of the decision which would normally (by which we mean in association with the acquisition of physical products) occur in the pre-purchase phase. In goods marketing, this includes all behaviour up to and including the physical acquisition of the product. In the case of pure services, physical acquisition is not relevant and purchase can take place post consumption. Therefore, for the sake of structure we will confine the discussion to behaviour that takes place before contact with the service provider. This includes behaviour related to collection and processing of information, comparison of the available alternatives and the derivation of expectations. It is also important to point out, however, that consumers do not come to a purchase situation as a 'blank slate' and that individuals cannot be considered to be similar in anything but the broadest sense. The first characteristics which we consider are those resources which the consumer has at his or her disposal.

CONSUMER RESOURCES

Consumers do not enter into the consumption of any product from an equal startpoint. Each of us differs in terms of our personality, our memory of past consumption, the amount of money we have to spend and the time we have to spend it. This can be conceptualised as having access to different resources which constrain the purchase decision. The primary resources can be broadly categorised as:

- economic
- temporal
- cognitive.

This is not to say that other resources, for example personality and experience, do not affect the purchase, but these three can be seen as the primary resources. However, these resources can not be viewed as absolutes—it is how they are perceived by the individual that is relevant. For example, an individual may regard themselves as a novice consumer of a product when—relative to other consumers—they are an expert.

Economic Resources

The clearest discriminator between consumers is the amount of disposable income they have. In this respect services are no different from disposable goods. Clearly the relevance of economic resources is in relation to price, in that price has meaning relative to disposable income. When we consider the pricing of physical products, it is possible in advance of purchase to establish total price and as such price becomes a choice criteria. In the services context it is unusual to be able to establish the price precisely in advance, therefore it is difficult to allocate precise levels of income to the purchase of services.

In understanding this relationship between income and price, it is necessary to take account of the possibility of consumers providing certain services themselves. In times of economic restraint consumers are more inclined to do this. For example, a consumer may decide to colour their hair themselves rather than go to a hairdresser, or to decorate their own room rather than use a decorator, or to change the oil in their car themselves rather than pay for the services of a garage. However, most consumers do not have the requisite skills to carry out services such as surgery, flying a plane or even plumbing. Therefore in terms of income allocation, purchase decisions in relation to services are more complicated than a buy/not buy dichotomy.

This self-delivery option can be extended to add a further continuum for services ranging from impossible to self-deliver, to possible to self-deliver. Equally, we identify services at an atomistic level, and within a particular service we can also identify components such as form filling, room cleaning before decoration, self-packing before house removal, and so on where a consumer can trade off their own time relative to the price of the service.

Services are also subject to a variety of pricing strategies such as value-based pricing, seasonal pricing or demand pricing, many of which are characterised by high price variability. For example, in the case of airline seats, no one, not even the most regular traveller, could accurately predict the price of a particular seat on a particular flight. Coupled with the difficulties in establishing price before consumption, consumers are often faced with a price range rather than a price point, which may vary across transactions with the same service provider. This considerably increases the perception of financial risk associated with services (Murray and Schlacter 1990). Clearly perceptions of uncertainty over price will impact upon consumer perceptions of their economic resources in relation to services.

Temporal Resources

A second resource that varies between consumers is time. Historically consumers' time budget was regarded as having two dimensions, work time and leisure time. However recent research has shown that this is an inadequate way to conceptualise time. Hornik (1982), Holbrook and Lehmann (1981), Graham (1981), Lane and Lindquist (1988) all point toward a more complex time allocation process which includes committed and uncommitted time, planned and non-planned time and obligated and non-obligated time. Perceptions of time are culturally, socially and economically defined. For example we can point to linear, circular and procedural meanings of time:

- *Linear:* characterised by western cultures where time is viewed as a continuum and can be divided into past, present and future. The objective is to spend time appropriately in the present in order to ensure benefits in the future.
- *Circular:* characterised by an affinity with the natural cycle of the seasons. People only do today things that have to be done today with little interest in future benefit or the value of 'lost' time.
- *Procedural:* perception of time governed by task. Time is measured in terms of task rather than money or benefit. Tasks will take as long as they take, without an externally imposed time frame.

Graham (1981)

Services, as a product class, are particularly time sensitive both in their production and consumption and can even be classified by time. For example, services purchased in order to save time, which can then be allocated to other activities such as cleaning or gardening, as compared to services which use time, such as hairdressing, education or travel. This distinction is based on the inseparability of production and consumption. For 'time using' services it is necessary for the purchaser to be present when the service is provided. Individuals may not have a choice about when to consume the service, or how long it will take, therefore it is difficult for a consumer to allocate time to the service. Considerable dissatisfaction with services can be traced to the unpredictability of the time taken to deliver a service. Consumers often allocate a notional expected time span which is used to structure events or subsequent activities. Services which promise fast cycle services and deliver slow service are at the greatest risk of time-prompted dissatisfaction.

Services are also a production in real time. If the service fails it is not possible to restore that time, for example if a teacher does not turn up for a class, that time is lost. Accordingly some organisations now offer time guarantees (see Fram and DuBrin 1988; and Jacoby, Szybillo and Berning 1976).

Cognitive Resources

A third relevant resource can be termed cognitive, or the ability of an individual consumer to process information and to draw upon that information in the form of product-specific knowledge. As consumers we are only able to process a limited amount of information at any one time (Miller 1956; Jacoby, Speller and Kohn 1974; Bettman 1975). This ability will vary between consumers depending upon their innate capacity to process information and their involvement with the product or product class. The issue of cognitive capacity has received considerable attention in the consumer behaviour literature which has considered the possibility of an information threshold for consumers, which once passed can lead to 'information overload' (see Bettman 1979; Punj and Stewart 1983). It is also apparent that consumers of different ages have different abilities to process information. As such, processing capacity is relevant in the evaluation and consumption of complex services such as health, financial and some professional services and may require the service organisation to consider signage, instructions and pre-encounter briefings to enhance knowledge.

Within the marketing literature the concept of consumer involvement has been shown to be important in understanding consumer information processing and the decision-making process. As a social psychological construct, consumer involvement is considered to be an individual difference variable and has been identified as a causal or motivating factor with direct consequences upon consumers' purchase and communication behaviour (Sherif and Cantril 1947; Krugman 1965 and 1967; Rothschild 1979; Mitchell 1981; Greenwald and Leavitt 1984; Batra and Ray 1985; Petty et al. 1983; Kassarjian 1981; Zaichowsky 1985; Mittal 1989). As a general definition, involvement is said to be a motivational variable reflecting the extent of personal relevance of the decision to the individual, in terms of basic goals, values, and self concept (see for instance Zaichowsky 1985; Celsi and Olson 1988). In practice, depending upon their level of involvement, consumers are likely to differ with respect to a number of decision process dimensions. As an extension to this work, a number of authors have presented distinctions between different types of involvement associated with the situation, the product, the person and the communication (Bloch and Richins 1983; Antil 1984; Muncy and Hunt 1984) as a means of explaining different observed behaviours. Both Laurent and Kapferer (1985) and Mittal and Lee (1989) suggest that the use of the term involvement with such qualifying prefixes, e.g. situational involvement or ego involvement, suggests that the source of the involvement is the most important factor. In fact, the importance of the construct is in the ability to conceptualise involvement as having many facets or dimensions which contribute to an individual response, rather than arriving at an index of high or low involvement on any single facet. If we consider the nature of the service product this is likely to include involvement with the provider, the environment, the process and the outcome. As such, involvement may provide a useful additional variable in understanding the consumers' relationship with the service product.

Other Resources

A number of other resources can be identified as relevant in understanding consumer purchase behaviour. These include enthusiasm, affinity for interaction and ability to vocalise. However we will concentrate upon two further general resources: personality and experience.

Personality

An individual's personality develops over a lifetime of interactions with people, places and ideas. As such it is an enduring dimension associated with the individual and is expressed in the way the individual interacts with the environment. When purchasing goods and services, personality can be reflected in a variety of ways. The important point for services is that an individual's personality is a key determinant of how they interact with the various parts of the service, such as provider and environment. Because the production and consumption of services is simultaneous, an individual's personality will impact directly on their participation in the service. For example, personality may affect the way that consumers react towards service technology, service providers and other customers as well as specific elements of the service product (see Gabbott 1996; Haugveldt et al. 1987; and Pervin 1984).

Experience

All consumers learn from their experiences and therefore build a bank of experience-based information behaviours and roles upon which to draw when purchasing or evaluating goods and services. This reservoir of experience will contain information which relates to specific products as well as general product classes. Where a purchase involves a product which the consumer has not encountered before he or she will draw upon existing experiences to provide a basis for product expectations. For example, a person who had never had experience of a particular restaurant would nevertheless draw upon their experience in other restaurants to inform their behaviour and evaluation. Experiences are a very powerful resource, but they are also subject to diminishing usefulness, for instance where the product has changed since the last purchase, or where products (such as services) vary to a high degree. As product variability increases the value of previous experience decreases except at the most general level.

It is possible to identify 'domain specific' experiences as those applicable to specific consumption situations, and 'global experiences' which are generalisable across many consumption situations. For example, an individual may know how to use a telephone as a global experience yet be unable to use a telephone banking service which requires domain-specific knowledge.

According to Bettinghaus and Cody (1987) the best way of predicting how an individual will act in the future is to consider how they have acted in the past and, therefore, experience is a resource which we will return to later in this book.

It is clear that the resources available to the consumers, in real or perceptual terms, vary considerably and as a consequence, it is inappropriate to view consumers as approaching the consumption of any product from an equal standpoint. From a service perspective, the characteristics of the product and the central role of the consumer in shaping the service make the consideration of consumer resources central to understanding the nature of the individual service experience. It is also evident that differences in resources will impact upon every stage of the consumption process, in the collection and processing of information pre-purchase, the service encounter, and the evaluation of the product post consumption. Before considering the first stage in this model, information acquisition, it is necessary to discuss the processes by which we, as consumers, utilise the resources available to us.

CONSUMER PROCESSES

In order to achieve any particular consumption outcome our resources are combined with the resources available in the environment through a series of mechanisms which we refer to as processes. Processes allow us to organise both internal and external information in such a way as to be relevant to intended and actual behaviour. The most important processes are perception, learning, and attitude formation. Each of these are important in understanding how consumers relate to the various components of the service product and incorporate this external information into their behaviour.

Perception

As an individual we respond to our environment at a very basic level by processing sensations received through our five senses. The originators of the sensations are referred to as stimuli, which can originate in verbal, visual or physical form. Of interest to consumer behaviourists and to marketers, are the changes which take place between our sensation of the stimuli and our assigning of meaning or explanation to them, this process is known as perception (see for example Statt 1997). Clearly, this process is entirely subjective and we allocate meanings and explanations to stimuli according to schema, or heuristics. These are simple rules or networks of belief and feelings derived from fundamental beliefs and experiences which group things together which are similar.

In allocating particular sensations to a grouping Bruner (1957) suggests a simple progression. First a primitive allocation of the sensation is made. This is followed by a 'cue check' where additional information is used to test the veracity of the primitive classification. The third stage is the selection of the group to which the stimuli belongs and finally a confirmation check to ensure all the information is consistent. Such a simple process hides an enormously complex task. The full complexity is fundamental in explaining how consumers form initial reactions. For instance, why consumers distrust certain service providers or find them surly and unhelpful when other consumers see them in a very positive light. Similarly, why some consumers feel comfortable and relaxed in some service settings while others find the same setting unreal and contrived. Certain stimuli have been shown to encourage a similar perceptual response from most consumers, such as colours, sounds and smells. The subjective and individualist nature of perception, coupled with the myriad of stimuli received before, during and after a service experience make generalisations both difficult and dangerous. One explanation of these individual differences in perception are perceptual selection and sensory thresholds.

Perceptual selection refers to the fact that the ability to process information is limited and the response by consumers is to be very selective in allocating their valuable processing abilities. Perceptual selection is, therefore, a mechanism for limiting information. In reality consumers will attend to some stimuli more than others. The stimuli they choose to attend to is governed first by whether the stimuli is noticed, either in terms of its existence or non-existence or any change in it. Both of these circumstances relate to sensory thresholds, simply whether the stimuli itself or the change to the stimuli is sufficient to 'break through' into consciousness. As an example, some consumers do not notice the background music in a restaurant at all, because their sensory threshold for this stimuli is high or their selective perception is to ignore it. Assume that the restaurant turns up the volume. This could have a number of consequences; those consumers who didn't notice it before, now notice the music either because their threshold is exceeded and they hear it for the first time, or the actual increase in volume gains their attention. Equally the consumer may decide that he/she can't ignore it any more and they have to listen to it.

Clearly the inter-relatedness of these two effects is an important dimension in both the design and the delivery of service products. It has implications for small changes in process, the activities of service personnel and alterations to outcome. Indeed one could argue that perception is at the heart of the consumption process, both in terms of its effect upon choice, the experience of service consumption and parallel evaluation.

Learning

The second process which binds together perception, experience and behaviour is that of learning. As a consumer behaviour process, learning is defined as a relatively permanent change in behaviour that is caused by experience. An understanding of how consumers learn is the result of evaluating a number of different perspectives and models. These fall into two main camps, the cognitive school and the behaviourist school.

The cognitive perspective views learning as a mental activity. Consumers form links and relationships between items of information which Krugman (1965) indicates form learned 'chunks' of information. This process is active, in the sense that the consumer is involved to a degree in conscious reasoning. It is also dynamic, such that as new information is assimilated the process alters to account for it and forges links with existing information, comparing and updating information from memory. In all, the process of cognitive learning is a hypotho-deductive process where the new data is assimilated and beliefs and actions altered to adapt to new information.

The central dynamic of cognitive learning is the attribution of meaning to data, the consequent associations drawn between stimuli, the impact of associations upon beliefs and subsequently actions. In its simplest form the service organisation will be attempting to associate good and enjoyable service experience with the company name, through location, staff and service outcomes. As consumers experience services over time they are engaged in what Hoch and Deighton (1989) refer to as learning through experience. This form of learning is particularly influential as consumers repeat the process of collecting data, forming the same associations and thereby reinforcing recall and retrieval routines as well as beliefs. It also suggests that learning is relatively complex and relies upon a significant degree of reasoning to cope with complex products and environments.

The alternative camp to the cognitive school is characterised as the behavioural learning school where the process of learning and the subsequent 'relatively permanent change to behaviour' is more a function of a reaction to the environment than of the dispassionate processing of specific chunks or items of data. Most expositions of this approach to learning describe three related forms of 'conditioning' in which the consumer is 'taught' to respond to particular stimuli. There has been much discussion about the use of conditioning in advertising and communication, but the consensus is that the empirical evidence using animals has less applicability to humans than first thought.

Following from the work of Foxall (1990) and the radical behaviourist perspective he describes it is clear that behavioural explanations of consumer behaviour hold particular interest for service marketers. Operant conditioning, for example, is a process where behaviour is conditioned through punishment and reward. Simply, if the behaviour is reinforced through reward it has a higher likelihood of repetition than behaviour which is punished. While consumer behaviourists talk of punishment and reward in very managerial terms, we also need to be aware that punishment and reward is an individual reaction and a dynamic state when associated with the consumption of a product like a service.

Operant in this context is any interaction with the environment and is an appropriate consideration for services as a product requiring high degrees of consumer involvement. The reinforcers and punishers can occur in many forms such as the social relationship with the provider, other consumers, the process of delivery or the outcome. Many of these will be outside the control of the service marketer, such as the actions of other customers, the short-tempered employee or some 'backroom' failure. We believe that behavioural learning perspectives on the consumer of services show some affinity with service product characteristics and the high degree of customer/product interaction. This would suggest that the service environment is a particularly appropriate context for further research in this area.

Similarly, observational learning, which is usually categorised as a behavioural learning phenomenon, also has an affinity with services. Many service products require consumers to participate in fairly complex and well scripted behaviours in public. Self-service restaurants, for instance, require a degree of experience before all activities and facilities are mastered. Fitness classes and educational services all have elements of the product which require the consumer to fulfil certain basic behaviours, for example, class formation, moving from class to class, and assessment. All these behaviours need to be mastered before the full service facilities can be accessed and perhaps before the full benefits associated with the service can be accessed. The process of learning by observing and copying behavioural routine, directed through the application of punishment and reward, would appear to be wholly consistent with a product which engages the consumer both physically and mentally in the delivery process.

Attitudes

The last issue in this section is associated with attitudes and how the attitudinal process relates to service products. Classic studies of consumer behaviour have pointed to the interaction between three key processes; beliefs, attitudes and behaviours. Accepting that attitudes are a central component of the information processing school, attitudes are viewed as a mediating construct between what the consumer believes about an object, (person, place, product, idea, etc.) and the behaviour exhibited towards the object (usually constructed in 'for or against' or in 'approach–avoidance' terms).

Attitudes embody summary evaluations of information which are dynamic representations of how the consumer feels on a relatively long-term basis and are framed on a continuum from positive to negative. The simple attitude models are based upon the premise that attitudes were developed sequentially, the CAB or tri-component model talked of a hierarchy of effects starting with beliefs about an object (cognitions) which are then followed by an evaluation (or affect) and ultimately some action (behaviour).

Clearly consumers can have many attitudes towards different objects and a central component of our understanding of attitudes is the need for consistency between attitudes. This is an essential component of a number of theoretical perspectives including dissonance theory, balance theory and congruity theory. For example, a consumer may believe that a particular company is one which emphasises good service and therefore has a positive attitude. However, when dealing with the company they experience bad service and this causes a conflict. As a result the consumer may decide that their beliefs about the company are wrong, or that the episode is not typical since the attitudes need to be consistent.

When we consider individual consumers in a social setting, the absence of any accommodation for 'social others' in the development of attitudes looks to be a shortcoming. In order to recognise this and present a number of technical refinements, Fishbein and Ajzen (1975 and 1980) presented the first of a sequence of multi-attribute models of attitude which included social dimensions and grappled with the definition of object. While the assumptions of the model are constraining it does provide a useful integration of a number of concepts when considering evaluation, social setting and intention in consumer buying behaviour.

INFORMATION ACQUISITION

Having identified the resources consumers have available to them and the processes by which they exploit these resources, we can turn to the first stage in the model of consumer decision making—information acquisition. Faced with any purchase decision, it is assumed that the consumer requires information with which to inform product choice. This is usually referred to as an information acquisition phase which commences with a search of already held information. Bettman (1979) and Jacoby, Chestnut and Fisher (1978) characterise this process as a scan of memory for experiences which constitute a body of knowledge about, or an attitude towards, a product or a product class, as previously discussed. Once it has been determined that this information is insufficient by virtue of its volume, age, specificity or accuracy, the information acquisition phase progresses towards the identification of desired information from external sources.

The extent of external search is said to be dependent upon a number of factors, such as product category experience, product complexity or the degree of buyer uncertainty and on each of these dimensions, services are likely to prompt significant external search effort. The literature on consumers' external information activity is large and concentrates upon classifying the various sources of information, (e.g. Beales et al. 1981; Engel et al. 1986; Westbrook and Fornell 1979; Fletcher 1987), the ability to assimilate information from these sources (e.g. Jacoby, Speller and Berning 1974; Miller 1956; Keller and Staelin 1987; Summers 1974; Wilkie 1974; Jacoby 1984; Muller 1984), the motivation for external search behaviour and the extent of that behaviour (e.g. Johnson and Russo 1984; Urbany, Dickson and Wilkie 1989; Bucklin 1996; Moore and Lehmann 1980). In considering the degree of information search in services it is inadequate to merely analyse the absolute number of sources used, but more productive to assess source effectiveness. Murray (1991) suggests that this approach is particularly appropriate for services because of the additional information burden on consumers. This burden is associated with the sources of information, the nature of information available from each source and the consumers' response to that information.

Information Effectiveness

The effectiveness of information available from external sources is related to the nature of services and the credibility of the source, that is the value assigned to information is in part governed by the source from which it came. For example, third party or impartial sources are more credible than partisan views, hence the popularity of restaurant and theatre reviews in newspapers and magazines. Whilst third party sources can be very subjective, they are assumed to provide an indication of the potential of the service to satisfy and are often used to confirm opinions. Similarly sales staff are assumed to have a vested interest in recommending their company's products although they are often seen to be an extremely credible source of information about other company's products in certain situations. Everyone will have experienced the sales assistant who suggests that you would be better off buying a competitor's product.

In order to discuss the information demands of services, Zeithaml (1981) after Nelson (1974) and Darby and Karni (1973) suggests a framework based on the inherent qualities of products. The framework was first applied in the economic regulation literature and uses three categories of product qualities: *search qualities*, which are attributes a purchaser can determine prior to purchase; *experience qualities*, which are attributes which can only be determined after purchase or during consumption; and *credence qualities*, characteristics which purchasers may find impossible to evaluate even after consumption. All products, it is suggested, can be described in terms of the proportions of the three qualities. Services are characterised as being low in search qualities but high in experience and credence qualities (see Zeithaml 1981).

However, whilst this tripartite conceptualisation of service information demand is useful, there are a number of deficiencies in this framework which have not been adequately addressed to date. Apart from the conceptualisation of products possessing 'qualities' as opposed to attributes or characteristics, the main criticism is associated with buyer response terminology, in particular the term 'search'. This term does not describe information search behaviour as such, but a characteristic of the information, that is that the information is searchable, or as Nelson (1974) refers to it 'inspectable prior to purchase' (p. 312). In the case of services, searchable qualities are said to be those which are associated with tangible sources of information, for example a tender or a price list. This searchable information may not necessarily describe the nature of the service experience which remains intangible.

A second problem with this framework is the blurred distinction between search and experience qualities. For instance, Zeithaml (1981) argues that purchasers can obtain information about experience qualities in the pre-purchase phase by using the vicarious experience of others. In this sense experience becomes 'searchable', since the source is tangible and can be consulted prior to purchase. Finally, the importance of the credence characteristics and the difficulties in evaluating certain services even after consumption, means that purchasers are likely to find some way of approximating the missing information.

In relation to goods, two key responses have been identified: first, the reliance upon product cues which are used to approximate missing information or predict likely outcomes, and second, the reliance upon inertia or loyalty built upon satisfaction in order to routinise the consumption decision. However, both these responses need to be examined in the light of the characteristics of services.

Searchable Information

Search qualities are defined by Nelson (1974) as attributes that can be determined prior to purchase. They are generally associated with factual information which is common to all consumers and verifiable in advance of purchase. These would include location, features of the premises, qualifications of service providers, or descriptions about how the service will be delivered. The key issue is that they do not directly describe the experience which the consumer will actually receive which is at the heart of the pre-consumption phase problem. However there is very little consistent evidence concerning consumer responses to this situation. For instance, it is generally accepted that consumers are seeking ultimately to simplify or routinise their purchase decisions at the same time as minimising the level of risk attached to the outcome by collecting or searching for as much information as possible.

A possible explanation of this apparent contradiction is that the consumer is continually trying to increase the value of the information held whilst at the same time reducing its volume (Bettman 1975). One means of achieving this outcome is to use information which *is* available to approximate information which is not. That is, use the searchable characteristics of services to estimate experience or credence characteristics. This can be explained further using an intrinsic/extrinsic distinction to examine product information such as that used by Zeithaml (1988).

By drawing a distinction between intrinsic information (objective product features) and extrinsic product information (part of the product value but which can be changed or removed without fundamentally altering the product), the relationship between searchable and non-searchable attributes can be explored. Extrinsic or subjective attributes are used to approximate missing intrinsic information, for example price to approximate quality or brand to approximate reliability.

In services there is very little intrinsic information, but there is likely to be a large amount of extrinsic information that can be used to infer product performance such as the appearance of the service provider, the premises, or quality of equipment. This extrinsic information is searchable within the definition provided by Nelson (1974), and as a consequence we can say that services do have searchable qualities, but these qualities are not intrinsic to the product. For instance, in describing the service which the company can or will provide, this searchable information may be used by the consumer to give indications or cues as to the likely service experience. However, an important consideration associated with the argument in favour of product cues for services, is in their predictive reliability.

Tangible cues vary from provider to provider and consumer to consumer. As such, the effectiveness of cues is likely to vary between transactions. Product cues in relation to goods are used pre-purchase and their value assessed post purchase. Where services are concerned, the actual delivery may take place at a different time, with a different provider, with different tangibles or in a different place to the purchase transaction. As a result cues used to evaluate a service pre-purchase may be different from those used in evaluation during delivery or even after delivery has taken place.

The second assumed response of consumers to an information shortage is brand or product loyalty, one form of routinising purchase behaviour. In the case of services, loyalty can only be placed with the provider of the service rather than the service itself. Individual loyalty is built up from a series of successful service encounters with the same provider. Aggregating consumers with successful encounters builds the reputation of the service provider. An important aspect of loyalty in relation to services, which is different from that of goods, is the potential to cement a relationship between customer and provider. Subsequent service encounters allow needs and expectations of the consumer to be synchronised with the abilities and performance of the provider. This process of repeat purchasing is likely to result in the continued and incremental strengthening of the service relationships, allowing the consumer to take full advantage of the potential benefits offered. In the case of goods, the relationship is likely to plateau once all benefits have been experienced and may in some circumstances start to decline.

It is evident that the continued relationship in the case of services also produces a sense of ownership over the service, with consumers referring to 'my accountant', 'my hairdresser', or 'my mechanic'. Equally this may have an impact upon attribution in the case of failure. The amount of investment in the relationship may lead consumers to rationalise failures on the basis of 'just a bad day' since they have experienced better, or that it is their own fault in not correctly communicating needs. Either way, relationships are likely to be more stable in the case of services than goods, not only because of the personal nature of the exchange, but also because of the implied switching costs associated with risk reduction. The implications of loyalty and relationship building in services are discussed in more detail in the following chapters.

Experience-based Information

Experience is regarded as the most effective source of consumer information in the pre-consumption phase. Although by the very nature of services a repeat performance can not be guaranteed, experience-based information is extremely credible and may relate to the service provider, the service class or similar service experiences. The problem for the consumer is that experiential information is the most difficult to obtain pre-purchase. The only sources of this type of information, other than having used the service provider before are pre-purchase trial, observation, and/or reliance upon the experiences of others (see Locander and Hermann 1979). Pre-purchase trial is not a common option in the case of services although it is possible to try one service episode to establish whether you will purchase a full service or a sequence of episodes. For example, it is possible to have a trial flying lesson or to have a free initial consultation with a lawyer. However, unlike a physical product where the trial is exactly equivalent to the actual product, in services there is no guarantee that the rest of the service bears any relation to the experience of the trial.

Observation is equally unreliable as a source of information, since the service is intangible and the participation of any other individual gives no guarantee of a repeated performance. As a consequence, a number of authors suggest that consumers look towards personal sources of information, that is the vicarious experiences of others (see for example Murray 1991). This position is supported by Zeithaml (1981), who suggests that the need for experience information of the service prompts a reliance upon word of mouth sources as they are perceived to be more credible and less biased. In addition the work of Robertson (1970), Eiglier et al. (1977) and Urbany and Weilbaker (1987) indicate that word of mouth sources are pivotal in relation to services. As a consequence we can say that where service is a dominant element of a product, consumers face a number of problems in acquiring and using experience, and that the likely response is an increased reliance on personal sources of information.

Expectations

As a result of the information acquisition phase consumers draw together information obtained from both memory and the environment as a summary of what is known about the likely service experience. This concept has been operationalised by a number of authors as 'expectation' (see for instance Olson and Dover 1976). In their definition of 'expectation', Olson and Dover describe expectations as pre-purchase beliefs about a service. A number of different expectations have been identified in the literature. Miller (1977) for example, proposed four different types of expectation: ideal, expected, deserved and minimum tolerable. The ideal is the 'wished for' level of performance, expected is an objective calculation of the probability of performance, whilst deserved is the customer's subjective opinion of their investment. Minimum tolerable is obviously the bottom level of performance acceptable.

Parasuraman, Berry and Zeithaml (1991) suggest that expectations have two levels, desired and adequate. The desired level is the service the customer hopes to receive; a blend of 'can be' and 'should be'. Adequate is based on a prediction of what the service will be. They suggest that separating the desired from the adequate is the 'zone of tolerance' (see Figure 2.1) within which they expect the service to be carried out. This zone varies from customer to customer and potentially

Figure 2.1
Service Level Expectations

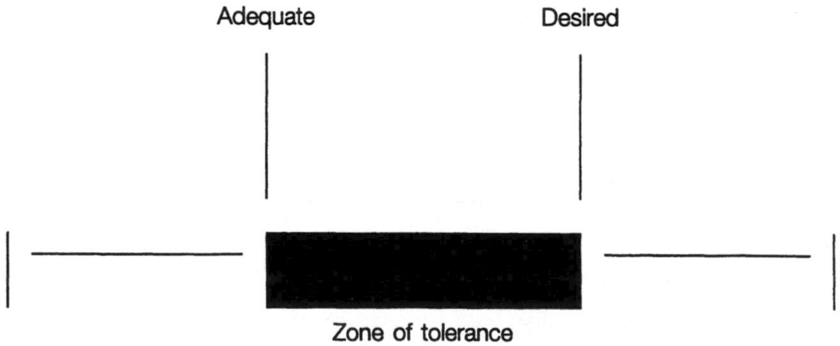

from one situation to the next, mediated by individual consumers' experiences. However, Rust et al. (1993) suggest that there is a minimum level of service provision which comprises the 'bottom line' expectations. These 'bottom line' expectations are those which must be achieved in a service delivery and are common across consumer groups, for example working light bulbs in hotels, or adequately heated food in a restaurant.

In their research Boulding et al. (1993) discuss ideal expectations and suggest that they are unrelated to what is reasonable/feasible and/ or what the provider tells the consumer to expect. They represent enduring wants and needs that are unaffected by marketing and as such are more constant over time. In contrast expectations of what should happen, namely normative expectations, are more likely to be influenced by service providers and are a dynamic concept changing over time. Therefore researchers referring the fact that consumer expectations of the quality of service they receive are increasing (see for instance Lewis 1991) are discussing their normative expectations of what will happen in the service encounter, rather than their ideal expectations.

Comparison

Information search leads the consumer to an evoked set of alternatives that are likely to fulfil their expectations which form the basis of comparison and choice. The difficulties of obtaining effective pre-purchase information about services is likely to result in a smaller evoked set in services than goods. Zeithaml (1981) suggests that because of the nature of services and these difficulties in obtaining effective information, consumers tend to be more loyal once they have found an acceptable alternative. For instance in the case of professional services such as solicitors, there is very little switching. Indeed, if the consumer has previous experience of a service the evoked set may be as small as one (Johnston and Bonama 1981). If the experiential infor-mation is negative, however, or the consumer does not have experi-ence on which to base the choice, then the size of the evoked set will be dependent upon the effectiveness of the external information available. There are various models of how consumers choose between available alternatives in different situations, such as Bettman (1979), Grether and Wilde (1984), Wright (1975), Fletcher and Hastings (1983). The common component of these models is a set of attributes. There are two identifiable problems for consumers in defining attribute sets in relation to services: problems of identifying attributes, and problems of making comparisons on the basis of these attributes.

All products have attributes or defining characteristics. In the case of goods these attributes are tangible, can be determined in advance of purchase and are common to all consumers purchasing the product. By contrast in the case of services, the attributes of provision are intangible, can not be determined in advance of purchase, and are not common to all consumers. That is to say, the individual consumer's needs are accommodated by their involvement in the service delivery. For example in the case of hairdressing the consumer is involved in describing and modifying the service outcome. In the absence of any tangible indications of what the service will be like, consumers must use other means of comparing services in the pre-purchase phase. Shostack (1977) and Berry (1980) point to the subsequent reliance upon peripheral tangible cues to predict the likely quality of the service.

The more intangible dominant the service the fewer clues are likely to be available. Levitt (1981) suggests that in these circumstances it is necessary for consumers to establish metaphors for tangibility or cues that help them to 'tangibilise the intangible', in order that they may create a credible expectation. Various authors have pointed to the role of the environment in which the consumption of the service takes place in providing these metaphors or cues such as Bitner (1992) or Lewis (1991). These would include corporate wear, decor, appearance of service providers, and the standard of equipment or furnishing, and all may be used to approximate the missing tangible product information. The key problem for the consumer is identifying the cues which will most accurately predict the nature of the service experience.

The second issue for consumers is in comparing service alternatives on the basis of common attributes. Services can not be compared simultaneously, but can only be compared in series, not parallel, that is a consumer can not put two services side by side at any one time. Added to this time dimension is the problem of heterogeneity. The absence of truly common attributes implies that services are non-comparable products. Johnson (1984) suggests that faced with non-comparable product alternatives the consumer will search for the basis of a comparison by moving to more abstract product attributes, for example necessity, social status or entertainment value. In the case of services, non-comparability is likely to evoke a reverse form of abstraction where services are compared on increasingly material or tangible criteria until there is little left to compare other than the service provider as the ultimate physical embodiment of the service.

Another characteristic of service dominant products is that some attributes are bargainable, in the sense that they are determined between provider and consumer. Brucks and Shurr (1990) define bargaining as a process whereby two or more parties mutually define one or more attribute values for a product. For instance, in the case of insurance services the terms of the offering are negotiated before delivery. The bargainable nature of some service attributes serves to emphasise the uncertainty of the comparison process. This factor also has implications for the number of alternatives compared, where bargainability reduces the number of alternatives as well as significantly reducing the number of attributes used in the comparison process.

That which is being assessed in the case of a service is the perceived benefit from the service, rather than the service itself. The consumer is choosing between their own subjective assessments of the likely service outcome. Comparison is hampered further by the hetero-geneity of service provision and the difficulties in identifying or generating attributes upon which to base a choice.

CONCLUSION

This chapter has investigated the implications for consumers in the pre-consumption phase of services products. Drawing upon the body of knowledge which explains consumer behaviour in relation to goods, this suggests problems for consumers in making consumption decisions in services. It is our contention that consumer responses to the problems associated with service require specific consideration due to the nature of the service product. Without this consideration service managers may be in danger of pursuing provider-orientated solutions to the problems perceived to be faced by consumers, rather than truly understanding the nature of consumer decision processes. In the following chapter we examine the consumption phase of services, conceptualised as the service encounter.

REFERENCES

Antil, J.H. (1984) 'Conceptualization and Operationalization of Involvement', in Kinnear, T.C. (ed.) *Advances in Consumer Research*, 11, Provo UT: Association for Consumer Research, pp. 203–209.

Assael, H. (1981) *Consumer Behaviour*, (New York: Wadsworth).

Batra, R. and Ray, M.L. (1985) 'How Advertising Works at Contact', in Alwitt, L. and Mitchell, A. (eds) *Psychological Processes and Advertising Effects: Theory, Research and Applications.* (New Jersey: Erlbraum), pp. 13–39.

Beales, H. et al. (1981) 'Consumer Search and Public Policy', *Journal of Consumer Research*, 8 (June), pp. 11–22.

Berry, L.L. (1980) 'Services Marketing is Different', *Business* (May–June), pp. 24–29.

Bettinghaus, E. and Cody, M. (1987) *Persuasive Communication* (New York: Holt, Rinehart & Winston).

Bettman, J. (1975) 'Issues in designing consumer information environments', *Journal of Consumer Research*, 2 (Dec), pp. 169–177.

Bettman, J. (1979) *An Information Processing Theory of Consumer Choice*, (Mass: Addison Wesley).

Bitner, M.J. (1992) 'Servicescapes: The Impact of Physical Surroundings on Customers and Employees', *Journal of Marketing* 56, pp. 57–71.

Bloch, P.H. and Richins, M.L. (1983) 'A Theoretical Model for the Study of Product Importance Perceptions', *Journal of Marketing*, 47, pp. 69–81.

Boulding, W. et al. (1993) 'A Dynamic Process Model of Service Quality: From Expectations To Behavioral Intentions', *Journal of Marketing Research*, 30 (February), pp. 7–27.

Brucks, M. and Schurr, P. (1990) 'The Effects of Bargainable Attributes and

Attribute Range Knowledge on Consumer Choice Processes', *Journal of Consumer Research*, 16 (March), pp. 409–419.

Bruner, J. (1957) 'On Perceptual Readiness', *Psychological Review*, 64 (March), pp. 123–152.

Bucklin, L. (1996) 'Testing Propensities to Shop', *Journal of Marketing*, 30 (January), pp. 22–27.

Celsi, R.L. and Olson, J.C. (1988) 'The Role of Involvement in Attention and Comprehension Processes', *Journal of Consumer Research*, 15, pp. 210–224.

Darby, M.R. and Karni, E. (1973) 'Free Competition and the Optimal Amount of Fraud', *Journal of Law and Economics*, 16 (April), pp. 67–86.

Eiglier, P. et al. (1977) 'Marketing Consumer Services: New Insights', (Cambridge MA: Marketing Science Institute).

Engel, F. and Blackwell, R.D. (1982) *Consumer Behaviour*, 4th ed., (New York: The Dryden Press).

Engel, F., Blackwell, P. and Miniard, P.N. (1986) *Consumer Behaviour*, 6th ed., (New York: Dryden).

Fishbein, M. and Ajzen, I. (1975) *Attitude, Intention and Behaviour: An Introduction to Theory and Research*, (Mass: Addison Wesley).

Fishbein, M. and Ajzen, I. (1980) *Understanding Attitudes and Predicting Behaviour*, (Englewood N.J.: Prentice Hall).

Fletcher, K. (1987) 'Consumers' Use and Perceptions of Retailer Controlled Information Sources', *International Journal of Retailing*, 2, 3, pp. 59–66.

Fletcher, K. and Hastings, W. (1983) 'The Relevance of the Fishbein Model to Insurance Buying', *Service Industries Journal*, 3, 3, pp. 296–307.

Foxall, G. (1990) *Consumer Psychology in Behavioral Perspective*, (New York: Routledge).

Fram, E. and DuBrin, A. (1988) 'The time guarantee in action: some trends and opportunities', *Journal of Consumer Marketing*, (Fall), pp. 53–60.

Gabbott, M. (1996) 'Don't Just Sit There – Stand up and Talk to Me: Interpersonal Orientation and Service Technology Marketing Theory and Applications', AMA Winter Educators Conference, Edward Blain and Wagner Kamakura (eds), (Chicago: AMA), pp. 324–332.

Graham, R. (1981) 'The Role of Perception of Time in Consumer Research', *Journal of Consumer Research*, 7 (March), pp. 335–342.

Greenwald, A.G. and Leavitt, C. (1984) 'Audience Involvement in Advertising: Four Levels', *Journal of Consumer Research*, 11, 1, pp. 581–592.

Grether, D. and Wilde, L. (1984) 'An Analysis of Conjunctive Choice: Theory and Experiments', *Journal of Consumer Research*, 10 (March), pp. 373–385.

Haugveldt, C., Petty, R. and Cacioppo, J. (1987) 'Need for Cognition and Advertising: Understanding the Role of Personality Variables in Consumer Behaviour', *Journal of Consumer Psychology*, 1, 3, pp. 239–260.

Hoch, S. and Deighton, J. (1989) 'Managing What Consumers Learn From Experience', *Journal of Marketing*, 53 (April), pp. 1–20.

Holbrook, M. and Lehmann, D. (1981) 'Allocating Discretionary Time: Complementarity Among Activities', *Journal of Consumer Research*, 7 (March), pp. 395–406.

Hornik, J. (1982) 'Situational Effects on the Consumption of Time', *Journal of Marketing*, 46 (Fall), pp. 44–55.

Jacoby, J. (1984) 'Perspectives on Information Overload', *Journal of Consumer Research*, 10 (March).

Jacoby, J., Chestnut, R. and Fisher, W. (1978) 'A Behavioural Process Approach to Information Acquisition in Nondurable Purchasing', *Journal of Marketing Research*, 15, 3 (August), pp. 532–544.

Jacoby, J., Speller, D. and Berning, C. (1974) 'Brand Choice Behaviour as a Function of Information Load: Replication and Extension', *Journal of Consumer Research*, 1, pp. 33–42.

Jacoby, J., Speller, D. and Kohn, C. (1974) 'Brand choice as a function of information overload', *Journal of Marketing Research*, 11 (Feb), pp. 63–69.

Jacoby, J., Szybillo, G. and Berning, C. (1976) 'Time and consumer behaviour: An interdisciplinary overview', *Journal of Consumer Research*, 2 (March), pp. 320–339.

Johnson, E. and Russo, J.E. (1984) 'Product Familiarity and Learning New Information', *Journal of Consumer Research*, 11 (June), pp. 542–550.

Johnson, M. (1984) 'Consumer Choice Strategies for Comparing Noncomparable Alternatives', *Journal of Consumer Research*, 11 (December), pp. 741–753.

Johnston, W. and Bonama, T. (1981) 'Purchase Process for Capital Equipment and Services', *Industrial Marketing*, 4, pp. 253–264.

Kapferer, J.N. and Laurent, G. (1985) 'Consumer Involvement Profiles: A New Practical Approach to Consumer Involvement', *Journal of Advertising Research*, 25, 6, pp. 48–56.

Kassarjian, H. (1981) 'Low Involvement—A Second Look', in Monroe, K.B. (ed.) *Advances in Consumer Research Vol VIII*, (MI: Ann Arbor), pp. 31–34.

Keller, K. and Staelin, R. (1987) 'Effects of Quality and Quantity of Information on Decision Effectiveness', *Journal of Consumer Research*, 14 (September), pp. 200–213.

Krugman, H.E. (1965) 'The Impact of Television Advertising: Learning Without Involvement', *Public Opinion Quarterly*, 29 (Fall), pp. 349–356.

Krugman, H.E. (1967) 'The Measuring of Advertising Involvement', *Public Opinion Quarterly*, 30 (Winter), pp. 583–596.

Lane, P. and Lindquist, J. (1988) 'Definitions for the fourth dimension: a proposed time classification system', in K. Bahn (ed.), *Developments of Marketing Science*, 11, (Blacksburg: Virginia AMS), pp. 38–46.

Laurent, G. and Kapferer, J.N. (1985) 'Measuring Consumer Involvement Profiles', *Journal of Marketing Research*, 22, 1, pp. 41–53.

Levitt, T. (1981) 'Marketing Intangible Products and Product Intangibles', *Harvard Business Review*, 59 (May/June), pp. 94–102.

Lewis, B. (1991) 'Service Quality: An International Comparison of Bank Customers. Expectations and Perceptions', *Journal of Marketing Management*, 7, pp. 47–62.

Locander, W. and Hermann, P. (1979) 'The Effect of Self-confidence and Anxiety on Information Seeking in Consumer Risk Reduction', *Journal of Marketing Research*, 19, pp. 268–274.

Miller, G. (1956) 'The magical number seven, plus or minus two: some limits on our capacity for processing information', *The Psychological Review*, 63, 2 (March), pp. 81–97.

Miller, J. (1977) 'Studying Satisfaction, Modifying Models, Enciting Expectations, Posing Problems & Making Meaningful Measurements', in Hunt, H.K. (ed.) *Conceptualisation & Measurement of Consumer Satisfaction & Dissatisfaction*, (Indiana: Bloomington).

Mitchell, A.A. (1981) 'Dimensions of Advertising Involvement', in Monroe, K.B. (ed.) *Advances in Consumer Research*, 8, (MI: Ann Arbor, Association for Consumer Research), pp. 25–30.

Mittal, B. (1989) 'Measuring Purchase-Decision Involvement', *Psychology & Marketing*, 6, pp. 147–162.

Mittal, B. and Lee, M. (1989) 'A Causal Model of Consumer Involvement', *Journal of Economic Psychology*, 10, pp. 363–389.

Moore, W.L. and Lehmann, D. (1980) 'Individual differences in Search Behaviour for a Nondurable', *Journal of Consumer Research*, 7 (December), pp. 296–307.

Muller, T. (1984) 'Buyer Response to Variation in Product Information load', *Journal of Applied Psychology*, 69, 2 (May).

Muncy, J.A. and Hunt, S. (1984) 'Consumer Involvement: Definition Issues and Research Directions', in Kinnear, T.C. (ed.) *Advances in Consumer Research*, 11, (Provo UT: Association for Consumer Research), pp. 193–195.

Murray, K. (1991) 'A Test of Services Marketing Theory: Consumer Information Acquisition Activities', *Journal of Marketing*, 55 (January), pp. 10–25.

Murray, K. and Schlacter, J. (1990) 'The impact of goods versus services on consumer's assessments of perceived risk and variablility', *Journal of the Academy of Marketing Science*, 18, 1, pp. 51–65.

Nelson, P. (1974) 'Advertising as Information', *Journal of Political Economy*, 81 (July/August), pp. 729–754.

Oliver, R.L. (1989) 'Processing of The Satisfaction Response in Consumption: A Suggested Framework and Research Propositions', *Journal of Consumer Satisfaction, Dissatisfaction and Complaining Behaviour*, 2, pp. 1–16.

Olson, J. and Dover, P. (1976) 'Effects of Expectation Creation and Disconfirmation on Belief Elements of Cognitive Structure', in Anderson, B. (ed.) *Advances in Consumer Research*, 3, (Chicago: ACR).

Parasuraman, A., Berry, L. and Zeithaml, V.A. (1991) 'Understanding Customer Expectations of Service', *Sloan Management Review* (Spring), pp. 39–48.

Pervin, L. (1984) *Personality*, 4th edn, (New York: John Wiley).

Petty, R., Cacioppo, J. and Schumann, D. (1983) 'Central and Peripheral Routes to Advertising Effectiveness: The Moderating Role of Involvement', *Journal of Consumer Research*, 10, 3 (September), pp. 135–146.

Punj, G.N. and Stewart, D. (1983) 'An Interaction Framework of Consumer Decision Making', *Journal of Consumer Research*, 10 (September), pp. 181–196.

Robertson, T.S. (1970) *Innovative Behaviour and Communications*, (New York: Holt Rheinhart).

Rothschild, M.L. (1979) 'Advertising Strategies for High and Low Involvement Situations', in Maloney, J.C. and Silverman, B. (eds) *Attitude Research Plays for High Stakes*, (Chicago: AMA), pp. 74–93.

Rust, R., Zahorik, A. and Keiningham, T. (1993) 'A Decision Support System For Service Quality Improvement', paper presented to AMA Frontiers in Services Marketing Conference, Vanderbilt University, Nashville (October).

Sherif, M. and Cantril, H. (1947) *The Psychology of Ego-Involvement* (New York: John Wiley).

Shostack, G.L. (1977) 'Breaking Free From Product Marketing', *Journal of Marketing*, 41, pp. 73–80.

Statt, D. (1997) *Understanding the Consumer*, (Basingstoke: Macmillan Press).

Summers, J. (1974) 'Less Information is Better', *Journal of Marketing Research*, XI (November), pp. 467–468.

Urbany, J. and Weilbaker, D. (1987) 'A Critical Examination of Nelson's Theory of Information and Consumer Behaviour', in Douglas, S. et al., AMA Educators Conference Proceedings (Chicago: AMA).

Urbany, J., Dickson, P. and Wilkie, W. (1989) 'Buyer Uncertainty and Information Search', *Journal of Consumer Research*, 16 (September), pp. 208–215.

Westbrook, R.A. and Fornell, C. (1979) 'Patterns of Information Source Usage Among Durable Goods Buyers', *Journal of Marketing Research*, 16 (August), pp. 303–312.

Wilkie, W.L. (1974) 'Analysis of Effects of Information Load', *Journal of Marketing Research*, XI (November), pp. 462–466.

Wright, P. (1975) 'Consumer Choice Strategies: Simplifying or Optimising', *Journal of Marketing Research*, 12 (February), pp. 60–67.

Zaichowsky, J.L. (1985) 'Measuring the Involvement Construct', *Journal of Consumer Research*, 12, pp. 341–352.

Zeithaml, V. (1981) 'How Consumer Evaluation Processes Differ Between Goods and Services', in Donnelly, J.H. and George, W.R. (eds) *Marketing of Services*, (Chicago: AMA).

Zeithaml, V. (1988) 'Consumer Perceptions of Price, Quality and Value: A Means End Model and Synthesis of Evidence', *Journal of Marketing*, 52 (July), pp. 2–22.

CHAPTER 3

CONSUMING SERVICES

INTRODUCTION

In the previous chapter we examined the nature of information in relation to services, and how the characteristics of the service product impact upon consumers' pre-purchase behaviour. The analysis was concentrated at the pre-purchase stage of consumption where the consumer is evaluating alternatives and making choices. In this chapter we move forward to the actual consumption of the service product, akin to the consumer of physical goods walking into the store. For service marketers, the situation where the consumer comes into 'contact' with the service company is critical for it provides what Carlsson (1987) refers to as the 'moment of truth', the instance when the consumer's expectations, past experiences, and previous information about the service product are validated by first hand experience. This contextualised event has been described as a 'service encounter' and has been traditionally defined as 'the interaction that occurs between customer-contact employees and customers' (see Lutz and Kakker 1976, Evans 1963, and Shostack 1977).

This interaction has a number of components, all of which make up the 'bundle of benefits' referred to by Enis and Roering (1981). A number of authors have addressed elements of this bundle, for example Bitner et al. (1990) have concentrated on the physical environment, on the effect of other customers, on contact personnel and the role of the employee (Bitner 1992, Bitner et al. 1994, Hui and Bateson 1991). The servuction model of Bateson (1995) attempts to draw these elements

Figure 3.1
The Servuction System

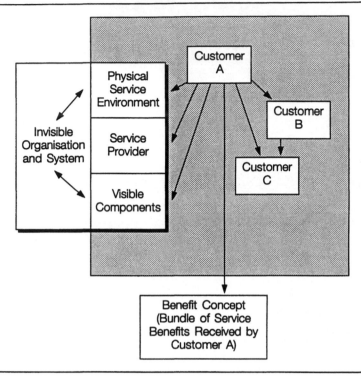

Source: Adapted from Bateson, J.E.G. (1995). Managing Services Marketing (2nd Edition). Dryden: London.

together diagrammatically and makes a distinction between parts of the organisation that are either visible or invisible to the consumer (see Figure 3.1), an image which is repeated in the dramaturgy model of Grove and Fisk (1983) who refer to front stage and back stage of service environments. However, the core of service consumption is the exchange between purchaser and provider, the service encounter.

THE NATURE OF SERVICE ENCOUNTERS

The use of the term service encounter implies that there is some form of interpersonal interaction between the employees of the service firm and the customer. However, in order to be considered a service encounter as opposed to any other form of interaction a number of conditions or descriptors have been established. These assumptions about the nature of the exchange were originally identified by Czepiel et al. (1985) and have been summarised as:

1. *The service encounter is purposeful and non-altruistic.* The effect of this condition is to remove interactions between individuals which are non-goal orientated, i.e., encounters with family and/or friends are not service encounters as they occur outside the context of a purposeful non-altruistic market exchange. However it must be recognised that there are degrees of 'task' as opposed to 'non-task' social interaction which varies by service. For example non-purposeful and altruistic social exchange is common in hairdressing services and some restaurant situations. In these situations one must examine the encounter as a whole. Finally, in order to firmly place a 'service' encounter within the business exchange domain, this assumption also implicitly associates the service encounter with the maximisation of rewards for both parties with the minimisation of costs.

2. *The service encounter does not require prior acquaintance.* The service encounter is a context in which the interacting parties do not necessarily know each other, i.e. strangers can interact within the boundary of the exchange. In a service encounter it is accepted that strangers can be approached (from either a customer or employee perspective) and engaged in social discourse without threat.

3. *The service encounter provides behavioural boundaries.* The precise detail of the encounter is constrained by the service being delivered and behaviours are bounded by information and actions associated with the product. This also applies to the roles adopted by the service encounter participants. For instance within the encounter, roles normally associated with the individuals are suspended in favour of an alternative hierarchy which in turn is dependent upon the service context. You may not like your bank manager as your neighbour, but you are necessarily polite and friendly when asking for a loan.

These conditions are meant to guide service marketers in identifying service 'occasions', but the nature of the service act is so varied that they are necessarily very general. An additional common assumption which is almost implicit in the service literature is that the interaction is personal, i.e. between people. However it is clear that the 'personal' component is a sufficient but not a necessary condition to characterise a service encounter. For instance, an encounter between a machine and a customer may fulfil all the conditions identified by Czepiel above and may therefore be a service encounter, but it is definitely not a personal interaction. As a means of accommodating the increasing instances of 'person/machine' encounters, an alternative definition provided by Shostack (1985) allows for a broader perspective—'a period of time during which a consumer directly interacts with a service'. This definition allows all aspects of the service firm to be included, including not only personnel but physical facilities, and other visible elements of the encounter. This approach includes everything that happens within the time frame during which the consumer directly interacts with the service firm. An alternative, perhaps more operationally based, is the time frame within which the consumer forms a first-hand impression of the service provider.

There is little debate that service encounters are central to the service experience, and consequently have been the subject of extensive research (see for instance Bitner et al. 1990, Czepiel 1985, Suprenant and Solomon 1987). Most of this research has concentrated upon interactive exchanges, i.e., face-to-face encounters between two persons, although Bateson (1985) talks of a three-cornered fight between partially conflicting parties; the customer, the server and the service firm as embodied in the environment and rules and procedures it creates for the service encounter. As a consequence understanding service encounters involves an appreciation of a complex set of behaviours from all parties and interactions which vary significantly from service to service. According to Klaus (1985) the service encounter should be defined as an 'epiphenomenon', a consequence of a delicate configuration of elements which taken together comprise the experience. From this perspective it is impossible to define all the attributes of a good and bad encounter, except that as individuals we

64

know them when they are experienced. This is similar to defining what is attractive about a landscape or a work of art, but we know what we like when we see it. Despite this characteristic of the encounter, in this chapter we attempt to identify a number of dimensions which can be used to characterise service encounters and consider some of the common components. This analysis provides a basis for exploring situated consumer behaviour in services, but is clearly not exhaustive.

DIMENSIONS OF THE SERVICE ENCOUNTER

As a starting point for discussing consumer behaviour in this context, various dimensions of the service encounter will be examined which impact upon consumption behaviour. Clearly in such a complex consumption situation including interpersonal behaviour, differences in process and alternate environments, it is invidious to have to categorise or identify commonality for it loses some of the richness of service provision. However, we can identify five common dimensions applicable to all encounters as: temporal duration (see Lovelock 1995), the physical proximity of the participants (see Bitner, Booms and Tetrault 1990, Zeithaml and Bitner 1996), participation (Zeithaml and Gilly 1987), the degree of emotional or cognitive involvement (see Price, Arnould and Tierney 1995 or Murray 1991), and the degree of customisation (Lovelock 1985). The effect upon consumers of each of these dimensions will be considered in turn.

Time

Across the range of service products we can identify service encounters which are both short and discrete on the one hand, and long and repetitive on the other. This defines the first continuum upon which the service encounter can be discriminated. There has been a tendency in published research to date to concentrate upon short and discrete encounters simply because they offer less methodological and conceptual challenges, but increasingly it is the long encounters with many interactions with service personnel which characterise many of the most important consumer services such as health care, travel, financial services and education. However, it is important that the encounter (the direct interaction between service provider and customer) is also seen in context. To enable the position of the encounter to be understood it is worth distinguishing single encounter and multiple encounter services. In single encounter services, for example dry cleaning services or hairdressing, a single transaction is bounded by a single encounter—indeed one could argue that the encounter is the transaction from the customer's point of view. The consumer is experiencing the purchase of a service product in much the same way as they would experience the acquisition of a physical good. By contrast, some services are multiple encounter, for example an estate agency or lawyer. In these services the transaction is completed over a number of service encounters and the consumer may interact with either the same or a different service provider several times before the exchange is complete. However, even in these cases the exchange relationship is finite and it is assumed to stop at some point. This view has been presented as multiple service experiences or episodes which can take place within the context of a single encounter, for instance at a hair salon, the consumer may interact with the reception staff, the person who washes their hair, the person who brings coffee, the stylist and the person who takes their money. In total all these individual interactions (or episodes) offer different and distinctive experiences within a short space of time even though the exchange relationship with the service organisation is finite. These individual micro-encounters may hold the key in understanding individual consumer experiences as well as providing some contribution to perceptions of service quality and satisfaction.

Finally, a number of services can be considered to be latent, i.e. where the service is activated either by the consumer or the service provider at certain times when necessary. Examples are utilities such as gas and electricity, car breakdown services and GP services. For consumers of these services the number of encounters is likely to vary from none to many, but the exchange relationship is assumed to be infinite. The distinguishing characteristics of these latent services are that the service organsiation and the consumer maintain some form of economic relationship.

If we consider these three forms of service relationship two alternative levels of analysis present themselves. First, to ignore the relationship dimension and concentrate upon the single transaction encounter, or second, to consider encounters as micro exchanges. In the first case, the encounter may be very short even though the relationship with the service provider is long term. For example, in GP services the actual encounter may be only minutes, although the exchange relationship is continuous. Equally, some single encounter transactions can extend over a considerable period of time even though the exchange relationship is short and finite, for example the experience of a holiday or river rafting trip (Arnould and Price 1993).

By contrast, concentrating upon micro exchanges emphasises the diversity of the consumer's experience within the transaction. In airline travel, for example, at the first level of analysis, the single encounter service, the product is a single transaction encounter with the airline company. At the second level of analysis the encounter extends over a relatively long period of time involving multiple exchanges. At the third level of analysis the encounter involves many episodes such as check-in, boarding, in-flight service and baggage reclaim. We can nominally categorise these levels of time analysis as the generic, specific and atomistic.

- *The Generic Level*:   Travelling to destination with a particular airline
- *The Specific Level*:   Finding out about flight times and costs
  Booking the flight
  The flight itself
- *The Atomistic Level*:   Understanding flight information
  Finding the right flight
  Check in
  Walking to the airplane
  Service from air steward

Arrival on time
Disembarking
Baggage reclaim

Clearly, in order to examine service encounters from a consumer perspective the level of analysis must be appropriate to the task. Generic level analysis may provide common components but not enable the identification of specific stages in the service process, equally only atomistic analysis will allow for the identification of the full range of experiences which comprise the encounter. Similarly, when studying or researching the service encounter it is important to clearly delineate the level of analysis before comparisons or benchmarks are pursued as every service will have particular encounter characteristics.

Physical Proximity

As was pointed out above, a service encounter has been defined as occurring every time a customer interacts with a service organisation, although the level of detail will vary according to the level of analysis adopted. These interactions, however, may or may not involve the parties to the exchange actually meeting. Zeithaml and Bitner (1996), identify three general types of encounter, distinguished in terms of the physical proximity of the consumer and provider: face to face encounters, remote encounters, and telephone encounters (or remote personal encounters).

Face to face encounters are central to service delivery, in fact Surprenant and Solomon (1985) define encounter in terms of this dyadic interaction. Bitner, Booms and Tetrault (1990) point out that a close examination of much of the service quality literature reveals that the majority of items relate directly to the human interaction element of service delivery. A number of other researchers have also identified the human interaction component as being of central importance to service satisfaction (see Quelch and Ash 1991, Brown and Swartz 1989, Surprenant and Solomon 1987). Where the participants in an encounter are human and physically proximate during a service transaction they are involved both consciously and sub-consciously in social action defined by Blumer (1953) as 'taking each other into account'. The richness of communication in this context is indicated by Blumer as 'being aware of him [sic], identifying him, making some judgement or appraisal of him, identifying the meaning of his action, trying to find out what is on his mind, trying to figure out what he intends to do'. From a service delivery perspective these verbal and non-verbal behaviours are akin to tangible cues identified in the previous chapter such as equipment, dress and physical setting. An additional effect of having both provider and consumer physically proximate is the facility for participation, and therefore customisation, of the service product. It could be argued that face to face encounters offer consumers the broadest access to the service product. In this realm of consumption behaviour, services become merely a context in which to study human interaction and to investigate components of individual behaviour applicable in a wide range of social contexts.

By contrast, remote encounters do not involve any direct human contact. The interaction between consumer and service organisation is mediated in some way by a representation of the service provider usually in the form of technology, such as an ATM (automated telling machine), vending machine or information console. These remote and non-personal encounters do not have the richness of interpersonal communication identified above and present different challenges to both consumers and organisations alike. From the consumer's perspective the non-personal interaction presents a number of behavioural boundaries presented by the facilities offered by the technology. The exchange boundaries are defined by a set of regularised behaviours within which the intermediary technology can cope. The consumer is self reliant in this form of mediated encounter, and must formulate service episodes into behavioural sequences. For instance in order to obtain cash from an ATM, the process must be broken into components such as 'insert card' then 'enter number' etc. The remoteness of the encounter and the restricted form is especially appropriate for highly standardised, routine transactions. Of interest are some of the explanatory variables for understanding technology use by consumers such as perceptions of self efficacy, personality and confidence which impact upon the consumer's experience of the remote impersonal encounter.

The third form of encounter is the remote personal encounter where personal interaction does occur but without the physical proximity. In the past this form of encounter has almost entirely been restricted to the use of telephones where two parties can interact verbally but at a distance. The advantage of the remote personal transaction over the remote non-personal transaction is that the consumer is able to participate verbally in the exchange without being limited by the boundaries presented by intermediary technology. Consumers are able to negotiate, customise, monitor service performance etc. However, it is clear that telephones are restricted forms of social action since they only allow the consumer access to verbal information such as tone of voice, delay or inflection and they do not allow access to the full range of facial expressions and body language that we normally rely on in interpersonal exchange. Indeed as Argyle (1994) points out, the distinction between verbal and non-verbal does not equate to vocal/non-vocal as verbal communication includes prosodic (i.e. timing, pitch and emphasis) and paralinguistic (i.e. emotional tone of speech) signals as well as the speech content itself. Increasingly new technology is allowing for other forms of real time communication at a distance. For instance, the introduction of video conferencing, internet cameras and virtual reality systems allows for quasi personal remote interaction, since a wider set of visual and verbal cues are available although still restricted when compared to person to person encounters.

Participation

Closely related to the concept of proximity is the notion of customer participation. Service encounters by their very definition involve the customer in the creation of a service product. However, we can distinguish different degrees of involvement in the creation process. This can be characterised as participation which may vary from passive

70

to active. For example, cinema audiences are a required part of the core service product yet play no active part in the service other than observation. By contrast consumers of legal services are actively involved in the service. The participation dimension is very closely associated with both customisation and physical proximity since both will have an impact upon the actual degree of participation. From a slightly different perspective, participation can also be seen to be an integral part of service product innovations, such as the self-service restaurant, the automated telling machine and express airline check-in facilities, all of which rely upon the consumer co-producing the service. This is especially true where technology is introduced to the service encounter.

The increasing alteration to the role of the customer in service delivery where some form of participation is required has been researched by a number of authors including Lovelock and Young (1979), Langeard et al. (1981), Bateson (1985), and Stern et al. (1993). In a traditional service delivery system the customer is placed in a particular context or physical environment and interacts with the service delivery personnel and the physical tangible elements of the product to produce a service. Where technology is present customers are being asked to participate more with the physical tangible aspects of the service environment and have much less interaction with the provider. Since one of the most important characteristics of the service product is the role of the customer in its delivery (Levitt 1976, Bitner et al. 1990, Parasuraman et al. 1985, Gronroos 1978, and Shostack 1977), the reduction or loss of a 'person' element to the service may be much more fundamental than merely an alteration in role. Indeed, it could be argued that the nature of the service itself has changed dramatically because of the need for greater participation by customers in the form of punching buttons, entering information, or the swiping of cards. This close integration of customer and provider in generating the product has also been described by Kelley et al. (1990) in terms of partial employment of the customer by the service in a relationship without sanction or control. Clearly such a shift in the mode of participation presupposes that consumers are both able and willing to become partially employed. Research by

Zeithaml and Gilly (1987), Gabbott (1996), Davis et al. (1989), Ellen et al. (1991) and Hiltz and Johnson (1990) all suggest that participation is as much a consumer variable as it is a product attribute and that participation may have a number of as yet unidentified benefits and costs for consumers.

Engagement

From a consumer behaviour perspective engagement with a product, whether cognitive, emotional or behavioural is presented as consumer involvement. This construct has been widely used in explaining different degrees of cognitive and behavioural activity in relation to product choice and consumption. While there has been little exploration of this construct in relation to service products it can be assumed that the degree of personal relevance of the service to the consumer will effect cognitive and behavioural activity in a similar way. The involvement construct has already been reviewed in the previous chapter but in terms of the service encounter we can identify a number of important dimensions associated with involvement which have particular relevance: interest, by which we mean the appeal of the service to the individual; pleasure, which refers to the amount of enjoyment associated with the service; and finally elements associated with the situation.

As with all products, consumers will display different levels of interest in the services they consume. This would apply both within and between services, i.e. one service product may require encounters with a number of different people. Encounters with reception staff will command less interest than encounters with the key professional or the specific service provider. Equally certain services will command a higher level of interest than others, for example entertainment services compared to utility services. This degree of interest may be mediated by individual characteristics such as mood, personality and individual resources as well as the situation in which the service is delivered. According to Laurent and Kapferer (1985) there is a strong conceptual link between interest and pleasure. For service encounters the degree of pleasure experienced is likely to be associated with a heightened level of sensory or cognitive activity which is also associated with interest. A particular aspect of service consumption not fully reflected in existing conceptualisations of consumer involvement is pleasure associated with elements of the experience unassociated with the service product, e.g. other consumers. As a consequence pleasure can be considered a dimension of the service delivery process, the service outcome, and the encounter setting. As has already been stated service encounters do not necessarily require the customer and service provider to be physically present nor to meet at a particular place. However, every encounter will involve a context or physical setting which then becomes an integral part of the service encounter experience whether or not it is intended to be so. For example, retailers have invested heavily in ensuring that store environments are controlled in the belief that they can affect the service experience by increasing or decreasing the level of engagement. Service atmospherics have not attracted much attention in the literature other than the article by Bitner (1992), but clearly the atmosphere of the service encounter will have a major impact upon both the consumption and post-consumption experience.

Degree of Customisation

One of the distinguishing characteristics of service products is that the product is created and consumed at the same time. Unlike physical goods where products are homogeneous, i.e. one tin of peaches is pretty much the same as another from the same producer, in services the participation of the customer, the immediacy of production and consumption and the natural variability of behaviour associated with people means that each service product is different. Schmenner (1984) following Chase identified two dimensions associated with customisation: the degree to which the consumer interacts with the service process and the degree to which the service is customised for the consumer. The former case describes the ability of the consumer to intervene in the service process, to alter the service being delivered by asking for variation or demanding additional or less service. The latter describes the degree to which the service is capable of being individually customised to satisfy particular preferences. For example a package holiday offers a standard level of service. The consumer is able to alter only small specific parts of the service product such as excursions, timing and room facilities, therefore the customer's ability to intervene is fairly limited. Compare this with a service where holiday travel can be almost entirely customised by being able to change itinerary and destination without hindrance. The distinguishing characteristic from the consumer's perspective is the degree to which the service personnel are able or willing to respond to customisation requests. This dimension of the service encounter is typically associated with the degree of personal interaction between customer and provider although specific instances suggest that such an association is misleading. For instance travel agency services are characterised by both high interaction and low customisation whereas certain computing support services offer high customisation with low interaction.

Service customisation is most often presented as a positive product attribute although the act of customising a service presents consumers with a number of challenges. First, in order to impose customisation upon a service product the consumer must have a degree of product knowledge, to know how much customisation is required to meet their demands. This includes timing of the process to ensure customisation is delivered. For instance, when receiving a hairdressing service the scope for customisation is greater at the beginning of the process rather than the end. Second, the consumer must have sufficient confidence to intervene while the service is being delivered, especially where the service provider is an expert. For example, health care or car maintenance services where the individual is highly reliant upon the expertise of the provider. Finally there is a significant risk in initiating customisation, for instance where the provider advises against it, where the provider refuses outright (affecting the service relationship through the destruction of goodwill), and finally the possibility of retribution from the provider for making their task more complex or less standardised. While service customisation is presented as a consumer benefit in relation to services, in reality it presents both challenge and risk.

These dimensions of the service encounter describe the components of the 'epiphenomenon'. They are not prescriptive nor are they definitive since much of interaction between customer, service provider and service organisation is so ephemeral. However, by way of a summary to this part of the chapter, these dimensions can be presented as a means of characterising service encounters from a customer perspective (see Figure 3.2).

Depending upon the positioning of each dimension and the perception of each encounter one could provide a map of each encounter comprising the dimensional scoring. Such a map has proved to be useful in exploring different perceptions among service providers and consumers and may provide a key to one of the enduring research questions in services consumption: the nature of consumers' reaction to the service encounter.

Figure 3.2
Service Encounter Dimensions

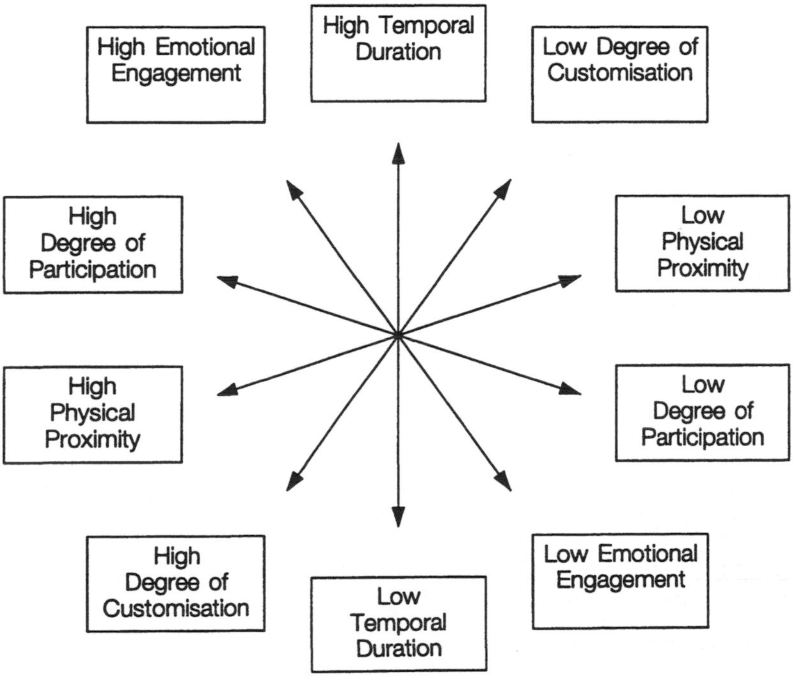

COMPONENTS OF AN ENCOUNTER

Having considered the dimensions of the service encounter and a consumer-orientated perspective on service encounter dimensions it is possible to point towards two additional elements in the consumption experience that have yet to be considered explicitly; the employee (or individual service provider), and the service setting.

Employees

One of the distinguishing characteristics of the service product is the role of people in creating the service experience for the consumer. Both front-line employees and staff who support front-line employees are critical in creating the consumers' service experience. In many services the encounter takes place with a single service provider and that individual will undertake all the tasks associated with the creation of the service, for instance in dental services, photographic services or financial advice. As Zeithaml and Bitner (1996, p. 304) point out 'the offering is the employee'. This approach can be expanded to include situations where there are many front-line employees who may each undertake different tasks, each of whom is an integral part of the offering and characterise the organisation. This role of the employee in embodying the attributes of the organisation occurs whether or not the employees are 'on duty' or whether they happen to be serving a particular customer. In a supermarket situation customers may over-hear a conversation between checkout assistant and another customer through which they will gain an impression of the company. Equally staff who are present but not active, whether on staff breaks or wearing a distinctive uniform home on the bus, will still be conveying messages about the company they work for. As such the selection, training and motivation and management of employees has a direct impact upon the perceptions of customers. This is especially true when examining specific face-to-face interaction with employees. At the moment of the interaction, two human beings are engaged in a quasi-social exchange. They will both be indulging in elements of interpersonal behaviour both visual and verbal to establish power, competence, interest and respect.

According to Czepiel et al. (1985) employees posses three characteristics which directly impact upon the consumer's experience. The first characteristic is expertise which refers to the employee's effectiveness in securing the desired service outcome. Expertise may be associated in some services with the exercise of particular skills which can be assessed via formal qualification, but an increasingly important component of expertise from the consumer's perspective are abilities which are associated with creativity, flexibility, and response to the customer. The second characteristic is what the authors refer to as attitude. This characteristic is associated with the character traits of the individual employee such as their openness, friendliness, empathy etc. The demeanour of the employee, their performance in this social exchange will impact upon the consumer's experience directly. An employee who is sullen, disinterested, inattentive or unable to empathise provides a completely different experience to the individual consumer than one who is attentive, interested and empathetic. This characteristic is defined by Hochschild (1983) as emotional labour, 'the act of expressing socially desired emotions during the service transaction' and by Ashforth and Humphrey (1993) as 'display rules'. Clearly it is difficult to provide training in this employee characteristic and in some instances may cause employee stress through the requirement for them to act out emotions which they do not feel. The final characteristic is the demography of the service provider. While today the term has become very value laden it is clear that issues such as gender, age and educational level of the service provider all have a direct effect on the consumer experience. For instance in healthcare services the availability of same gender practitioners is an important consideration for some groups of consumers.

If the employee is the service product as Zeithaml and Bitner suggest, marketers should be investing as much in developing their employees as their products. However, employees can not be considered as commodities, nor are standardised approaches to employee development possible. As individuals employees need to be able to express their individuality and it is the actions of individuals which are consistently associated with exemplary service in the eyes of the consumer. Currently, 'employee empowerment' (see below) is seen to hold an answer to these conflicting pressures, allowing the exercise of individuality within a supportive organisational environment (see Bowen and Lawler 1995). Given the importance of the employee both within and beyond the immediate encounter, coupled with the inability and undesirability of applying standardised approaches to their development, the relationship between front-line employees and customers will always be the subject of attention. Perhaps as the relationship marketing paradigm becomes more talked about in relation to consumer services, the focus will again be placed upon the efforts by and qualities of individual employees in initiating, building and sustaining extended exchange relationships on behalf of their employers.

Clearly, employees can not be considered as a commodity. Natural and advantageous differences between employees have to be recognised and effectively managed but increasingly the literature is turning to the issue of employee empowerment. The service encounter is shaped in the main by the activity of employees who interact with individual customers. The service companies' employees are in a very privileged position since it is they who mediate between company and customer. Where employee/customer contact is relatively high, a good employee will be able to monitor and control the service delivery process in 'real time', anticipating customer's needs and providing the necessary customisation to enhance customer experience. To achieve this end, the employee should be empowered to act in the customer's best interests. Specifically, to achieve a total customer focus, through culture and organisational structure, they should be able to make decisions without having to refer to supervisors, to be individually accountable for the service they provide and not to be risk averse in breaking away from standard operating procedures to pursue customer satisfaction. The literature of producing the empowered employee/organisation and management considerations associated with the concept is large and not appropriate for discussion in this text but readers may wish to refer to the work of Bowen and Lawler (1992) Conger and Kanungo (1988), Thomas and Velthouse (1990).

Service Context

The second implicit component of the service encounter is the service environment. A number of authors have indicated that the environment in which the service takes place will have a direct impact upon the consumer's perception. Both Bitner (1992) Zeithaml and Bitner (1996) and Bateson (1995) quote Mehrabian and Russell's work (1974) on approach avoidance behaviour as well as the subsequent work by Donovan and Rossiter (1982). This later work categorises retail environments as either encouraging positive approach responses (enjoyment, returning, attraction, exploration) or negative avoidance responses (not to enjoy, not to return, not to explore etc.). Despite the adoption of the term 'servicescape' to summarise the elements of the service environment, there has been little explicit research conducted by services researchers outside retailing on the impact of environment on consumer behaviour (see for example Markin et al. 1976, Granbois 1968, Belk 1975). One of the reasons for this is the difficulty in isolating environmental effects from other variables associated with the encounter. In such a rich environmental context, physical design, smell, sound, activity of service providers, etc. environmental influence becomes very confused. For the consumer, service environments can be described in terms of their layout (see Hui and Bateson 1991, Bitner 1992, Sundstrom and Sundstrom 1986), their ambient conditions (see for example, Baker 1987, Milliman 1986), and their physical content:

Layout: This factor would include the arrangement of desks, entrance and waiting areas, size and shape of furniture, and obvious process paths (such as those associated with self service delivery).
Ambiance: This includes physical ambiance such as temperature, humidity, as well as lighting, colour, sound and smell.
Content: This aspect would include whether the space contained complex equipment or not, whether it contained office furniture or trolleys, tools or food, was sterile or dirty etc.

One way to consider environments is to examine the main influence upon their design. In this respect three domains can be identified: the consumer dominant domain, the employee dominant domain and the exchange dominant domain, each of which will have a different emphasis in terms of layout, ambiance and content.

As illustrated above, encounters can be distinguished by the degree of physical proximity between provider and consumer. As a consequence, service encounters take place in a service facility (also referred to as a service factory). The facility may contain the employee only (for instance a telesales office), both the employee and the customer (for instance a hotel), or just a customer (such as a mail order booth, computer terminal room, or the consumer's own home). These three environments specify different domains of the service experience and can be shown diagrammatically (Figure 3.3).

Figure 3.3
Domains of the Service Environment

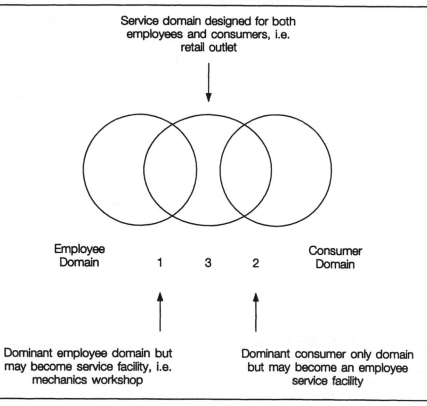

In the first identified domain the employee is the dominant consideration and for the purpose of this text is of little concern. This would include purely office environments or 'back stage' facilities which consumers would not see or experience. Of more significance are those service domains which are primarily employee orientated in design but in which consumers will often find themselves consuming a service, for example the car mechanic's garage or the quick-fit exhaust workshop (indicated in Figure 3.3 by the numeral 1). These environments are characterised by layouts determined by the nature of service task and designed to facilitate service outcomes. There will be little consideration given to those ambient conditions of importance to the customer such as temperature, cleanliness or lighting, and the content of the service environment will be highly functional. In these environments there will be little difference between front and back stage areas. By contrast, environments indicated by the numeral 2 are designed primarily according to consumers' interests but where employees will often find themselves delivering a service, for instance a theatre, or executive lounge at an airport. In these circumstances the layout may be less functional (but this will depend upon the service), and the ambience will be directed entirely towards the customer perspective, especially in the case of lighting, seating and temperature. Finally, the content of the service space will be far more decorative than functional. Between these two extremes are domains in which both customers and employees operate and this characterises the majority of service contexts. Retail outlets, personal services, education and so on inhabit a middle ground, with individual variation on the formality of layout, accommodation for employees and customers in terms of temperature and facilities.

There have been many studies on the impact of environment upon consumer behaviour but they tend to amount to snippets of unrelated information which, while of interest, have limited generalisability. For instance, Maslow and Mintz (1953) suggested that the aesthetic appeal of physical surroundings can affect individual mental states, Sommer (1969) cites research which indicates that raising light levels can increase interpersonal communication, and increasing natural light levels can enhance mood. Markin et al. (1976) present a summary of what is known: that space modifies and shapes behaviour, and affects consumers through the stimulation of the senses, thereby affecting perceptions, attitudes and images which can be managed through careful space utilisation. In total this is very little for marketers to exploit but for service marketers the importance of environment should encourage the extension of this work to understand more fully the impact of physical environment or setting upon consumer behaviour.

EXPLANATORY PARADIGMS

Having explored some of the dimensions of the service encounter it is now time to move to a more holistic approach and consider two of the main explanatory paradigms which have been used to explore service encounters. These are Symbolic Interactionism and Dramaturgy (Role Theory).

Symbolic Interactionism

This approach, which has been developed in application to sociological studies in the 50s and 60s has found increasing relevance to the study of services and service consumption. As a perspective, Symbolic Interactionism can be summarised as a concentration upon interaction between people. Clearly this approach rejects many of the central tenets of our understanding of consumer behaviour since it is not focused upon the individual, their personality, motivations or even their past experiences. This rejection of the passive consumer in favour of the socially interactive consumer comprises a radical shift in approach to consumer behaviour in general and services consumption in particular. The first implication is that people are constantly changing: as they interact with each other consumers are influenced by what other people are doing and are influencing other people in what they are doing. In this way the consumer becomes more dynamic rather than reactive, which sits comfortably with the idea of customer participation in service delivery. A second component of the interactionist perspective is that durable constructs such as attitudes, values, motivations etc. have less of an impact than real time cognitive activity, i.e. the process of thinking defines and interprets the situation and therefore the way we act. This too is reminiscent of the role of signs, symbols and artefacts in the service environment which provide consumers with information cues. These will change according to the social construction put upon them during social interaction. A third component of the perspective is the concentration upon the present rather than the past. This is perhaps the major challenge to accepted consumer behaviour theory for it asserts that we are not controlled by what has happened in the past, i.e. consumers are not acting out predetermined consumption routines, or personality traits. This assertion of behaviour being reliant upon present activity and being influenced primarily by current interaction and interpretation presents a picture of the consumer as far more unpredictable and active.

Of particular interest in decoding symbolic interactionism is the concern with language and symbol. Insights from linguistics and literary theory have meant that simple reporting of interaction in the form of narrative text has been rejected as narrative constructions of a partial reality. Language itself has become symbol and therefore as symbolic interactionism becomes known and used within services marketing we are likely to see service encounters reported in radical forms such as poetic discourse, self voices and extended stories (Charon 1995). The second concern is for the nature of symbols and here the interaction perspective makes a connection with semiotics. The discourse on the difference between sign, artifact and symbol is long yet the basis of the discussion is how objects are defined, interpreted and incorporated in interaction. Both these concerns should be of interest to service marketing researchers and practitioners.

For service consumption, this perspective provides a number of interesting questions. For example, at a fundamental level are consumer behaviour theories appropriate for the analysis of a product form so dominated by social interaction? Further, this approach implies that service marketers have at their disposal a 'service laboratory' in which consumers find both the motivation and the influence for their actions.

This implies that the study of interpersonal interaction between employees and customers, customers and other customers is at the root of the service experience. It also implies that methodological tools suited to the observation of consumers in purchase situations are crucial to decoding the process of service delivery. If the concept of past and present is considered it would imply that far from having idealised scripts for a service encounter, the consumer will alter perceptions and behaviours within an encounter by reference to others. The reciprocity implicit in the interaction approach places a heavy burden upon the service employee and would re-emphasise the need for 'empowered employees' in the service setting able to rely upon their own social skills when interacting with customers.

Role Theory

The second persuasive perspective upon the service encounter is that of Role Theory. The idea of roles in marketing research is not new and has been reviewed by a number of authors (see Lutz and Kakkar 1976, Solomon et al. 1985, Fisk, Grove and Bitner 1992). Developed from the sociological tradition, role theory is concerned with the cues that guide and direct individual behaviour in a social setting. People are considered to be social actors who learn and adopt behaviours appropriate to the positions they occupy in society. In this respect role theory and symbolic interactionism are closely associated. For role theorists, individuals adopt or learn roles by reference to a socially constructed position and by examining the roles adopted one can infer the social construction of their actions. Once the central idea of individuals acting out certain roles is accepted, there are extensions in the form of confidence in one's role, the competence of the performance, the commitment to role, and role identity. The most persuasive use of this theory in services marketing is in combination with a drama metaphor developed from the work of Goffman (1959, 1967, 1974) and presented by Grove and Fisk (1983). This particular approach to understanding service encounters has become known as 'dramaturgy'.

The dramaturgical approach depicts social behaviour as a theatrical performance in which actors perform, to an audience, certain roles. The action takes place within a theatre where the audience inhabits a front region and roles are rehearsed away from the audience in a back region. The basis of the metaphor for services is that the performance of the service requires actors, audience, script, setting, rehearsal, appearances, and authenticity. Further, that by using the theatrical metaphor the roles of individual customers, and employees can be better understood and managed. Of crucial importance to service marketers are four aspects to the drama: the actors, the audience, the setting and the performance.

The Actors

Continuing the drama metaphor, just as a theatrical performance relies to a great extent upon the people on stage, a service performance relies upon the actions of service employees. As the audience, the consumer makes evaluations about the service product through the technical and functional expertise of the employee. Just like players in a drama, the service employee must be cognisant of the need to concern themselves with presentation and communication in their role. In particular three dimensions have been identified by Fisk, Grove and Bitner (1992):

1. their appearance and manner, which includes dress, grooming and general demeanour, all of which contribute to communicated attitudes/mood etc.;
2. their skill in playing their parts or performing their routines, which refers to considerations such as knowledge, efficiency communication ability; and finally
3. their commitment to the service performance which is evidenced by the employees commitment to learn and perform their part correctly and sustain the service performance.

It is clear that industries and individual services vary in the importance of the actor and also of the performance. Industries with high personal interaction, regular frequent contact and which don't rely upon technology are indicated.

The Audience

The second strand of the metaphor refers to the audience in whose presence the service is delivered. Just as an audience at a theatre has to adopt certain norms and rules of behaviour, sitting quietly, knowing when to applaud and when to participate, so do service consumers. They have to learn how to participate in order that they can gain the full benefits associated with the service, for instance being able to describe symptoms to a doctor, obtain a self-service meal or outline what is required to a builder. Clearly consumers will have to learn these roles and scripts and companies may be concerned to ensure that consumers are taught them. This is especially true where the service requires completely new behaviours unlike anything the consumer has previously experienced. Often in such a situation consumers can be disorientated and confused, lacking cues as to what behaviour to adopt. An important component of this part of the metaphor is the recognition of an intra-audience effect, that consumers can affect the experience of other consumers by their actions such as talking, shouting and arguing, by their volume, making the service setting crowded and by their mere presence where confidentiality is required. Finally, one can imagine situations where consumers having different scripts and behaviours may interact, such as at an airport where first class customers may interact with charter flight customers in airport buildings. In these circumstances it is important for the service organisation to manage audience groupings so as to avoid deleterious interaction.

The Setting

The third component of the service performance metaphor is the setting for the service often referred to as the backdrop, props or scenery. Following Bitner (1992), Booms and Bitner (1982), Zeithaml (1981) and Zeithaml, Parasuraman and Berry (1985) it is evident that the physical setting can have a direct impact upon consumer behaviour and experiences associated with service consumption above and beyond the physiological impact of atmospherics such as heat, light and sounds etc. Settings are used to distinguish services both in terms of broad classification and also between similar services. By looking at a service setting it is clear whether it is an office or workshop or other business just by the arrangement of the decor. Equally we can distinguish between top class and seedy hotels or prestigious lawyers' offices from back street offices, merely by the decor. As a consequence physical setting can align expectations, help in the identification of role and contribute toward service identity.

The Performance

This final part of the metaphor is used to describe a situation where the actors, audience and setting are present and combine to achieve service production. Clearly the performance has to be managed by the service organisation to ensure that actors and setting are in concert, for instance ensuring that food services are delivered via hygienic and clean staff and premises. The coordination of the elements goes further to incorporate audience response in the design and delivery of the performance. For instance monitoring staff and customer reaction to new settings and new services. At a fundamental level this would not present too much of a challenge to the consumer-orientated organisation but it relies to a great extent upon the ability of front-line service personnel to detect subtle changes in audience satisfaction. This may require immediate alteration to the performance, an adjustment of the setting, the provision of guidance in terms of role, empathy and support. These dimensions are said to reflect the truly adaptive and reflective nature of the service performance.

In total the drama metaphor highlights a number of important characteristics of the service experience for consumers. On the positive side it encourages a concentration upon testing, rehearsal, coordination and staff training but it also holds some dangers, in particular the importance of authenticity; the underlying duplicitousness of service providers acting out roles which are merely representations of good providers rather than reality. This can easily be identified, as providers are tempted by the nature of human interaction to move out of their scripts and ad lib. Equally performances have to be tailored to the audience. The metaphor gives the impression of multiple consumers where in fact the performance is to one individual at a time and getting the performance wrong can have greater long-term effect than getting it right. One of the drivers of this subtle alignment of performance and audience is the ability to sense and identify mood. Research into mood and mood states has been receiving increased attention in recent years as a significant mediating variable in a number of consumption activities and is therefore included here in the interests of completeness.

Mood

While at first sight a consideration of mood may have been included in the pre-consumption of services, mood is perhaps more pertinent in isolation when considered in relation to the service encounter. Until the work of Gardner (1985, 1987), mood was not considered explicitly as a consumer behaviour variable. Once the link had been made to earlier literature such as Srull (1983) and Westbrook (1980) it became apparent that mood had a major impact upon aspects of consumption behaviour. Broadly defined as a transient mood state, the empirical research was first applied to services by Knowles, Grove and Pickett (1993) who state that consumers' moods are believed to play an important role along a number of dimensions in what transpires during and after a service encounter. In particular these authors point to the potential for mood research including the impact of *a priori* mood states upon encounter responses, the effect of mood state upon recollection and evaluation, as well as the quantity and nature of the information recalled. General findings from the mood literature can be grouped into four areas. The first consideration is whether the mood is positive or negative. Consumers in positive moods tend to exhibit more efficient information processing, and better search and decision-making behaviour. Avoiding the controversy over the subjective nature of the measurement protocols used in the study by Isen (1984), subjects with negative moods tends to exhibit limited decision making.

According to Gardner (1985) the consumer's mood state may directly affect an individual's recall of a previous encounter and affect their evaluation of the service experience both during and after consumption. As Belk (1975) pointed out, situational variables such as mood can moderate responses to different phenomena across the consumption experience and as such mood is considered to be particularly pervasive in relation to service consumption. Knowles, Grove and Pickett (1993) identify three aspects of service consumption where mood is hypothesised to have significant effect: memory, evaluation and behaviour. In considering memory and specifically information recall it is evident that positive and negative mood states will effect both the accuracy and efficiency of recall. As a consequence consumers in a good mood display more efficient recall and better search than those with a negative mood. In terms of service evaluation, mood comprises an antecedent state (i.e. consumers will approach with a mood state) a consumption variable (i.e. consumers' moods will alter during the service encounter depending upon their experience) and finally it is relevant in a post-consumption context (the consumption of some services may put you in a good or bad mood). Finally mood is associated with behaviour although the direction of the relationship is not clear. It is suggested by Forest et al. (1979) and Gardner (1985) that consumers in positive moods are more likely to engage in behaviours with perceived positive outcomes, but that is as far as the research is prepared to go. We can surmise that consumers in positive mood states would seek to engage in congruent behaviour, engage more with the encounter, perhaps be easier to please and serve, prefer human interaction above technologically mediated transactions and so on. Unfortunately, mood is such a volatile and dynamic consumer characteristic and is dependent upon such a variety of inputs that service marketers will find it difficult to manage. All that can be said perhaps is that mood as a consumer variable may hold the key to our understanding of dynamic service encounters and the variation in behaviour, outcome perception and evaluation that are often displayed in relation to services. While we continue to look at encounters as slices of time rather than longitudinally, mood is unlikely to feature prominently.

CONCLUSION

In this chapter we have considered the nature of the consumers' experience within the service encounter. A distinction was drawn between dimensions of the encounter, components of the encounter, and explanatory paradigms which synthesise dimensions and components. We believe the case has been made that the service encounter is central to the consumption experience, and as such is central to the management and marketing of service companies. A number of issues have also been highlighted which are worthy of restatement. First, the issue of time, which so far has had only a peripheral place in services research. As the relationship marketing perspective becomes more widely reviewed, concentrating as it does upon building relationships through subsequent and sequential encounters, time becomes fundamental. From a service management point of view, time dictates opportunities for developing, recovering, cross selling, up-selling and maintaining customers. For the consumer time offers opportunities to develop trust, commitment, knowledge, participation and value. While discrete analysis offers us a glimpse of service consumption, longitudinal research into extended encounters will become indispensable. The second issue is that the service encounter is inextricably linked to what precedes it and what follows it in terms of consumer behaviour. The process of searching for information, learning about service offerings and evaluating different services provides a context for the encounter embodying expectations, learned responses, scripts and agendas. Equally, how the encounter was experienced, emotional and cognitive responses, to people and service will impact upon how the service organisation is viewed. While separation of the encounter into a discrete process serves both analytical and conceptual facility there is no doubt that in terms of consumer behaviour, actual purchase is a very small part of the consumption process. In the next chapter we consider some of the main post-encounter constructs such as quality, satisfaction and recovery/complaint behaviour.

REFERENCES

Argyle, M. (1994) *Bodily Communication*, (London: Routledge).

Arnould, E. and Price, L. (1993) 'River Magic: Extraordinary Experience and the Extended Service Encounter', *Journal of Consumer Research*, 20 (June), pp. 24–45.

Ashforth, B. and Humphrey, R. (1993) 'Emotional labor in service roles: the influence of identity', in Blake, E., *Academy of Management Review* (Jan 1993), 18, 1, p. 88(28).

Baker, J. (1987) 'The Role of the Environment in Marketing Services: The Consumer Perspective', in Czepiel, J., Congram, C. and Shanahan, J. (eds) *The Services Challenge: Integrating for Competitive Advantage*, (Chicago: AMA), pp. 79–84.

Bateson, J. (1985) 'Perceived Control and the Service Encounter', in Czepiel, J., Solomon, M. and Surprenant, C. (eds) *The Service Encounter*, (Lexington Mass: Lexington Books).

Bateson, J. (1995) *Managing Services Marketing*, (London: Dryden Press).

Belk, R. (1975) 'Situational Variables and Consumer Behaviour', *Journal of Consumer Research*, 2 (December), pp. 157–164.

Bentham, J. (1907) *An Introduction to the Principles of Morals v Legislation*, (London: Clarendon Press).

Bitner, M. (1992) 'Servicescapes: The Impact of Physical Surroundings on Customers and Employees', *Journal of Marketing*, 56, pp. 57–71.

Bitner, M., Booms, B. and Tetrault, M. (1990) 'The Service Encounter: Diagnosing Favorable and Unfavorable Incidents', *Journal of Marketing*, 54 (January), pp. 71–84.

Blumer, H. (1953) 'Psychological Import of the Human Group', in Sherif, M. and Wilson, M. (eds) *Group Relations at the Crossroads*, (NY: Harper and Row), pp. 185–202.

Booms, B. and Bitner, M.J. (1982) 'Marketing services by managing the environment', *The Cornell and Hotel and Restaurant Administration Quarterly*, 23 (May), pp. 35–39.

Bowen, D. and Lawler, E. (1992) 'The Empowerment of Service Workers: What, Why, How and When', *Sloan Management Review* (Spring), pp. 31–39.

Brown, S. and Swartz, T. (1989) 'A Gap Analysis of Professional Service Quality', *Journal of Marketing*, 53 (April), pp. 92–98.

Carlsson (1987) *Moments of Truth*, (Cambridge, MA: Ballinger (US edition)).

Charon, J. (1995) *Symbolic Interactionism*, 5th ed. (NJ: Prentice Hall).

Conger, J. and Kanungo, R. (1988) 'The Empowerment Process: Integrating Theory and Practice', *Academy of Management Review*, 13, 3, pp. 471–482.

Czepiel, J., Solomon, M., Surprenant, C. (1985) *The Service Encounter*, (Lexington, Mass: Lexington Books).

Davis, F., Baggozzi, R. and Warshaw, P. (1989) 'User Acceptance of Computer Technology: A Comparison of Two Theoretical Models', *Management Science*, 35 (August), pp. 982–1003.

Donovan, R. and Rossiter, J. (1982) 'Store Atmosphere: An Environmental Psychology Approach', *Journal of Retailing*, 58 (Spring), pp. 34–57.

Ellen, P.S., Bearden, W.O. and Sharma, S. (1991) 'Resistance to Technological Innovations: An Examination of the Role of Self Efficacy and Performance Satisfaction', *Journal of the Academy of Marketing Science*, 19, 4, pp. 297–307.

Enis, B.M. and Roering, K.J. (1981) 'Services Marketing: Different Products, Similar Strategy', in Donnelly, J. and George, W. (eds) *Marketing of Services*, (Chicago: AMA).

Evans, F. (1963) 'Selling as a Dyadic Relationship – A New Approach', *American Behavioural Scientist*, 6 (May), p. 216.

Fisk, R., Grove, S. and Bitner, M.J. (1992) 'Dramatizing the Service Experience: A Managerial Approach', in Swartz, T., Brown, S. and Bowen, D. (eds) *Advances in Services Marketing and Management*, 1 (JAI), pp. 91–121.

Forest, D., Clark, M., Mills, J. and Isen, A. (1979) 'Helping as a Function of Feeling State and Nature of the Helping Behaviour', *Motivation and Emotion*, 3, 2, pp. 161–169.

Gabbott, M. (1996) 'Don't Just Sit There – Stand Up And Talk To Me – Understanding Interpersonal Orientation and Service Technology', Proceedings of American Marketing Association Winter Educators Conference, Hilton Head, pp. 321–324.

Gardner, M. (1985) 'Mood States and Consumer Behaviour – A Critical Review', *Journal of Consumer Research*, 12 (December), pp. 281–300.

Gardner, M. (1987) 'The Effect of Mood States on Consumer Information Processing', *Research in Consumer Behaviour*, 2, pp. 113–135.

Goffman, E. (1959) *The Presentation of Self in Everyday Life*, (New York: Doubleday).

Goffman, E. (1967) *The Interactional Ritual*, (New York: Doubleday).

Goffman, E. (1974) *Frame Analysis: An Essay on the Organization of Experience*, (New York: Harper and Row).

Granbois, D. (1968) 'Improving the Study of Customer In-Store Behaviour', *Journal of Marketing*, 32 (Oct), pp. 28–33.

Gremler, D., Bitner, M. and Evans, K. (1994) 'The Internal Service Encounter', *International Journal of Service Industry Management*, 5, 2, pp. 34–56.

Gronroos, C. (1978) 'A Service Orientated Approach to Marketing Services', *European Journal of Marketing*, 42, 8, pp. 589–601.

Grove, S. and Fisk, R. (1983) 'The Dramaturgy of Services Exchange: An Analytical Framework for Services Marketing', in Berry, L., Shostack, L. and Upah, G. (eds) *Emerging Perspectives on Services Marketing*, (Chicago: AMA), pp. 45–49.

Hiltz, S. and Johnson, K. (1990) 'User Satisfaction with Computer Mediated Communication Systems', *Management Science*, 36, 6, pp. 739–764.

Hochschild, A. (1983) 'The Managed Heart: Commercialisation of Human Feeling', (Berkeley: University of California Press), referenced in Czepiel et al. (1985), op cit.

Hui, M. and Bateson, J. (1991) 'Perceived Control and the Effects of Crowding and Consumer Choice on the Service Experience', *Journal of Consumer Research*, 18, 2, pp. 174–184.

Isen, A. (1984) 'The Influence of Positive Affect on Decision Making and Cognitive Organisation', in Kinnear, T. (ed.) *Advances in Consumer Research*, XI ACR, Provo UT, pp. 534–537.

Kelley, S., Donnelly, J. and Skinner, S. (1990) 'Customer Participation in Service Production and Delivery', *Journal of Retailing*, 66, 3, pp. 315–335.

Klaus (1985) 'Quality Epiphenomenon: The Conceptual Understanding of Quality in Face to Face Service Encounters', in Czepiel, J., Solomon, M. and Surprenant, C. (eds) *The Service Encounter: Managing Employee/Customer Interaction in Service Businesses*, (MA: Lexington Books), pp. 17–33.

Knowles, P., Grove, S. and Pickett, G. (1993) 'Mood and the Service Customer', *Journal of Services Marketing*, 7, 4, pp. 41–52.

Langeard, E., Bateson, J., Lovelock, C. et al. (1981) 'Marketing of Services: New Insights From Consumers and Managers', *Marketing Science Institute*, Report No. 81–104.

Laurent, G. and Kapferer, J.N. (1985) 'Measuring Consumer Involvement Profiles', *Journal of Marketing Research*, 22, 1, pp. 41–53.

Levitt, T. (1976) 'The Industrialisation of Services', *Harvard Business Review* (September–October), pp. 63–74.

Lovelock, C. (1995) *Services Marketing*, (New York: Prentice Hall).

Lovelock, C. and Young, R. (1979) 'Look to Consumers to Increase Productivity', *Harvard Business Review*, 57 (May–June), pp. 168–178.

Lutz, R. and Kakkar, P. (1976) 'Situational Influence in Interpersonal Persuasion', in Anderson, B.B. (ed.) *Advances in Consumer Research*, 3 (Cincinnati: Association for Consumer Research), pp. 370–378.

Markin, R., Lillis, C. and Narayana, C. (1976) 'Social-Psychological Significance of Store Space', *Journal of Retailing*, 52 (Spring), pp. 43–54.

Maslow, A. and Mintz, N. (1953) 'Effects of Aesthetic Surroundings', *Journal of Psychology*, 14, pp. 247–254.

Mehrabian, A. and Russell, J. (1974) 'An Approach to Environmental Psychology', (Cambridge MA: MIT Press).

Milliman, R. (1986) 'The Influence of Background Music on the Behaviour of Restaurant Patrons', *Journal of Consumer Research*, 13 (September), pp. 286–289.

Mills, P., Chase, R. and Margulies, N. (1983) 'Motivating the Client/Employee System as a Service Production Strategy', *Academy of Management Review*, 8, 2, pp. 301–310.

Murray, K. (1991) 'A Test of Services Marketing Theory: Consumer Information Acquisition Activities', *Journal of Marketing*, 55 (January), pp. 10–25.

Parasuraman, A., Zeithaml, V. and Berry, L. (1985) 'A Conceptual Model of Service Quality and its Implications for Future Research', *Journal of Marketing*, 49 (Fall), pp. 41–50.

Price, L. and Arnould, E. (1993) 'River Magic: Extraordinary Experience and the Extended Service Encounter', *Journal of Consumer Research*, 20 (June), pp. 25–45.

Price, L.L., Arnould, E.J. and Tierney, P. (1995) 'Going to extremes: Managing service encounters and assessing provider performance', *Journal of Marketing*, 59, 2, pp. 83–97.

Quelch, J. and Ash, S. (1991) 'Consumer Satisfaction with Professional Services', in Donnelly, J. and George, W. (eds) *Marketing of Services*, (Chicago: AMA), pp. 82–85.

Shostack, L. (1977) 'Breaking Free From Product Marketing', *Journal of Marketing*, 41 (April), pp. 73–80.

Shostack, L. (1985) 'Planning the Service Encounter', in Czepiel, J., Solomon, M. and Surprenant, C. (eds) *The Service Encounter*, (Lexington, Mass: Lexington Books).

Solomon, M.R. et al. (1985) 'A role theory perspective on dyadic interactions: The service encounter', *Journal of Marketing*, 49 (Winter), pp. 99–111.

Sommer, R. (1969) *Personal Space: The Behavioural Basis of Design*, (NY: Prentice Hall).

Srull, T. (1983) 'Affect and Memory: The Impact of Affective Reactions in Advertising on the Representation of Product Information in Memory', in Bagozzi, R. and Tybout, A. (eds) *Advances in Consumer Research*, X, (ACR: Ann Arbor), pp. 520–525.

Stern, B., Gould, S. and Tewari, S. (1993) 'Sex-typed Service Images: An Empirical Investigation of Self-Service Variables', *The Service Industries Journal*, 13, 3, pp. 74–96.

Surprenant, C. and Solomon, M. (1987) 'Predictability and Personalisation in the Service Encounter', *Journal of Marketing*, 51 (March), pp. 86–96.

Thomas, K. and Velthouse, B. (1990) 'Cognitive Elements of Empowerment: An Interpretive Model of Intrinsic Task Motivation', *Academy of Management Review*, 15, 4, pp. 666–681.

Westbrook, R. (1980) 'Intrapersonal Affective Influences on Consumer Satisfaction with Products', *Journal of Consumer Research*, 7 (June), pp. 49–58.

Zeithaml, V. (1981) 'How Consumer Evaluation Processes Differ Between Goods and Services', in Donnelly, J.H. and George, W.R. (eds) *Marketing of Services*, (Chicago: AMA).

Zeithaml, V. and Bitner, M. (1996) *Services Management*, (New York: McGraw Hill).

Zeithaml, V. and Gilly, M. (1987) 'Characteristics Affecting the Acceptance of Retailing Technologies: A Comparison of Elderly and Non Elderly Consumers', *Journal of Retailing*, 63 (Spring), pp. 49–68.

Zeithaml, V., Parasuraman, A. and Berry, L. (1985) 'Problems and Strategies in Services Marketing', *Journal of Marketing*, 49 (Spring), pp. 33–46.

CHAPTER 4

EVALUATING SERVICES

INTRODUCTION

The final part of the model presented in Chapter 1 is the evaluation of the service received. Once again, in comparison with physical goods, service evaluation is a complex phenomenon, primarily because there is no single post-consumption phase. Existing consumer behaviour literature points to a post-purchase phase comprising the steady depletion of the physical product. This reflects the normal course of events where the consumer purchases a product and then consumes it. In these circumstances the evaluation takes place post-purchase, by which we mean after the exchange transaction. With services, the purchase can take place at any time before, during or after consumption. Therefore the 'post-purchase' focus of consumer behaviour literature does not have ready application to service consumers as it concentrates explicitly upon the outcome of the exchange rather than the exchange itself. As a consequence we refer to evaluation, which is less time specific and is related to both the process of consumption as well as the outcome of service delivery. The basis of this is the consumer's constant evaluation of the process during the service delivery followed by an outcome evaluation after the service has been delivered.

Zeithaml, Parasuraman and Berry (1990), who point to an evaluative relationship between these two aspects of the service product, suggest that the service outcome is vital in determining consumer satisfaction, but that the 'process' will be re-evaluated in light of the 'outcome'. This implies that if a service fails to deliver what it is designed to achieve, getting the process of delivery right will not be enough. There is a suggestion from the physical goods literature of a process/outcome relationship between evaluation during the pre-purchase phase and the consumption/depletion phase. This is normally conceptualised as a feedback loop, where the process of selection is evaluated in terms of the satisfaction received from the purchase. Development of this approach has been almost entirely within the services literature. The identification of two evaluative dimensions to a product has intuitive appeal, for example if a mechanic fails to mend a car, the fact that the surroundings were pleasant is unlikely to compensate. However, it raises a number of interesting issues about the meaning of evaluation in the services context, what constitutes an outcome, the relationship between outcome and process, and how overall evaluations are determined.

As a way of structuring this chapter, and as a way of avoiding the need to describe the overall arrangement of the evaluative components repetitively, we present a summary diagram in Figure 4.1. The first point to note is the parallel, rather than sequential, positioning of service delivery (i.e. the process) and service evaluation (i.e. the evaluation). This implies that evaluation is taking place from the earliest part of the transaction, possibly before the encounter, and is likely to include specific encounters, elements of the process and outcomes. Secondly, an important distinction is made between evaluation of the outcome (i.e. the level of satisfaction) and evaluation of the process (i.e. perceived quality), which is the basis of the evaluative asymmetry referred to by Zeithaml et al. (1990). Finally, the model identifies complaint and service recovery activity as additional variables in determining intention to repurchase. This model provides the structure for the following discussion.

SERVICE EVALUATION

The first issue to be considered is the meaning of 'evaluation'. According to the *Oxford English Dictionary* the act of evaluation is 'to

Figure 4.1
Evaluation Model

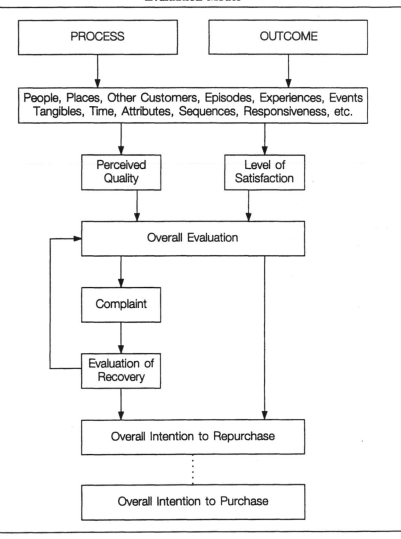

assess or appraise something in order to determine value'. The consumer behaviour literature treats evaluation of a physical good in precise terms as both a pre-purchase stage that occurs before the consumer experiences the product, and as a post-purchase phase where the consumer reflects upon the consumption. For services the bulk of the evaluation activity takes place between these two points, that is during the consumption process. Thus evaluation has two dimensions: what was received and how it was delivered. It is not suggested that this dichotomy is as distinct in the minds of the consumer, indeed in many services, such as entertainment or physiotherapy, the process of delivery is the outcome.

A review of the literature on service evaluation would suggest that consumers make two evaluative judgements about a service: 'Is it of good quality?, and 'Am I satisfied?'. The relationship between these two concepts has been the basis of considerable academic discussion. Some authors suggest customer satisfaction is an antecedent to service quality, which is seen as a meta-concept encompassing a general view of a service, i.e. an accumulation of satisfying or dissatisfying experiences creates an overall assessment of service quality (see Bitner 1990; Bolton and Drew 1991; Holbrook and Corfman 1985; Olshavsky 1985; Zeithaml, Parasuraman and Berry 1988). However, this viewpoint is at odds with other models suggested by satisfaction researchers which focus on transaction-specific assessments and suggest that high service quality leads to satisfied customers (see for example Kasper and Lemmink 1988; Lewis and Klein 1987). Cronin and Taylor (1992) argue that the distinction is important because service providers need to know whether their objective should be to deliver satisfied customers who will then develop a perception of high service quality, or to aim for high service quality as a way of increasing customer satisfaction. It has even been suggested that 'quality' is referred to in the service literature whilst 'satisfaction' has been used in the goods marketing literature and that it is acceptable to consider them as simply different operationalisations of the same construct.

An alternative perspective taken by Iacobucci, Grayson and Ostrom (1994) and Oliver (1993) is that the concepts are orthogonal, thus a consumer can be asked to evaluate quality or satisfaction for both individual encounters or for the long-term duration of a service. Certainly it is possible to imagine circumstances where a consumer can recognise that a service was of high quality, but was not satisfied with what he/she received. For example the first class air passenger may recognise the quality of the in-flight service but be dissatisfied with how it is executed. Indeed, some airlines are experiencing dissatisfaction due to 'over service' where passengers perceive that there is too much interference. Equally a bargain flight buyer may recognise that the plane and the service is poor, but be satisfied with the experience given the cheap cost of the seat.

Using the terminology of consumer behaviour, it can be suggested that quality is predominantly a cognitive response to attributes while satisfaction is predominantly an emotional or affective response (see Westbrook 1987; Dube-Rioux 1990). Accepting the distinction, there is evidence in both for some emotional or mood construct at work (see Westbrook and Oliver 1991). Iacobucci et al. (1994) suggest that quality is essentially external ('Was the experience of high quality?'), whilst satisfaction is more internal and personal ('Did I like it?'). It is clear that although satisfaction requires some direct experience, quality might be judged on the basis of external criteria. For example it is possible to know that a restaurant is of high quality without having eaten there, while it is not possible to be satisfied with the meal unless it has been consumed (Oliver 1993).

Although satisfaction and quality are considered distinct, they are undoubtedly related. For instance Bitner and Hubbert (1995) distinguish between hierarchical levels of satisfaction which are related to a quality judgement. They use encounter satisfaction, that is satisfaction with a particular service incident; overall satisfaction with the provider, which is dependent on the number of encounters with different parts of the organisation or different employees within the organisation over multiple service experiences; and service quality, which is an overall attitude or global value judgement about the service organisation. Anderson and Fornell (1991) in their review of the satisfaction/quality debate draw parallels with transaction-specific and brand-specific judgements. They suggest that it is consumers' satisfaction with the service brand that is important, and that consumers evaluate brands as a composite judgement across product attributes and specific transactions, to arrive at the brand assessment. Service quality, on the other hand, is viewed as a higher order construct representing the consumer's overall impression of the relative superiority or inferiority of the organisation and its services. Before considering how either of these constructs can be operationalised it is worth considering the meaning of the words as this throws some light on the discussion.

QUALITY

Despite the amount of discussion in both academic and popular publications, the meaning of the term 'quality' remains elusive. Holbrook (1994) suggests that 'issues regarding the meaning of "quality", appear to pose formidable barriers to clear thinking'. The original meaning of the word, as a defining characteristic, carried no overtones of worth. However, the use of the word has evolved to the point where it is now commonly used to imply some form of value judgement. The semantic confusion associated with 'quality' can be traced throughout the management literature. Zeithaml (1988) calls it 'superiority', Juran (1988) refers to quality as 'fitness for the purpose . . .', and Crosby (1979) defined it as 'conformance to requirements, not elegance'. What all of these definitions have in common is an acknowledgment that the quality of a product in some way rates it against a standard, whether it be real or implied. This standard may be defined by the producer, defined by the consumer, either explicitly or implicitly, or set by other similar products with which it is compared.

Steenkamp (1989) points to semantic confusion within the term which encompasses the metaphysical concept of innate excellence, the economic view of attribute quantity and product differentiation, a production management view of conformance, performance at an acceptable cost, and an understanding of the consumer's preference formation. In fact, Steenkamp (1989) suggests that it is the coexistence of these four approaches which is largely responsible for the confusion surrounding quality. This point is reflected in the paper by Holbrook and Corfman (1985) who blame the difficulty in arriving at an acceptable definition of quality on the tendency to define it in isolation without placing it in context as a type of customer value. To this end Oliver (1993) suggests that quality encompasses the attribute set, in the correct weighting, from the standpoint of the observer. Quality is, therefore, the form of value purchasers receive in consumption events.

There are two broad approaches to evaluating the quality of a product which consumers have at their disposal. These can be loosely characterised as 'hard', i.e. there exists objective quality, measured against a standard by a third party in some way, and 'soft', i.e. the quality is based on subjective perceptions, operationalised in terms of consumer value. For example, how can a 'good' haircut be measured? While some hard service quality standards can be determined in relation to services, such as the speed of telephone answering, the response time for enquiries, queuing times, scripts, delivery characteristics etc., the definition is very dependent upon a measurable 'soft' dimension marginal to the product attributes. In practice most are associated with time.

Service consumers are faced with problems associated with 'soft' quality. That is, determining quality in industries which are inherently heterogeneous, are inseparable from both purchaser and provider, and where the requirements of the product are intangible and therefore do not lend themselves to measurement. In the case of goods which are tangible, attributes are concrete common to each consumer and can be assessed and compared on the basis of actual physical features. For example it is comparatively easy to judge whether a washing machine meets the criteria laid down, as its features can be compared with other similar products and the mechanical parts inspected and demonstrated to be in working order.

The subjective assessment is made by the consumer of the machine in deciding whether it washes clothes to the standard that the individual expects. This will in turn be dependent on how the consumer formed their expectations, including essentiality, technical complexity, value of the purchase both in monetary terms and sacrifice of alternatives, consequence of failure, or the degree of perceived risk involved, the novelty or frequency of purchase, and the knowledge or experience of the individual consumer.

This approach reflects Enis and Roering's (1981) argument that consumers do not purchase goods or services but a bundle of benefits that the buyer expects will deliver satisfaction. This is a user based assessment of quality, an evaluation of the benefits of the purchase rather than the technical superiority of the product. This led Kathawala and Elmuti (1991) to suggest that quality in service is a function of what the consumer of the service expects that service to provide, rather than a fixed objective standard that can be assured on the basis of statistical techniques. The essential feature is the consumer's belief that the 'offering' will deliver satisfaction. The implication' of this approach is that the quality of a product, either a good or a service, is associated with the value that the purchaser ascribes to the product and is therefore a discriminating element in the determination of satisfaction.

SATISFACTION

As Oliver (1993) points out, the word 'satisfaction' comes from the Latin *satis* (enough) and *facere* (to do or to make). Thus the original meaning of satisfaction is linked to an adequacy construct. However, as with the word 'quality', the meaning of satisfaction has evolved to imply gratification and fulfilment. Within the concept labelled satisfaction, Rust, Zahorik and Keiningham (1996) suggest that there are many satisfaction states. For instance contentment (the plumber arrived), surprise (the plumber arrived quickly), pleasure (the meal was superb) and relief (the dentist has finished drilling). Spreng, MacKenzie and Olshavsky (1996) drew attention to the fact that satisfaction must incorporate both the needs and the desires of the consumer. They argue that it is the failure to include consumer desires that has caused the logical inconsistencies in·satisfaction research. Indeed, if satisfaction is to be defined in terms of an emotional response, the consumers' desires and their individual goals must play a part in determining satisfaction.

Several researchers have drawn attention to the fact that satisfaction occurs at multiple levels within and during a service encounter. Consumers may be satisfied or dissatisfied with the contact person, the core service product or any of its attributes, the surroundings or any part of the servicescape, and with the service organisation overall. As a result, satisfaction can be conceptualised as a state of mind that can constantly change and be reassessed over the encounter, or a series of encounters, and is not static even within one encounter. For example a healthcare consumer may be dissatisfied because they have been kept waiting, but then be satisfied because the doctor is friendly. As the consumer moves through the service encounter their perception of satisfaction may change several times before arriving at a final and aggregate response to the experience. The precise format of this incremental contribution is yet to be determined.

The final point to consider in discussing satisfaction is that it is not always necessary to be either satisfied or dissatisfied—the consumer may in fact be totally neutral to aspects of the service. This idea of 'no dissatisfaction' is discussed in more detail below in relation to the different aspects of service delivery and their contribution to evaluation. However, while most of the research in this area has been focused on the definition and measurement of satisfaction, very little attention has been paid to neutral evaluation. For example in the case of public utilities consumers are generally neither positively satisfied or dissatisfied with the service they receive; it is a latent service and as such consumer satisfaction is dormant. Dissatisfaction is only activated by specific incidents which prompt complaint or query. It is also quick to dissipate once the immediate circumstances have been resolved.

REPURCHASE BEHAVIOUR

The implicit assumption in the quest for consumer satisfaction/quality is that there is a link between positive evaluations and repurchase behaviour. That is, that the consumer will favour, or pay more for, one product or provider above another because they perceive it to be 'better' or more 'likeable'. By creating customer satisfaction and a perception of service quality, an organisation can retain their existing customers and attract new business thus improving market share. On this basis what is interesting from a consumer behaviour perspective is not the relationship between quality and satisfaction, but the overall evaluative judgement that the consumer makes about the service. In the following discussion the term 'evaluation' will be assumed to consist of both quality and satisfaction. Despite the above discussion, there is some justification for considering the two constructs together because as Parasuraman points out they have both been operationalised using the same paradigm, the disconfirmation of expectations.

Disconfirmation of Expectations

Disconfirmation theory in services is based on the idea that consumers evaluate services by comparing their expectations of what will happen during service delivery with their perceptions of the performance of the service. This is conceptualised as a 'gap' (Zeithaml et al. 1990, 1985; Oliver 1993, 1980, 1977). When an experience is better than expected there is 'positive disconfirmation' of the expectation and consumer satisfaction/good perceived quality is predicted. When an experience is worse than expected there is 'negative disconfirmation' and dissatisfaction or poor perceived quality is predicted. There is some ambiguity in the literature about the effect of expectations being simply confirmed (rather than better or worse), however the basic premise is of a gap between what is expected and what occurs.

In fact Zeithaml et al. (1990) go further in their discussions of quality and identify five locations for the application of the discon-firmation procedure. These were termed 'gaps' between expecations and service delivery that affected evaluation. The first gap is between the customer's expectations of superior service and the management's perception of customers expectations. This gap has been explored in numerous research projects (see Lewis 1989) and has been proved to be pivotal in ensuring a perception of high service quality. If the service supplier does not understand the customer's expectation of the service it is unlikely that they will be met.

The second identified gap is between management's correct per-ception of expectations and the service quality specifications that are made to meet those expectations, which is a failure to operationalise customer expectations. The third gap is between service quality specifications and service delivery, or the ability of the supplier to deliver the quality that is necessary. This relates to the inseparability of services from both purchaser and provider and the high personal contact between service providers and their customers. To meet requirements service providers must be able to provide adequately trained staff and be backed up by appropriate resources.

The fourth gap is between service delivery and the way in which the supplier communicates with the customers. This gap between the actual and the promised service will affect quality by raising expectations that can not be delivered, or conversely by not communicating all that has been achieved to the customer, thereby missing an opportunity to raise customers' perceptions.

These gaps are summed in gap 5, that between the customer's expectations of service and the perceived service delivered:

$$\text{evaluation of service quality} = \text{fn (Experience} - \text{Expectations)}$$

$$\text{(Zeithaml, Parasuraman and Berry 1990, 1985)}$$

According to Zeithaml, Parasuraman and Berry (1990), operationalising the concepts of service quality and customer satisfaction depends upon examining this central gap by establishing customer expectations, understanding how these expectations are used to assess customer perceptions of the service, and finally how this influences consumer behaviour. The problem with using expectations as the basis for understanding how consumers evaluate services is in the logic of their application. The model predicts a consumer's evaluation of the service as long as their expectations are met or exceeded, regardless of whether their prior expectations were high or low and regardless of whether actual or absolute performance was high or low. Iacobucci et al. (1994) suggest that this is illogical and uses the example of two restaurants, a fine expensive restaurant and a 'greasy spoon diner'. If a customer visits the diner with low expectations of the food and service and in fact receives poor food and indifferent service their expectations have been confirmed, or at least there has been no disconfirmation. This does not lead to satisfaction or a perception of quality. If the same customer has their expectations of the fine restaurant met, this does not imply that both meals were of similar quality, in fact theoretically in this model it would be easier to please people whose expectations were low. This is not necessarily an empty argument as Peters (1987), for example, suggests 'under promise, over deliver' as a way of managing expectations.

In an attempt to meet criticisms of this comparison of expectation and experience, Oliver (1993) and Tse and Wilton (1988) adapted the model to include some absolute level of quality so that consumer experience is conceptualised as being judged relative to some standard or level. Iacobucci et al. (1994) propose this as a way of distinguishing between satisfaction and quality. It is possible to be satisfied if low expectations of the diner are met, whilst still acknowledging that the fine restaurant is superior in terms of quality. This returns to the idea of there being 'hard' quality standards and suggests that quality is relative to an absolute standard, while satisfaction is relative to expectation. Identifying this absolute standard causes logistical and conceptual problems and is perhaps analogous to the CL and CLalt standards proposed by Thibaut and Kelley in 1959. 'CL' is the comparison level based on current options and 'CLalt' is the comparison level for alternatives based on accumulated past experiences, which would include an industry standard, and equates to a quality judgement. The combination of the two results in the consumer's overall evaluation.

One of the problems the expectations—gap model fails to consider is that expectations are a dynamic concept. The model would predict that as better than expected performance became the norm it would become more difficult to meet, let alone exceed, the consumer's expectations, until even near-perfect service would fail to exceed expectations. Logically in these circumstances consumers would be dissatisfied with this very high level of service. In fact it would be impossible to satisfy them, and expectations would fall again. This is referred to by Gronroos (1988) as the 'expectation paradox'. In addition consumer expectations do not necessarliy rise over time, in reality they can fall. For example in healthcare where patients have come to expect long waits, the gap model would imply that when these expectations are confirmed they are satisfied. In fact the typical reaction to this type of confirmation is dissatisfaction.

The Effect of Price on Evaluation

As was discussed in Chapter 2, consumers are affected by price which has been operationalised as both cost and as a measure of value (Zeithaml 1988). Most consumers are price sensitive and when evaluating services make simultaneous judgements about value (Crosby and Stephens 1987; Swartz and Brown 1989). Expecations are, therefore, mediated in some way by the price of the service, either actual or anticipated. Within the gap model this would imply that the cheaper the service the lower the expecations of it, and consequently, the easier to satisfy/deliver quality service. This is patently not true. Consumers must therefore incorporate some form of value judgement, an assessment of what is received for what is given (Bolton and Drew 1991), which is similar to the price–quality relationship that has been identified in goods. From the consumer's perspective price is what is given up or sacrificed to obtain a product (Zeithaml 1988) and in the purchase of tangible goods there has been shown to be a positive relationship between price and quality, i.e. the more a consumer pays the higher their expectations of the good. There is little empirical evidence for such a relationship in services. Zeithaml et al. (1991) suggest that in general price is positively correlated to expected quality, that is the more you pay, the more you expect. However low price is not seen as an excuse for poor service. The role of price in the evaluation of services requires further investigation, but it is likely that it is related to both absolute and affective evaluations (high price = high expectation: high price = high standard).

The Evaluation of Process and Outcome

As we have already pointed out, whether discussing satisfaction or quality, the nature of services suggests that there are likely to be several evaluative judgements made by the consumer related to both the process of delivering during the service and its outcomes. The relationship between process and outcome has been discussed by a number of authors, and has been variously referred to as 'core-peripheral', 'technical-functional', 'intrinsic-extrinsic', 'motivation-hygiene', 'rational-trigger', 'instrumental-expressive' and 'what-how' (see Gronroos 1990; Berry, Zeithaml and Parasuraman 1985; Zeithaml 1988; Lawson 1986; Swan and Comb 1976; Swartz and Brown 1989). The word pairs are not exactly interchangeable but there are strong conceptual parallels between them.

Outcomes relate to the objectives of the service, what is expected to be achieved. Research carried out by Zeithaml et al. (1990) has shown that the minimum expectation of a service is that it fulfils the fundamental promise, i.e. the service provider does what he undertakes to do. Gronroos (1991) calls this the technical quality dimension, 'what' is received. Zeithaml et al. (1991) identify this dimension as the reliability of the delivered service or outcome. In many cases the outcome of the service may be specific—the outcome of an accountancy audit is audited accounts. In other services the outcome may be more difficult to define, for example management consultants may deliver a report, but the key outcome may be the advice given which is abstract and conceptual.

Even when the outcome is specific the consumer does not always know if the service has been delivered in the most effective or efficient way. In healthcare, for example, it is possible for the patient to know that his/her symptoms have been relieved, but not that they have been 'cured' or even that they have been treated in the most effective way. Similarly in legal services the consumer does not have the technical knowledge to know whether they have been given the best advice. In these circumstances the consumer has to rely on the process of service delivery.

The process elements of the service relate to how the service is delivered, what Gronroos (1991) calls the 'functional aspect' and what Swan and Comb (1976) refer to as 'expressive performance'. These process elements of the service experience comprise the peripheral tangible parts of the service, the facilitating goods that enable the service to be performed, the relationship aspects, for example the willingness to help, the knowledge and courtesy of staff and the individualised attention to customers. These have been described by Zeithaml et al. (1990) as:

Responsiveness:	Willingness to help
Competence:	Possession of the required skill to do the job
Courtesy:	Politeness, respect, consideration and friendliness of contact personnel
Tangibles:	Appearance of facilities, personnel and communication facilities
Credibility:	Trustworthiness, believability, honesty of the provider
Security:	Freedom from danger, risk or doubt
Access:	Approachability, ease of contact
Communication:	Keeping customers informed and listening
Understanding:	Making the effort to know customers and their needs.

Added to the reliability of 'what' was delivered, these form the ten dimensions of service quality, which they later refined to five principal dimensions: reliability, assurance, tangibles, empathy and responsiveness (RATER). These five dimensions form the basis of the SERVQUAL scale for the measurement of service quality (Zeithaml et al. 1990). The SERVQUAL scale has been comprehensively discussed in innumerable articles about the management of services and quality and its validity challenged on the grounds of detailed theoretical and operational criticisms. These draw on the general inherent problems of the 'gap' approach, on the dimensionality of the actual scale and on the validity and reliability of the scale itself (see Buttle 1995). What we are concerned with in this text is not the measurement of consumer satisfaction or quality, but understanding consumer response, although the popularity of the SERVQUAL scale means that it does merit some discussion here.

In accepting the five RATER dimensions as a basis for understanding consumer evaluation we must be aware that when the SERVQUAL scale has been used in modified form up to nine distinct dimensions of quality have been found according to the sector under investigation (Carman 1990; Saleh and Ryan 1992). One explanation for this proposed by Carman (1990) is that customers are partly context specific in the dimensions they employ to assess quality and that different dimensions are more prevalent in certain situations.

Another problem with the SERVQUAL scale is that it uses differences in scores as the basis of measurement. Such scores are notoriously unreliable both statistically and methodologically in the way that questions are answered, as is demonstrated by Iacobucci et al. (1994), Buttle (1995), and Lewis (1993). Methodologically there are also difficulties in asking respondents what their expectations are after they have completed the experience. Clowes and Vorhies (1993) note that consumers who have negative experiences tend to overstate their expectations, thus creating a larger 'gap', whilst consumers who have a positive experience understate their expectations leading to smaller 'gaps'. Neither does it take account of the core/peripheral problem, especially as an aspect of choice. Returning to the airline example, if consumers are asked to rate the comparative importance of a number of aspects of an airline, it would be irrational to assume that a variable such as food, for instance, would be rated of greater importance than safety. However, if passengers are asked how they chose one airline over another, they may indeed make the choice on the quality of the food. The safety dimension is more important in absolute terms, but is not a factor in the choice as it is taken for granted. Clearly the criteria consumers use for comparative choice are not necessarily the same as for a one-off evaluation. To understand this it is insufficient to merely consider an overall quality/satisfaction rating, it is necessary to understand the components in the judgement and how they weigh against each other. Inevitably some aspects of the service will be more difficult or costly to improve than others, and similarly some aspects will be more directly affected. The next topic for discussion therefore is how these various product dimensions relate to each other.

Service Aspects and Evaluation

It is possible for consumers to evaluate components of the service product independently, for instance to be satisfied with the situation, but be dissatisfied with the attention of the provider. Equally a consumer may be satisfied with the service process, but be dissatisfied with the outcome. The components of the service product can be categorised according to whether they are part of the process of delivery, such as signs, symbols and artefacts, people, the situation and timing, or part of the outcome—what the service is designed to deliver.

If we accept that services are 'bundles of benefits', then the outcome dimension is based upon delivering the benefits that the consumer expects. However, in many cases the consumer may not know the extent of the benefits provided by the service or be able to evaluate the benefits in an objective manner. For example, the benefit of healthcare is not care *per se* but 'health' or 'well being'. These are difficult concepts for individual patients to assess. A patient may know that the symptoms have been relieved, but they are not able to assess whether they have been 'cured' or that they have been treated in the most effective manner. There is often time lag between the delivery of the service and the assessment of the benefits, especially in financial or legal services, indeed in certain circumstances the benefits may not be apparent until after the purchaser's death!

The idea of 'outcome', therefore, is service specific. The benefits must be evaluated according to what the consumer's requirements were of the service. It has even been suggested that in circumstances where the consumer can not, for whatever reason, evaluate the outcome the process factors will be used as proxies. This would imply that if consumers were not able to assess the success of the outcome of a technically complex service such as legal services, they will use the elements of the process such as the lawyer's manner, the way that he or she is dressed or the other cues that are available during the service encounter to approximate the outcome. The process and outcome are, therefore, interdependent and to discuss them as separate dimensions belies the relationship between them. The important point is that the consumer uses different aspects of the service as a basis for evaluation at different times according to the nature of the benefits expected from the service. An appreciation of the relationship between the different dimensions of the service is vital to understanding consumer evaluation.

Rust, Zahorik and Keiningham (1993) suggest that there is a minimum level of service provision which comprises elements which, if present, do not cause satisfaction, but if missing cause dissatisfaction.

These items are the bottom line aspects of a service which must be achieved prior to a consumer having a perception of quality. To these can be added elements in the service which enhance the evaluation because they are either unexpected or fall within the ideal, or deserved, bands of service expectations. To illustrate this point Rust and Oliver (1994) use the example of a hotel room. If a guest turns on a light and it works this does not lead to satisfaction. However, if the light bulb does not work the guest is disproportionately dissatisfied, as working light bulbs are a minimum requirement. This idea of a 'no dissatisfaction' situation is important when considering a consumer's evaluation and not one generally considered in the literature which focuses on the disconfirmation/gap model.

Inevitably there are certain elements in a service situation that are taken for granted if present and only affect the evaluation if absent. It can be argued that it is these aspects which form the core dimensions of the service, the fundamentals of the service product. Certain of these core dimensions are generic across service industries, for example, everyday courtesies in social interaction. Others are service specific and demand an understanding of how consumers view the purchase. For example lawyers and undertakers must present concern rather than flippancy, car mechanics and computer support staff must have an appreciation of urgency. Some of these core components may indeed be customer specific and provide a means of segmenting the customer base for a service, by customising and adjusting the core service to target particular customer groups.

To these core aspects are added 'non-core' or peripheral aspects of the service that enhance the core. It is important to note here that peripheral does not mean marginal, rather they form part of the augmented service. The distinction is important because it is likely that these elements will have a disproportionate effect on evaluation. These peripheral aspects are the basis of the augmented service offering, the enhancements of the core which lead to a perception of satisfaction if they are right but do not provoke the same levels of dissatisfaction if they are missing or fail in some way.

The important point for understanding how consumers evaluate services is that the relationship between aspects of the service is nonsymmetrical. That is, a situation where the positive evaluation of a particular core or intrinsic aspect of the service is not reflected in a similarly positive evaluation overall. The reason for this asymmetry is that in many situations the core of the service is taken for granted and its presence is a fundamental expectation. This puts an onus upon the peripheral or extrinsic elements of the service product in determining overall satisfaction. This is true in a variety of service settings, for example airlines, where safety is central but taken for granted, and evaluation is based upon hospitality factors such as food or comfort. This does not imply that the core product is unimportant (in airlines it is vital) but the effect upon overall evaluation is likely to be minimal if present and catastrophic if absent. The relationship between core and peripheral elements of the product, evaluation of particular aspects of the service and overall satisfaction is shown in Figure 4.2.

This model illustrates that there are fundamental or core attributes of the service whose presence is a required antecedent of satisfaction, but not a determinant of it. For instance in airline services the competence of the flight crew is a core aspect of the service, but the ability of the flight crew to fly the aeroplane is not in itself a determinant of passenger satisfaction. In addition, there are other aspects of the service which consumers perceive as peripheral to the core product (such as flight service and check-in arrangements). It is the evaluation of these aspects which have a direct impact upon how satisfied the passenger is with the service.

Figure 4.2
The Impact of Product Dimension upon Evaluation

		Product Dimension	
		Core	Peripheral
Evaluation	Positive	**Neutral**	**Satisfaction**
	Negative	**Extreme Dissatisfaction**	**Dissatisfaction**

However, if the core aspect of the service fails, positive evaluations of the peripheral aspects will be unable to compensate. The challenge for service managers is to identify which aspects of the service are core and which are peripheral. Research by Gabbott and Hogg (1996) has shown that it is inadequate to assume that these dimensions equate to process and outcome. This is due partly to the general problems consumers have with assessing outcomes described earlier, and partly due to the heterogeneous nature of service products. Whilst it may be possible to point to the outcome of dry cleaning services as clean clothes, it is not as straightforward in financial services, for example where the outcome may be life insurance, but the core benefit expected by the consumer is peace of mind. This approach can be applied to any service consumption context and provides a strong conceptual link between the process and outcome dimensions of the product and the evaluative process dimensions instigated by the consumer.

At this point we also need to consider what the outcome of the consumption/evaluation process is likely to be. Having already reviewed the literature on quality and satisfaction the outcome evaluation could be satisfaction, delight, non-response, dissatisfaction, or anger at any point following the service experience. Equally these responses could be reversed at some subsequent point after reflection, or a process of attribution or experience with other providers. In the next section we deal explicitly with the situation where a consumer is dissatisfied as the literature on complaint and service recovery is particularly relevant.

COMPLAINT AND SERVICE RECOVERY

As Bateson (1995) points out, service failures are an inevitable fact of life. The very nature of services means that some things will go wrong, either as a result of the delivery system, the actions of the employees or indeed the customers themselves. Service failure generally is assumed to lead to consumer dissatisfaction, however recent work on service recovery suggests that properly handled this dissatisfaction does not necessarily lead to customer defection. In fact Berry (1996) suggests that service managers should look on service failure as an opportunity and develop recovery strategies. However before a service organisation can institute a recovery strategy they must be aware that the service has failed. Whilst in some cases this may be obvious (for example if the plane is late), in many cases the only indication that the service organisation perceives a breakdown in the service is when the consumer is dissatisfied and he or she complains.

Alicke et al. (1992) suggested that complaining behaviour is ubiquitous: everyone complains sometimes. Complaining is distinguished from ordinary criticism in that it expresses a source of dissatisfaction, thus it is not merely a comment on what has occurred, it leads to an subjective judgement on the part of the consumer. Faced with an unsatisfactory incident not all consumers complain.

Day and Landon (1977) identify three responses from dissatisfied consumers: no action, private action and public action. No action implies that the consumer is willing or able to either accept that the service failure is not the fault of the provider or even that they themselves are implicated in it. Private action is of much more concern to the service provider because it implies that the consumer will change service provider and in all probability tell family and friends of their dissatisfaction. This creates a very powerful type of negative word-of-mouth information, without the service provider knowing. As a result most service management texts tell managers to encourage complaint and to look on consumer complaints as an opportunity to improve the service provision. So why do consumers not complain when they are dissatisfied? Three main reasons are generally cited for this. Firstly, that consumers do not think it would do any good. However Alicke et al. (1992) suggest that only a small percentage of complaints are 'instrumental', that is they are requests for redress. Many complaints are 'non-instrumental'—they are made as an emotional release rather than as a desire for any alteration and even these complaints are seldom made to the offending source.

Secondly, consumers do not complain because they do not feel that the service provider would be interested or take the complaint seriously. This source of dissatisfaction is a major problem within large organisations, where the consumer is dissatisfied because their individual problems or service failures appear to be treated as insignificant. This may be especially true when failure occurs in the type of peripheral service dimensions described above. Consumers faced with dissatisfaction with a peripheral part of the service may feel that as the core service is satisfactory it is churlish to complain about relatively minor aspects, yet in the overall evaluation these minor dissatisfactions may influence switching. In service situations consumers, as part of the service delivery process, are often face to face with the service provider and may feel uncomfortable or intimidated due to having to deal directly with the source of dissatisfaction. As Lovelock (1996) points out, there is also a cultural dimension to this type of non-complaining behaviour: in Japan there is a strong guest/host relationship between service providers and customers, making consumers feel that it is discourteous or embarrassing to complain about aspects of the service.

The third reason cited to explain why consumers do not complain is that they do not know how to or what to do. Whilst research showing that consumers who complain tend to come from higher-income, better educated backgrounds appears to support this statement, it is perhaps more likely that individual character traits are of more importance. We are constantly encouraged by charters, guarantees and consumer groups to be aware of our rights and to exercise them. However by complaining we are implicitly requesting that our view of events, people or processes is endorsed by the listener and our standards and expectations are accepted. This is in order to regain a measure of control over the situation. Some consumers lack the self confidence to make such an open expression of their opinion whilst others feel that they lack the technical or specific expertise to justify the complaint. For example, very few consumers have the knowledge to enable them to complain about car mechanics, despite their dissatisfaction with the work they carry out.

The fact that the alternative to non-complaining is described as 'public' action emphasises the open nature of complaining behaviour. Indeed, some consumers have been shown to complain precisely to

118

make a public impression and research has shown that complainers are often perceived as being more discerning than non-complainers (see Amabile 1983). Public action can be divided into voice action and third party actions. Voice action implies that the dissatisfied consumer communicates verbally with the service provider and can be divided into high voice, where the consumer communicates directly with the manager, and medium voice, where the communication is with the service deliverer. However, increasingly voice also includes written communication, either in the form of a letter or the completion of a customer comment card. This type of complaint allows the consumer a degree of anonymity—indeed, total anonymity if they prefer and do not seek recourse. The act of writing a letter implies that the consumer was so dissatisfied as to go to some inconvenience and expense to complain, but did not wish to enter into a public discussion.

Third party complaining is generally made in writing, as the complainer is so dissatisfied that they are invoking the intervention of an independent arbiter to intervene on their behalf or to prevent the type of service failure happening in future. Most service industries have some associations willing to pursue complaints on behalf of consumers, many with statutory powers, for example OFWAT in the privatised water industry, the National Health Service Ombudsman and local government Trading Standards and Environmental Health departments. Research has shown that the consumers' propensity to complain to this type of third party is affected by past experience with the service provider, knowledge of consumer rights and unfair practices, their previous experience of how complaints were handled, as well as the degree of 'upset' caused by the service failure in question (Singh and Pandya 1991). This type of complaining behaviour implies that the consumer is so dissatisfied that they are not content with complaining to the service provider direct, or that they do not feel that the provider has responded to their complaint in an appropriate manner, thus damaging the customer's confidence in the service provider.

Berry (1996) suggests that a single service problem is unlikely to completely destroy a customer's confidence in the firm except in circumstances where the service failure is extremely serious. For example, if dishonesty is involved, or it fits into a pattern of failure rather than an isolated incident or that the service provider in the final outcome does not attempt to recover the situation effectively. As Bateson (1995) points out, consumers expect services to fail occasionally, however they also expect service providers to take responsibility for the failure and to act to recover the situation. Hart, Heskett and Sasser (1990) and Berry and Parasuraman (1991) demonstrate that an effective response to service failure can have a positive influence on evaluation. However in order to recover a service failure, the provider must do more than the original service because consumer expectations of recovery are generally assumed to be higher than for the original service, i.e. the zone of tolerance (see Chapter 2) moves to the right. This means that the consumer's 'bottom line' or minimum tolerable expectations are greater in recovery situations, for example the consumer's original expectation may be that the plane will depart on time; if it fails to do so his/her expectations of recovery are that the airline will provide free refreshments as well as ensuring that the subsequent plane journey departs on time.

A key element in effective recovery is the consumer's deserved expectations, or the consumer's belief that they have been treated fairly. In reality this means that their complaints have been recognised and appropriate steps taken to solve the problem even if the service itself is not recoverable. For example, a passenger who misses a connection because the first plane was late, will be less dissatisfied if the airline responds by acknowledging that the passenger is not to blame and making appropriate alternative arrangements. In these circumstances legality is not the standard that providers should adhere to (Berry 1996). In a recent case two businessmen arrived at the airport to discover their plane had been cancelled and the next alternative did not leave until after their appointment. The airline's terms of carriage stated that they were within their rights to cancel or postpone flights without prior notice and as a consequence were only obliged to offer an alternative flight, not a refund. The case received publicity not because a flight had been cancelled, but because of the perceived unfairness of refusing to refund the price of the ticket, even though the airline were within their legal rights (You and Yours, BBC Radio 4, 5.3.97).

Attribution

One of the problems for service providers in understanding consumers' expectations of recovery is the concept of attribution. Attribution theory, first proposed by Heider (1958), is based on the assumption that individuals intuitively apply informal causal analyses in order to understand the relationships between events (Hogg and Abrams 1988). As Fiske and Taylor (1984) demonstrated, consumers are biased when assessing the causes of events. There is a natural tendency for people in all circumstances to take credit for success themselves whilst attributing blame for failure to someone else. Schneider (1995) suggests that this is because we tend to downplay the situational causes of the behaviour of others whilst seeing our own behaviour as situationally determined. This can be equated to the difference between internal and external attribution. Internal attribution implies that the consumer takes credit or blame for the outcome personally, whereas external attribution implies that the consumer sees the source of the outcome to be outside him- or herself, in either the product or other people. The nature of services and the inseparability of purchaser and provider suggests that this attribution will be focused on the individuals involved in the exchange.

Zeithaml (1981) suggests that in services where there is a high degree of credence qualities and an investment in the relationship between consumer and provider, the consumer may be more inclined to attribute blame internally. For example, if a doctor fails to make the patient better, he/she may feel that they didn't explain their symptoms clearly. This idea of 'forgiveness' and internal attribution of service failures is linked to loyalty and the degree of investment that the consumer has in the relationship with the service provider.

After making initial attributions about the cause of situations consumers then attempt to test their inferences by adding information that either confirms or disconfirms their assumptions. Kelley and Thibaut (1978) suggest four criteria that consumers use to determine attribution:

1. *Distinctiveness*: the event happens when a person is present and not when absent
2. *Consistency over time*: the reaction is the same whenever the person is present
3. *Consistency over modality*: the reaction is the same when the situation varies
4. *Consensus*: the action is perceived the same way by other consumers.

This self-enhancing/protecting behaviour is applicable to both service providers and consumers, however if service providers are to successfully recover situations of service failure then the service personnel must be trained to accept the attribution and respond to it rather than attempt to 'blame' the consumer. This is a precondition to service recovery—in order to be able to rectify a situation the service provider must acknowledge that they have a responsibility to the consumer to rectify the situation.

Effective service recovery is time dependent. Consumers who voice their complaints during the service delivery are more likely to be satisfied with the response if action is taken immediately. Although as Lovelock (1996) points out, real-time complaints may be demotivating for staff and interfere with the smooth running of the service organisation. On the positive side they give the possibility of limiting the damage and creating satisfied customers immediately, thus controlling the amount of negative word of mouth. As human beings we are reluctant to hear adverse information and have a tendency to exhibit 'defensive avoidance' (Janis and Mann 1977).

Just as consumers may be reluctant to complain, so service providers may be reluctant to hear complaints and their immediate reaction may be to adopt cognitive defences, to argue or challenge the consumer or to use procedural barriers to distance themselves from the problem. This can compound the service failure and add to the consumer's dissatisfaction by, in effect, making a bad situation worse, and will increase the likelihood that the consumer will switch. Whereas effective recovery can enhance satisfaction, ineffective recovery can severely increase dissatisfaction.

SERVICE LOYALTY

The theory that a satisfied customer or a customer who perceives high service quality, is more likely to return has been investigated by a number of authors (see Fornell 1992; Steenkamp 1989; Boulding et al. 1993). They suggest that customers who perceive higher levels of service quality (and satisfaction) will demonstrate greater commitment to the organisation and therefore repurchase behaviour and loyalty (see also Mazursky, LaBabera and Aiello 1987; Anderson and Sullivan 1993). Consumer loyalty has received a lot of attention recently, specifically as it has been shown to have a direct link to profitability (Reichheld 1993).

Within the physical goods literature the concept of loyalty is operationalised as brand loyalty, that is the degree to which the consumer holds positive attitudes towards the brand, is committed to it and whose behavioural response is the purchase of that brand repeatedly over time. From a transactional perspective, this makes loyalty measurable either in terms of the proportion of purchases over time or the extent of repeat purchase behaviour with additional input from attitudinal research. The key distinction is the degree of brand commitment within the target group which may well be dependent upon aspects of product and outlet availability. The problem for service marketers is that, as yet, the implementation of the service brand is at an early stage (see Fitzgerald 1988; Turley and Moore 1995), so understanding the concept of brand loyalty in services in the same terms as brand loyalty for physical goods is not well founded.

According to Gremler and Brown (1996) the concept of service loyalty is distinct in a number of ways from the characteristics of loyalty displayed in relation to more tangible product offerings. Their case is the result of several observations which can be summarised as:

1. Service organisations have the opportunity to create stronger loyalty bonds with their users through direct interaction and simultaneous presence allowing for loyalty to develop (Parasuraman et al. 1985; Berry 1985; Czepiel and Gilmore 1987; Zeithaml 1981);
2. There is evidence that loyalty is greater or more prevalent among service consumers, due for instance to higher switching costs (Snyder 1986; Zeithaml 1981);
3. Because perceived risk is often greater when purchasing services this provides an atmosphere with a higher propensity to customer loyalty as a risk-reducing device (Murray 1991; Zeithaml 1981).

As a result, in addition to the already identified constructs of loyalty in relation to more tangible goods such as behavioural, attitudinal and cognitive loyalty, services loyalty differs on at least three further antecedents—the satisfaction experienced, the nature of switching costs, and the degree of interpersonal bonding which is present. This approach is very close to that pursued by a number of relationship marketing scholars such as Wilson and Jantrania (1994) and a more detailed review of the literature would indicate that the bonding characteristics identified above by Gremler and Brown (1996) are incomplete.

In examining service loyalty, the key to the transition from tangible based conceptualisations of brand loyalty to service lies in the examination of the bonding arrangements between the parties. The bonds identified by Wilson and Jantrania (1994), described as the 'glue' which holds a collaborative arrangement together over time, were used to examine business-to-business markets. The beauty of the bonding thesis is that it can also be used without significant reconceptualisation to examine consumer service markets. Bonding is considered to be of six forms acting in concert: goal compatibility, trust, satisfaction, investment, social, and structural.

The first bonding variable identified is goal compatibility, where both parties view the achievement of benefits from a continued association. For service consumers this would include elements of process and outcome characteristics that comprise the fundamental reason to return. While the construct relates to collaborative synergy we would suggest that spatial considerations, i.e. locality, and convenience could be included here as well. The second bonding characteristic is trust between the partners. For service consumers this bond could be easily examined in relation to household cleaners, doctors and and some professional services. It is associated with perceptions of ability, competence, honesty, motives and intentions that together builds a mutual respect and closeness.

The third bonding characteristic is the degree of investment. For business-to-business markets this is clearly a consideration for collaborative ventures although in consumer markets investment may include the foregoing of alternatives, emotional investment such as in the case of doctors, financial investment perhaps in the form of access fees, previous expenditure or the procurement of items associated with transactions such as specialist carriers, adaptors or sports, educational equipment etc. The fourth bonding arrangement, social bonding, is one which is particularly appropriate for the consideration of consumer services.

Social bonding describes the relationship between the supplier and the buyer and has been associated with higher levels of committment. An interesting characterstic is the difference between relationships where parties are forced into a situation (associated with industrial business-to-business marketing) as opposed to situations where there is a degree of choice. In the first instance, the parties may not be socially compatible, leading to a very fragile kind of committment sustained through functional or investment considerations. In the latter situation where one party chose to enter the relationship the opportunities for social bonding are much greater. Consumers often relate the exemplary service they have received from one person, or refer indirectly to a particular service provider. In services which are multi-transaction, social bonding has an opportunity to develop in a natural way (for human relationships) rather than being overburdened by other exchange considerations.

Structural bonding from a business-to-business perspective refers to intertwined technology and sunk cost investment, a development of the transaction cost framework. This concept needs a little adjustment for the consumer market context. The basis of the argument is some kind of pressure to maintain the relationship, whether external (i.e. from one partner to another) or internal (i.e. self analysis of costs associated with switching). For consumers, structural bonds mirror this analysis and we can identify situations where there is an external imperative to continue, such as single store credit cards, loyalty programmes, constraining technology such as Mac vs PC, or bought in (packaged) constraints such as having a car serviced at a particular garage, and the interval required to maintain the validity of a guarantee. One could argue that much of current marketing activity is an attempt to introduce and maintain structural bonding arrangements with consumers. At the internal level of analysis consumers may have reasons for remaining with a supplier regardless of level of service, for instance in situations decribed by inertia. Retail outlets which are physically very close, service providers in markets with high perceived risk can encourage internal perceptions of a structural bond.

Support for a special form of service loyalty and relationship building relative to traditional approaches would seem to be appealing. Not only are pure service offerings different in the nature of the consumption experience, but they offer different imperatives associated with bonding arrangments. Equally, the fact that physical goods suppliers are using associated service to build relationships with consumers (such as Nintendo, M&S, GM/Visa, etc.) would suggest at least some sympathy with the argument that services provide greater opportunities for building long-term loyalty and possibly relationships. One important outcome of this consideration of service loyalty is the need to consider evaluative activity in services in context. By this we mean that the evaluative process and its formal outcome are dependent upon what has happened previously and what the consumer expects to happen subsequently. As a consequence service evaluation provides a number of substantial methodological challenges in which studies concentrating upon single transaction analysis will have limited value unless validated by longitudinal research activity.

CONCLUSION

This chapter has considered the bases for the consumer's evaluation of a service by summarising the characteristics of the evaluation process in services. The figure presented at the beginning of this chapter suggested a number of components of the evaluation process both before, during and after delivery. The figure also identified one of the enduring complications of service research in this area: the continuous evaluation process. The discussion has pointed out the parallel nature of service evaluation and consumption rather than a sequential process associated with physical goods markets as one of the defining characteristics of the service evaluation. This chapter has also presented a summary of the quality and satisfaction literature as an aid in focusing upon the evaluation task and the cognitive vs emotional reaction to delivery. Finally this chapter presented an asymmetric evaluation model that would appear to offer an implementable approach which can link evaluative characteristics with managerial action.

The preferred outcome for marketing managers and an implicit assumption in the consumer behaviour literature is an outcome defined as repeat purchase, or in individual terms the creation of a brand loyalty. We assume that this desired outcome is similar for all market activity though it should also be considered that consumers may be very wary of entering 'relationships' with service provider companies. Since one of the definitions of a relationship is a state in which both parties recognise some continuing obligation, this would suggest that the relationship paradigm is still problematic in terms of current thinking. The idea of differential bonding is one which may be more intellectually comfortable for consumer marketers.

The central argument here is that for consumers of physical goods current perspectives would suggest evaluation post-purchase. A process of reflection and disconfirmation as the physical product is used or consumed. Clearly for service consumers such a post-transaction specific event is inappropriate as they move through the service experience, both contributing to its production and ultimately its outcome. Evaluation of the product can take many forms and occur at many stages, each impacting differently upon the overall deter-mination of service quality or satisfaction. If we add to this process the activities associated with service recovery, and the formation of particular bonds with service providers, what is being described is a remarkably complex form of human behaviour. Such complexity undermines a reliance upon a particular model of behaviour in favour of an examination of context in order that underlying commonality can be extracted to aid in the development of higher order constructs consistent with the characteristics of services. Such an approach requires the examination of specific service contexts and that is where this book now turns.

REFERENCES

Alicke, M. et al. (1992) 'Complaining Behaviour in Social Interaction', *Personality and Social Psychology*, 18, 3, pp. 286–295.

Amabile, T. (1983) 'Brilliant but Cruel: Perceptions of Negative Evaluators', *Journal of Experimental Social Psychology*, 19, pp. 146–156.

Anderson, E. and Fornell, C. (1991) 'The Impact of Product Performance on Customer Satisfaction', Working Paper, University of Michigan.

Anderson, E. and Sullivan, M.W. (1993) 'The antecedents and consequences of customer satisfaction for firms', *Marketing Science*, 12 (Spring), pp. 125–143.

Bateson, J. (1995) *Managing Services Marketing*, (Orlando: Dryden Press).

Berry, L.L. (1985) 'Hidden Benefits of a Bank Sales Program', *Bank Marketing*, 17 (May), pp. 13–16.

Berry, L. (1996) *On Great Service: Competing Through Quality*, (New York: The Free Press).

Berry, L. and Parasuraman, A. (1991) *Marketing Services*, (New York: The Free Press).

Berry, L., Zeithaml V. and Parasuraman, A. (1985) 'Quality Counts in Services, Too', *Business Horizons*, 28 (May–June), pp. 44–52.

Bitner, M.J. (1990) 'Evaluating Service Encounters: The Effects of Physical Surroundings and Employee Responses', *Journal of Marketing*, 54, pp. 69–88.

Bitner, M.J and Hubbert, A. (1995) 'Encounter Satisfaction v Overall Satisfaction vs Quality: The Customer's Voice', in Rust, R. and Oliver, R. (eds) *Service Quality: New Directions in Theory and Practice*, (London: Sage).

Bolton, R. and Drew, J.H. (1991) 'A Multi-Stage Model of Customers Assessments of Service, Quality and Value', *Journal of Consumer Research*, 17, pp. 375–384.

Boulding, W. et al. (1993) 'A Dynamic Process Model of Service Quality: From Expectations To Behavioural Intentions', *Journal of Marketing Research*, 30 (February), pp. 7–27.

Brown, S. and Swartz, T. (1989) 'A Gap Analysis of Professional Service Quality', *Journal of Marketing*, 53 (April), pp. 92–98.

Buttle, F. (1995) 'What Future For Servqual?', in *Marketing Today and For The 21st Century*, Proceedings of the XXIVth EMAC Conference, Paris, pp. 211–228.

Cadcotte, E., Woodruff, R. and Jenkins, R. (1987) 'Expectations and Norms in Models of Consumer Satisfaction', *Journal of Marketing Research*, 24, pp. 305–314.

Carman, J.M. (1990) 'Consumer Perceptions of Service Quality: An Assessment of the SERVQUAL Dimensions', *Journal of Retailing*, 66, 1, (Spring), pp. 33–35.

Clowes, K.E. and Vorhies, D. (1993) 'Building A Competitive Advantage For Service Firms', *Journal of Services Marketing*, 7, 1, pp. 22–23.

Cronin, J.J. and Taylor, S.A. (1992) 'Measuring Service Quality: A Re-Examination and Extension', *Journal of Marketing*, 56 (July), pp. 55–68.

Cronin, J.J. and Taylor, S.A. (1994) 'SERVPERF Versus SERVQUAL Reconciling Performance Based On Perceptions – Minus – Expectations Measurement of Service Quality', *Journal of Marketing*, 58, 1, pp. 125–131.

Crosby, L. and Stephens, N. (1987) 'Effects of Relationship Marketing On Satisfaction Retention and Prices in The Life Assurance Industry', *Journal of Marketing Research*, 24, pp. 404–411.

Crosby, P.B. (1979) *Quality Is Free*, (New York: McGraw Hill).

Czepiel, J. and Gilmore, R. (1987) 'Service Encounters: An Overview', in Czepiel, J., Congram, C. and Shanahan, R. (eds) *The Services Challenge: Integrating for Competitive Advantage*, (Chicago: AMA), pp. 91–94.

Day, R. and Landon, E. (1977) 'Towards a Theory of Consumer Complaining Behaviour', in Woodside, A., Sheth, J. and Bennet, P. (eds) *Consumer and Industrial Buying Behavior*, (NY: North Holland), pp. 425–443.

Dube-Rioux, L. (1990) 'The Power of Affective Reports in Predicting Satisfaction Judgements', in Goldberg, Gorn and Pollay (eds) *Advances in Consumer Research*, (ACR Provo UT), 17, pp. 571–576.

Enis, B.M. and Roering, K.J. (1981) 'Services Marketing: Different Products, Similar Strategy', in Donnelly, J.H. and George, W.R. (eds) *Marketing of Service*, (Chicago: American Marketing), pp. 1–4.

Fiske, S. and Taylor, S. (1984) *Social Cognition*, (MA: Addison Wesley).

Fitzgerald, T. (1988) 'Understanding the Differences between Services and Products To Exploit Competitive Advantage', *Journal of Services Marketing*, 2 (Winter), pp. 25–30.

Fornell, C. (1992) 'A National Customer Satisfaction Barometer: The Swedish Experience', *Journal of Marketing*, 56 (January), pp. 6–21.

Gabbott, M. and Hogg, G. (1996) 'The Glory of Stories. Using Critical Incidents to Understand Service Evaluation in the Primary Healthcare Context', *Journal of Marketing Management*, 12, pp. 493–503.

Gremler, D. and Brown, S. (1996) 'Service Loyalty: Its Nature, Importance and Implications', QUIS Proceedings, pp. 171–180.

Gronroos, C. (1988) 'New Competition in the Service Economy: The Five Rules of Service', International Journal of Operations and Product Management, 8, 3, pp. 9–18.

Gronroos, C. (1990) Service Management and Marketing: Managing the Moments of Truth in Service Competition, (Maxwell Macmillan: Lexington Marketing Association).

Gronroos, C. (1991) 'The Marketing Strategy Continuums: A Market Concept For The 1990s', Management Decision, 1, pp. 7–13.

Hart, C., Heskett, H. and Sasser, W. (1990) 'The Profitable Act of Service Recovery', Harvard Business Review (July–Aug), pp. 148–156.

Heider, F. (1958) The Psychology of Interpersonal Relations, (New York: John Wiley).

Hogg, M. and Abrams, D. (1988) Social Identifications, (London: Routledge).

Holbrook, M.B. (1994) 'The Nature of Customer Value: An Axiology of Services in The Consumption Experience', in Rust, R. and Oliver, R. (eds) Service Quality: New Directions in Theory and Practice, (California: Sage).

Holbrook, M.B. and Corfman, K.P. (1985) 'Quality and Value in The Consumption Experience: Phaedrus Rides Again', in Jacoby, J. and Olson, J.C. (eds) Perceived Quality: How Consumers View Stores and Merchandise, (Lexington, MA: Heath), pp. 31–57.

Hunt, Keith (1977) 'Consumer Satisfaction/Dissatisfaction: Overview and Future Research Directions', in Hunt, K. (ed.) Conceptualisation and Measurement of Consumer Satisfaction and Dissatisfaction, (Cambridge: MSI).

Iacobucci, D., Grayson, K. and Ostrom, A. (1994) 'The Calculus of Service Quality and Customer Satisfaction: Theoretical and Empirical Differentiation and Integration', in Advances in Services Marketing and Management, 3, pp. 1–67.

Janis, I. and Mann, L. (1977) Decision Making: A Psychological Analysis of Conflict, Choice, and Commitment, (New York: The Free Press).

Juran, J.M. (1988) Quality Control Handbook, (NY: McGraw Hill).

Kasper, H. and Lemmink, J. (1988) 'Perceived Aftersales Service Quality and Market Segmentation: A Case Study', in Blois, K. and Parkinson, S. (eds) Innovative Marketing – A European Perspective, Proceedings of The XVIIth MAC Conference, Bradford, pp. 365–387.

Kelley, H. and Thibaut, J. (1978) Interpersonal Relations: A Theory of Interdependence, (NY: Wiley).

Kelley, S., Hoffman, K.D. and Davis, M. (1993) 'A Typology of Retail Failures and Recoveries', Journal of Retailing, 69, 4, pp. 429–452.

Lawson, R. (1986) 'Consumer Satisfaction: Motivation Factors and Hygiene Factors Marketing', Discussion Paper, (NZ: University of Otago).

Lewis, B. (1989) 'Quality in the Service Sector: A Review', International Journal of Bank Marketing, 7, 5, pp. 4–12.

Lewis, B.R. (1993) 'Service Quality Measurement', *Marketing Intelligence and Planning*, 11, 4, pp. 4–12.

Lewis, R. and Klein, D. (1987) 'The Measurements of Gaps in Service Quality', in Czepiel, J. (ed.), *Add Value To Your Service*, (Chicago: AMA).

Lovelock, C. (1996) *Services Marketing*, (NJ: Prentice Hall).

Mazursky, D., LaParbera, P. and Aiello, A. (1987) 'When Consumers Switch Brands', *Psychology and Marketing*, 4 (Spring), pp. 17–30.

Murray, K. (1991) 'A Test of Services Marketing Theory: Consumer Information Acquisition Activities', *Journal of Marketing*, 55 (January), pp. 10–25.

Oliver, R.I. (1980) 'A Cognitive Model of the Antecedents and Consequences of Satisfaction Decisions', *Journal of Marketing Research*, 17 (November), pp. 460–469.

Oliver, R. (1977) 'Effect of Expectation and Disconfirmation on Post-Exposure Product Evaluation: An Alternative Interpretation', *Journal of Applied Psychology*, 62 (April), pp. 480–486.

Oliver, R.L. (1993) 'A Conceptual Model of Service Quality and Service Satisfaction: Compatible Goals, Different Concepts', in Brown, S., Swartz, T. and Bowen (eds) *Advances in Services Marketing and Management Volume 2*, (JAI Press), pp. 65–85.

Oliver, R. and Swan, J. (1989) 'Consumer Perceptions of Interpersonal Equity and Satisfaction in Transactions', *Journal of Marketing*, 53 (April), pp. 21–35.

Olshavsky, R. (1985) 'Perceived Quality in Consumer Decision Making: An Integrated Theoretical Perspective', in Jacoby, J. and Olson, J. (eds) *Perceived Quality*, (Lexington: MA), pp. 3–29.

Parasuraman, A., Zeithaml, V. and Berry, L. (1990) 'An Empirical Examination Of Relationships In An Extended Service Quality Model', Report No. 90-122 (Cambridge, MA: Marketing Science Institute).

Parasuraman, A., Zeithaml, V. and Berry, L. (1985) 'A Conceptual Model of Service Quality and Its Implications for Future Research', *Journal of Marketing*, (Fall), pp. 41–50.

Peters, T. (1987) *Thriving on Chaos*, (New York: Harper Row).

Reichheld, F. (1993) 'Loyalty Based Management', *Harvard Business Review*, 71 (March), pp. 64–73.

Rust, R. and Oliver, R. (1994) *Service Quality: New Directions in Theory and Practice*, (California: Sage).

Rust, R., Zahorik, A. and Keiningham, T. (1996) *Service Marketing*, (New York: Harper Collins).

Rust, R., Zahorik, A. and Keiningham, T. (1993) 'A Decision Support System For Service Quality Improvement', Paper Presented To AMA Frontiers in Services Marketing Conference, (Vanderbilt University Nashville) (October).

Saleh, F. and Ryan, C. (1992) 'Analysing Service Quality in The Hospitality Industry Using The Servqual Model', *Services Industries Journal*, 11, 3, pp. 324–343.

Schneider, D. (1995) 'Attribution and Socal Cognition', in M. Argyle and A. Colman (eds) *Social Psychology*, (Essex: Longman).

Singh, J. and Pandya, S. (1991) 'Exploring the Effects of Consumers' Dissatisfaction Level on Compliant Behaviours', *European Journal of Marketing*, 25, 9, pp. 7–21.

Snyder, D. (1986) 'Service Loyalty and its Measurement: A Preliminary Investigation', in Venkatesan, Schmalensee, and Marshall (eds) *Creativity in Service Marketing: What's New, What Works and What's Developing*, (Chicago: AMA).

Spreng, R., MacKenzie, S. and Olshavsky, R. (1996) 'A Reexamination of the Determinants of Consumer Satisfaction', *Journal of Marketing*, 60, 3, pp. 15–32.

Steenkamp, J.B.E.M. (1989) *Product Quality: An Investigation Into The Concept and How It Is Perceived By Consumers*, (Assen/Maastricht, The Netherlands: Van Gorcum).

Swan, J. and Comb, L. (1976) 'Product Performance and Consumer Satisfaction: A New Concept', *Journal of Marketing*, 40 (April), pp. 25–33.

Swartz, T. and Brown, S. (1989) 'Consumer and Provider Expectation and Experiences in Evaluating Professional Service Quality', *Journal of the Academy of Marketing Science*, 17, pp. 189–195.

Thibaut, J. and Kelley, H. (1959) *The Social Psychology of Groups*, (New York: Wiley).

Tse, D.K. and Wilton, P.C. (1988) 'Models of Consumer Satisfaction Formation: An Extension', *Journal of Marketing Research*, 25 (May), pp. 204–212.

Turley, L. and Moore, P. (1995) 'Brand Name Strategies in the Service Sector', *Journal of Consumer Marketing*, 12, pp. 42–50.

Westbrook, R. (1987) 'Product/Consumption-Based Affective Responses and Postpurchase Processes', *Journal of Marketing Research*, 24 (Aug), pp. 258–270.

Westbrook, R. and Oliver, R. (1991) 'Dimensionality and Consumption Emotion Patterns and Consumer Satisfaction', *Journal of Consumer Research*, 18 (June), pp. 84–91.

Wilson, D. and Jantrania, S. (1994) 'Understanding the Value of a Relationship', *Asia-Australia Marketing Journal*, 2, 1 (August), pp. 55–66.

Zeithaml, V. (1981) 'How Consumers Evaluation Processes Differ between Goods and Services', in Donnelly, J.H. and George, W.R. (eds) *Marketing of Service*, (Chicago American Marketing), pp. 186–190.

Zeithaml, V. (1988) 'Consumer Perceptions of Price, Quality and Value: A Means-End Model and Synthesis', *Journal of Marketing*, 52 (July), pp. 2–22.

Zeithaml, V.A., Parasuraman, A. and Berry, L.L. (1985) 'Problems and Strategies in Services Marketing', *Journal of Marketing*, 52 (April), pp. 33–46.

Zeithaml, V.A., Parasuraman, A. and Berry, L.L. (1988) 'Communication and Control Processes in The Delivery of Service Quality', *Journal of Marketing*, (April), pp. 35–48.

Zeithaml, V., Parasuraman, A. and Berry, L. (1990) *Delivering Quality Service*, (New York: Collier Macmillan).

Zeithaml, V.A., Parasuraman, A. and Berry, L.L. (1991) 'The Nature and Determination of Customer Expectations of Service', Marketing Science Institute, Working Paper No. 91-113, (Cambridge, MA: Marketing Science Institute).

PART II

THE SERVICE CONSUMER IN CONTEXT

Introduction to Part II

At this point in the book it should be evident that we believe that consumer behaviour associated with service products is sufficiently distinct from that related to physical goods to demand attention. However, in an attempt not to fall into the same trap as previous writers who have assumed that current consumer behaviour literature is applicable to all product forms, this section of the book comprises a series of chapters which attempt to delineate distinct facets of behaviour associated with different service products. It would be desirable to include as many contexts in this section as there are service products since only then would all facets be covered. Given the limitations of space and the need to provide material which is indicative rather than conclusive, only a relatively small selection is included here which, it is hoped, will be of use to teachers and researchers in providing an insight into the different contexts of service consumption. Some may argue that the absence of chapters on industrial services, communications, airlines, education etc. is a fundamental error, but in making this selection we have looked to include chapters which have issues relevant to service products as a whole and those which are of interest to the specialist. It is hoped that the selected chapters on financial services, professional services, tourism, retailing, healthcare and charities, from authors in Europe and the US will provide sufficient material for thought. Clearly, in a book such as this we have attempted to ensure that the chapters have a common form and structure which we have identified as a problem/solution format. The chapters have varying degrees of explicitness in presenting this framework although we hope that the beginning and end points are at least consistent.

Part II of this book starts with an article by Monica Hanefors and Lena Larsson Mossberg who examine the tourism context for service consumption. The article starts with a definition of the 'tour' product, pointing out the complexity of the attribute bundling for both consumers and service marketers. In keeping with the flow of the book the chapter then moves on to examine motives for consumption as a preliminary stage to addressing the purchase process, the consumption process and the evaluation of tourist services. The authors conclude with a summary of the characteristics of the tourism consumer whose main assertion is that tourism is a form of escape and removal from everyday life, something which puts this work parallel to the consumption of extraordinary experiences.

From tourism, this section moves on to a chapter by Kitty Koelemeijer and Marco Vriens considering the professional services consumer. This chapter provides a link into the consumption of business-to-business services which we have deliberately avoided in the first part of the book. Clearly, within the definition provided by the authors both business and private consumers can purchase professional services but this chapter pursues the topic from a business perspective. After a review of the characteristics of professional services, the authors present two sections on business-to-business buying and the problems of evaluating quality in this sector. In sum these service products present high degrees of uncertainty and risk for buyers which emanate from the high credence qualities of the process and the outcome. In response the development of trust and long-term engagements would seem a necessary although perhaps over emphasised characteristic of this market.

The chapter by Ennew and McKechnie investigates the particular problems faced by consumers in the consumption of financial services. As one of the most important services sectors of most developed economies, this sector has always been approached by services researchers with some trepidation. Some would argue that financial services are sufficiently distinct to be able to dissent from current service marketing literature, while others would point to the characteristics of services as proof that financial products are no different from restaurant meals, airline travel or utilities. The characteristics of the product, in particular the extent of engagement between the service organisation and the consumer over the life of the product, are more akin to latent services as outlined in Chapter 3 and that in itself makes them unusual. However, the authors of this chapter have framed the discussion in two main parts which concern the problems faced by consumers and the responses made by service providers in this sector. As such it highlights many of the issues raised in Part I associated with evaluation and choice.

Healthcare is an issue on the agendas of most developed economies as a function of the value of this market sector and the political importance of the service. Increasingly, as an alternative to government allocation, consumers are being asked to make choices about healthcare. In this chapter by Joby John, Mark Gabbott and Gillian Hogg, two healthcare systems are compared pointing to both similarity and differences in the way consumers make healthcare choices. After a review of the two healthcare systems the authors summarise the main decisions faced by consumers and identify some of the problems that these present, in particular the issue of cost. In the US system cost is transparent while in the UK cost is still veiled by the intermediary institutions. The conclusion is that consumers expectations of other services are beginning to impinge upon the healthcare sector, demanding a concentration by providers upon convenience, access and availability.

A quick review of publications and conference papers around the world would point to an increasing emphasis upon the application of marketing to 'non-traditional' areas of the economy. One of these emerging areas is the non-profit sector and this chapter by Sue Horne and Sally Hibbert entitled 'The Charity Consumer', provides an indication of how consumers engage in the consumption of a service for which there is no direct outcome. This unusual exchange relationship has a number of characteristics of interest to those concerned with consumer behaviour, in particular the importance of motivation, the nature of competition, the quenching of guilt, and the apparent absence of a need to see the outcome in order to evaluate performance. While services marketing has struggled to be recognised in its own right, non-profit marketing is emerging with particular contextual issues. After a review of the sector and some of the drivers for charitable behaviour the authors use a pre-donation, donation, postdonation structure to consider some of the issues related to information search, behaviour and evaluation. The authors conclude that the exchange relationship in non-profit services requires considerably more attention from services researchers than is currently the case.

CHAPTER 5

THE TOURISM AND TRAVEL CONSUMER

MONICA HANEFORS AND LENA LARSSON MOSSBERG

INTRODUCTION

Modern tourists are far more complicated than in the past. It is important, therefore, at this stage of our understanding to use knowledge from a range of disciplines other than marketing to further our knowledge of the tourism consumer. As a result the importance of a sophisticated approach to marketing in this sector has become widely recognised within the world's fast growing tourism industry. The aim of this chapter is to discuss the tourism product and the tourists' specific characteristics in relation to their decision-making process, including their travel motives, preferences, perceptions, vacation behaviour, and service evaluation. Although, as Gilbert (1991) points out, people have always travelled, it was historically a life event, a pilgrimage, grand tour or health cure visit that motivated the individual to leave their home and experience another environment. The modern tourist's cultural or personal expectations of travel are far removed from the historical perspective in both ability and mobility, as well ultimately in their motivation to travel (Murphy 1985, Gilbert

Consumers and Services. Edited by Mark Gabbott and Gillian Hogg.
© 1998 John Wiley & Sons Ltd.

1991). This chapter discusses the motivation for consumers to become tourists, the tourism product itself and the consumption process or the way that the consumer adopts the role of 'tourist'.

THE TOURISM PRODUCT AND THE TOURIST

A tourism product is not a simple matter. A tour, for example, comprises a combination of several service components. The product that the tourist purchases often consists of a complex system of products in combination, i.e. accommodation, transportation, food service and activities. It should be seen as a bundle or package of tangible and intangible components perceived of by the tourist as a total experience. In most cases, these components are not competing, instead they are complements in the tourist product. In the tourist's mind this complex product is a mental construct—an idea, a set of expectations and a hope for fulfilment.

To be able to satisfy the tourist's expectations, it is vital for any tourism company to collaborate and coordinate with others. This is a reflection of the interdependent nature of the product, and the necessity of relying on other organisations for collaboration in market research, mutual product development and promotion activities. In common for all companies involved, there is no way that a single company can collect all necessary data of various target markets, potential segments (national and international), the image and attractions of all the various destinations, together with aspects such as seasonality and vulnerability. However, if the companies get an understanding of the tourist's general behaviour before, during and after the travel a lot of information can be gained for all types of individual and can inform collaborative marketing activities.

From the service consumption point of view, the tourist has bought a 'holiday experience' and soon he or she will leave home and spend some time elsewhere. The first issue at hand is how to conceptualise the tourism services consumer. Imagine the stereotypical 'tourist'—a loud-voiced foreigner in colourful clothes with a camera or two hanging around his or her neck—just like someone we do not want to know and never have been ourselves. This is a common mistake and like most stereotypes is misleading in its generality. Another way to describe the tourist is to say that he or she is someone leaving their natural habitat for more than 24 hours. Erik Cohen provides a more scientific, and useful, way to define the tourist:

> A voluntary, temporary traveller, travelling in the expectation of pleasure from the novelty and change experienced on a relatively long and non-recurrent round-trip.
>
> Cohen (1974) p. 529

There are several dimensions in Cohen's definition, concerning the trip itself, the tourist, and his state of mind. The most important part, however, is related to the tourist's travel motives; she/he wants 'pleasure from the novelty and change'.

The overall motive for travelling is to move in different ways, physically as well as socially. The physical move means that the tourist leaves his familiar surroundings and comes into contact with an environment which might be different in many respects from that which he is used to. The social move, on the other hand, means that the tourist, for a certain limited period of time, is leaving his everyday life behind—he takes a step '. . . beyond the bounds of ordinary social reality' Crick (1989) p. 332.

When travel motives are discussed, it is often in relation to human needs. Maslow's work (e.g. 1954), examining human motivation, is considered to be the most significant and widely quoted. He suggests that human needs are organised hierarchically, although embedded in each other. Physiological needs, such as food, water and a roof over one's head, are the basic ones. Safety needs, such as the wish for an orderly world, comes next, followed by the need for love and acceptance. When those needs are fulfilled Maslow talks about esteem needs, first of all in relation to oneself, but also to other people. Self-actualisation constitutes the top of Maslow's hierarchy. Much of the research on travel motives is based on Maslow, and the discussion has become progressively more complex, even if the development has been slow. In 1977 Graham Dann, one of the most prominent researchers on motivation theory, commented that an understanding of travel motives is very complicated. Ten years later Jafari is able to note that there is still no deeper understanding to be found. This might be a result of the interest of academics in listing motivational factors. Thomas (1964) for example, listed 18 reasons; Gray (1970) discussed just two distinct motivations—'wanderlust' and 'sunlust'; and Lundberg (1972) identified 20 factors, while Crompton (1979) recognised nine different motives. It is not until this stage of listing motives ends, and discussions such as that by Dann (1981), Iso-Ahola (1982, 1984), Mannell and Iso-Ahola (1987) take place, that we will find any real development in this field. Through these recent developments it is becoming clear that tourists' travel motives are complex; there are both expressed and subconscious motives at work simultaneously, in an individual and situational combination.

There are two characteristics which dominate the study of motives in this context: the tourist travels away *from* something (escape) and *to* something (compensation), at the same time. The escape motives, on the one hand, are characterised as motives dominated by the need to leave everyday life—'pleasure from change'. The trip offers a short break from the daily routines, bad weather, ringing telephones, from responsibility and too many bills. Dann says that these escape motives, or the push factors, deals with tourist motivation *per se* (1981). Neil Leiper (1983) adds that all travelling involves a temporary escape of some kind, i.e. that a holiday trip actually allows a change of several dimensions—for example place, speed, faces, lifestyle, behaviour and attitudes.

On the other hand, the compensation motives, also known as 'pull factors', help the tourist to decide where to go—'pleasure from the novelty'. A specific destination may attract a certain type of tourist. It might be the case that a tourist interested in history chooses to go to Athens, just to be able to see the Acropolis, while the next tourist, with an interest in botany, wishes to go to Madeira. Both of them want to get away from everyday life for a while, but to compensate in different ways for what they do not find at home.

In a recent study of Japanese package tourists (Hanefors and Larsson Mossberg 1995) it became obvious that even this elaborate way to think about travel motives is not sufficient. Instead, the escape motives must be seen to be linked together with individual characteristics and with the cultural background of a specific tourist. Likewise the compensation motives are linked together with the prerequisites of a specific destination and the activities offered there—what we may call the destination attributes.

As stated above, it has never been enough just to list motivational factors, and it is not enough to isolate either the tourist nor the destination, the escape nor the compensation motives. In order to understand the tourist's travel motives, there is a need for a more holistic approach.

Figure 5.1
Tourist's Travel Motives

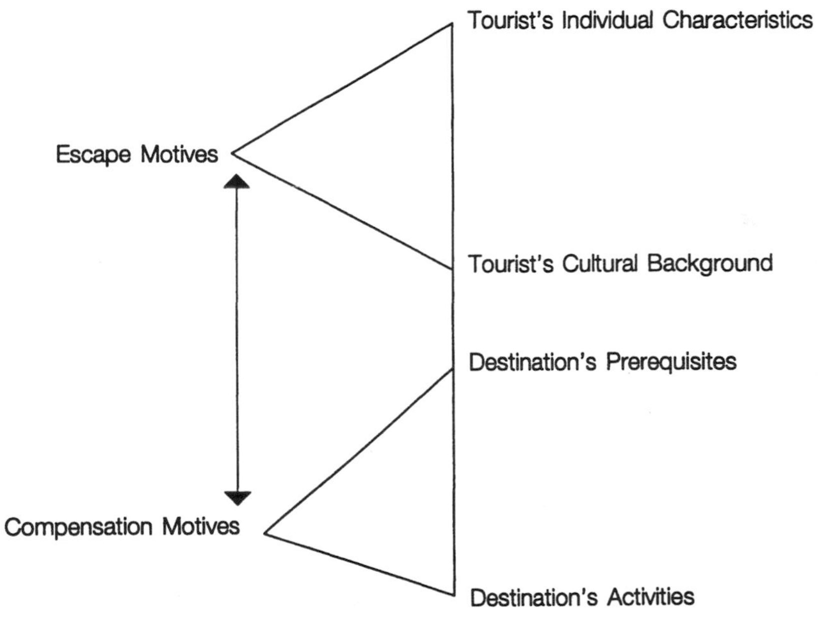

Source: M. Hanefors and L. Larsson Mossberg: 1995, Den paketresande japanen. Forskning Turism—Utbildning. Göteborg

THE PURCHASING PROCESS

The Tourist

Graburn (1983) characterises tourism not only as someone's physical movement away from home, but as one way for human beings to get necessary breaks from their ordinary lives. Tourism presents to the tourist

> a separation from the normal 'instrumental' life and the business of making a living, and offers entry into another kind of moral state in which mental, expressive, and cultural needs come into the fore.
>
> Graburn (1983) p. 11

Graburn also suggests that tourism is a kind of modern ritual, and refers to Hubert and Mauss (1898), when saying that the structure of tourism is '. . . basically identical with the structures of all ritual behaviour' (1983, p. 12). Rituals, which may be structured into three main parts—'separation', 'margin', and 'aggregation', mark the passages from one stage of a person's life to another. The first part—'separation'—signifies the detachment from routine everyday life. 'Margin', which constitutes the second part, means that the structured life of every day becomes transformed into an undifferentiated state of 'communitas': '. . . a cultural realm that has few or none of the attributes of the past or coming state . . . no status, property, insignia . . . indicating rank or role' (Turner 1969, p. 94f).

During the third part—'aggregation'—the individual passes back to structured life, where ordinary norms apply. A number of anthropologists lean towards Arnold van Gennep (1908) and Turner (1969, 1974a,b) they include, for example, Crick (1985, 1989) and Wilson (1993). Further examples are Moore (1980) who takes a special interest in the nature of Walt Disney World, or Lett (1983) on Caribbean charter yacht tourism, where '. . . tourists enjoy themselves in an exaggerated, unrestrained manner' (cf. Cohen 1988, p. 39), and Passariello who focused on Mexican holidaymakers, 'seeking to experience in a short time something different from their ordinary, daily lives' (1983, p. 120). Similarly Wagner (1977) studied Swedish charter tourists in The Gambia and, like Turner, discusses structure and anti-structure. She concludes that tourists go through a process of inversion during their tourist experience. Wagner shows the contrast between

> . . . ordered behaviour of role-playing and status holding and their enactment over time, and a temporal 'cut-out' typified by the negation of structure and noticeable emergence of a communitas type of behaviour.
>
> Wagner (1977) p. 39f

Tourists undergo a temporary status suspension. During the tourists' absence from home, time has a flowing or flexible quality and may be handled in any way the tourist wants. The differences between everyday life and tourist life—between the ordinary and the non-ordinary—is also discussed by Jafari (e.g. 1986, 1987).

> The ordinary is comprised of the mundane, profane, daily life whose procession loses strength due to its ordained rhythmic course; while the non-ordinary is the heightened position resulting from the departure from the ordinary ranks.
>
> Jafari (1986) p. 4

Jafari develops Turner's earlier discussion about ritual by adding two new components in his own tourist model—he prefers to talk about the five phases of the tourist experience: 'corporation', 'emancipation', 'animation', 'repatriation', and 'incorporation'. The first component, corporation, is composed by '. . . substances and conditions which incubates the motivation for travel to an outer zone' (Jafari 1986, p. 152), which is already discussed above. Together with the next component, emancipation, the basis for the tourist's mobility is formed—the tourist is distancing himself from the ordinary.

To reach the non-ordinary—the phase of 'animation'—there are a number of gates to pass for the tourist. The tourist continues to peel away the homebound cultural layers until he is ready to let go. The gates may be places like banks, passport authorities, insurance companies, vaccination centres and pharmacies, or events like dealing with the neighbourhood watch, a babysitter or kennels, and purchases of travel equipment. Another example is the family which had a 100 centimetre measuring tape and, starting 100 days before departure from home, cut one of the centimetres off every morning at the breakfast table. Different tourists spend various lengths of time becoming more or less absorbed into the animation phase of the trip.

Information Gathering and Purchase

The tourist's decision making is in most cases not a standardised process. When it comes to international tours it is a complex decision compared to, for example, purchasing a local bus ticket. The latter is instead routinised with low risk, low customer involvement, limited time consumption, and the customer has a good knowledge of available alternatives. Complex decision making, on the other hand, necessitates active information gathering, rational evaluation of various competing alternatives and a comprehensive post-purchase behaviour (Assael 1992). The tourist is strongly engaged in the purchase and can see differences between competing alternatives. He or she is actively seeking more information, developing criteria for the choice, forming attitudes to various offered alternatives, and arriving at preferences for certain tour operators etc.

The first stage in the decision-making process, after the tourist's recognition of a need, is the choice of either an independent tour or a package tour (related to the tourist's individual characteristics). Once a need is recognised the collection of information starts. Information collection consists of internal sources based on the person's earlier travel experiences, and external sources such as advertising and publicity, word of mouth, and studies of travel literature and brochures. In general, the travel brochures play an important role in the tourist's study of the country, holiday destination and in the choice of accommodation (Moutinho 1987).

Tourists' decision-making processes concerning choice of destination is a growing research area (see e.g. Moutinho 1987; Goodall 1991; Um and Crompton 1990; Crompton and Ankomah 1993). A number of models have been developed to explain how potential tourists collect and evaluate information about different destinations in order to finally be able to make a decision. Researchers within the area (Crompton and Ankomah 1993) suggest the choice of a specific tourist destination as a process including different phases:

1. Awareness set: an initial set of possible destinations
2. Evoked set: a limited set of destinations after reductions
3. Final destination selection.

Goodall (1991) also describes the decision process. All possible destinations form a number of possible alternatives, the 'initial opportunity set'. Some destinations are not considered, perhaps because they are unknown or are too expensive or too far away. Only the destinations of which the individual is aware will be considered. What is left forms a number of potential relevant alternatives. The number is probably large and must be further reduced. If the number is still too large, further evaluations will take place with regard to operative limitations (e.g. time and distance). The destinations are now evaluated depending on what the individual expects to benefit. Attributes offered by each destination are evaluated separately, and the number of possible destinations is decreased further. In general the number of destinations in the evoked set is a maximum of three. Thereafter the final evaluation occurs and a decision is made.

Besides the choice of tour and choice of destination a number of other decisions have to be made. For example, transportation, accommodation, activities and 'guiding', but this depends to a great extent on the type of tour. In many cases the tourist has a choice of these, in others they can not be selected and are instead already set (e.g. hotels and activities). The choice of tour operator depends, for instance, on the customer's earlier experience of the operator, attractive advertising, word of mouth, price or on other aspects of service delivery. In common with other services this decision also includes the option to organise the event oneself.

Besides motives, as previously discussed, how a person decides depends also on the tourist's sociodemographic characteristics such as age, sex, travel experience, willingness to take holiday, and price sensitivity. Other factors are family situation, risk perception and how many people are involved. In one family it might only be one decision maker, while in others a whole family may discuss the options. Decision making in families concerning choice of products can be described as 'syncratic', 'partially syncratic' and 'autonomic' (Moutinho 1987). Syncratic decision making implies a joint decision, partially syncratic means some decisions are made jointly, while others are made either by the husband or wife. Autonomic decision making is the case when the same number of separate decisions are taken by the husband and wife (Moutinho 1987). The degree of joint decision making tends to decrease after some time in the family life cycle and changes to one of the family members as the dominating decision maker. However, joint decision making dominates when the risk factor is high. An example of a high risk decision might occur when choosing a destination with a high incidence of HIV or AIDs, criminality or earthquakes. Other types of risks are financial (e.g. poor exchange rate), social (e.g. embarrassment), functional (e.g. the expectations are not fulfilled) and psychological (e.g. the risk of a bad product damaging the consumer's mental state).

The Consumption Process

The Tourist

> People go away because they no longer feel happy where they are (. . .). In order to be able to carry on, they urgently need a temporary refuge from the burdens imposed by the everyday work, home and leisure scene. (. . .) They feel the monotony of the daily routine, the cold rationalitites of factories, offices, apartment blocks and transport, shrinking human contact, the repression of feelings (. . .) life has been reduced to mere existence.
>
> Krippendorf (1987) p. xiv

According to Jafari the 'animation' phase means 'a life of non-ordinary flotation' (1987, p. 153), where the non-ordinary becomes the new reality for the tourists. Jafari calls it 'touristhood' and this component of the tourist model is a mental state, characterised as a state of non-responsibility by Hanefors (1979, p. 25). This is the phase for eventual anti-structural utterances, quite different from what the tourist is used to—the socially and culturally sanctioned everyday life—and the tourists accept and articulate this idea about freedom from everyday captivity.

Several studies have suggested that a destination is somewhat like a bubble, in a physical sense as well as in the way in which tourists themselves create meaning through their social makeup. Smith talked about a tourist or environmental bubble in her book *Hosts and Guests* (1978, 1989), as did Cohen (1972), and later Garcia (1988). Earlier than that Dumazedier called the bubble a region, that is '. . . "cooked" up solely for the benefits of tourists' (1967), while Sampson (1968) discusses what happens there by referring to a 'the cruise liner effect'. Cohen describes the bubble as an all-embracing 'tourist space' (1979) while Farrell (1979) calls it an 'enclave of familiarity'. According to Graburn this tourist enclave is a 'homegrown bubble of their [the tourists'] life style' (1978, 1989). The bubble offers nearly unlimited opportunities to tourists, and they tend to stay within its abstract borders to be able to experience them. The tourist might challenge and change any of the norms that usually control his or her life (see also Gorman 1979). He or she may try out new roles or even a new identity (see e.g. Gottlieb 1982), and may improvise any way he wants to, because '. . . while away from home, the real identity of the traveller is disguised' (Jafari 1986, p. 6). In short the tourist is anywhere rather than somewhere, articulating his escape motives in a tourist environment—the bubble.

The fourth phase of the model is 'repatriation', a 'return to the ordinary platform' (1987, p. 154). When the period of the extra-ordinary comes to an end, and the tourist returns home, he or she takes on his everyday clothing again. The suitcases are put away, and relatively abruptly he or she returns back to work, duties, studies, family and to behaviour mainly organised by others. Jafari describes a bank director shaving off his week-long beard before returning to work, and a female tourist from Des Moines hiding away her provocative bathing suit, which was her normal outfit during the holiday.

Incorporation, the fifth and last phase, signifies the tourist's total absorption into normal life again. The trip as such matters very little here, after the gifts are given out and the pictures have been shown to friends and relatives. No one seems to care a lot about what the tourist has experienced and to the tourist the trip does not make any great difference, not until next time this particular tourist starts to think about another trip—out of the ordinary.

The Service Encounter

One issue under debate is the applicability of the traditional marketing mix perspective (from the 1960s) to services marketing. Many authors argue that it is not relevant due to the characteristics of services (see e.g. Cowell 1984; Grönroos 1990; Gummesson 1991). Instead an interactive marketing function has been proposed. The concept was introduced by Grönroos (1979) to cover the customer's influence of marketing during the consumption process.

When the product is predominantly a service and the service delivery lasts a long time, as is the case with many tours, there are important questions to be asked about the marketing approach, in particular whether the marketing function be based on a traditional marketing approach in combination with an interactive marketing function (Larsson Mossberg 1994). In this way the service encounter can be focused on as a competitive tool. The reason is that the traditional tools as price, distribution and promotion mainly are used before the purchase in the decision-making process, as was discussed above. The interactive marketing, on the other hand, is not a function occurring between production and consumption, it appears mainly in the consumption phase and, more specifically, in the service encounter.

The interactive marketing approach focuses on the personnel as tacticians who are responsible for service delivery. The personnel give service and get immediate feedback from the customer. From this response the service can, if necessary, be modified within certain previously agreed limits. In package tours lasting a week or more, the interactive marketing function is of special interest. The tourist has bought the tour without being able to inspect in advance. The promises the tourist got when booking the tour should be fulfilled. During the consumption phase the traditional marketing function has a very limited chance to influence the tourist's preferences for the operator. Instead, the tour leader can influence tourist satisfaction through the activities occurring during the service encounters.

In the main, the tour operator is tested at two points, the travel phase and the destination phase. What happens during the trans-portation phase, such as delays due to bad weather etc. are not under the control of the tour operator but may be attributed to them. The personnel of the tour operator can only direct, control and manage events happening at the destination, such as bus excursions, fires, lack of electricity and water, epidemics etc. The activities of the personnel at the destination strongly affect word of mouth among the co-travellers. In a study by Webster (1991) in an evaluation of customers' expectations of various services, word of mouth had the strongest influence, followed by earlier experience, and thereafter advertising and sales promotion. Boulding et al. (1993) found a positive correla-tion between high perception of service quality and a willingness to give positive word-of-mouth recommendations. Other studies point to the importance of word of mouth to get new customers (for example File et al. 1992). The marketing effect of word of mouth is important—often more so than personal-, direct-, and mass-communication, writes Grönroos (1990). Word of mouth can be considered very important in the context of the purchase of tours due to the complex buying process, the high risk associated with it and the number of decisions involved. Moreover it is often costly, not spontaneous and involves a long planning process. Therefore, word of mouth spread via friends plays an important role, and may be perceived by the consumer as objective information.

As a service is intangible, service organisations can have difficulties differentiating their services towards competitors. While goods can incorporate differentiation advantages through product design, it can be strategy and flexibility in the service encounter which differentiates one service company from an other. For example, many tours offered by tour operators are essentially similar and distinct characteristics are hard to find. One way for a tourism organisation to differentiate the service is to use the personnel in the service encounter as a strategic resource to fulfil tourists' expectations while they are in the bubble. This can be done through strategic planning and service encounter construction (see e.g. Solomon et al. 1985; Surprenant and Solomon 1987; Schneider and Bowen 1984) considering that tourists challenge norms and try out new roles.

EVALUATION PROCESS

A variety of approaches have been used in order to explain the consumer's view of a company's service. Multi-attribute models are the most commonly used within the area of marketing. With such models a customer's assessment of service quality is often considered to be a result of a comparison between his expectations of the service and his actual perceptions of the service, based upon a number of attributes.

A number of interactive perspectives have been proposed, originating from a variety of behavioural sciences, primarily anthropology, psychology and sociology. These interactive perspectives are valuable because they allow a deeper understanding of behaviour. The participants' roles, status and the personality of the personnel are all assumed to influence the behaviour of those involved in the service encounters.

Depending on the complexity of the tourism product with often many organisations involved, it is necessary to distinguish the customer's perceptions on different levels. Service satisfaction can, for example, be evaluated in a specific service encounter, for one organisation or for a whole tour. Let us take a tourist's perception of a tour operator as an example to describe links between often used service evaluation concepts in a tourism context. Service encounter satisfaction can be defined as 'The customer's dis/satisfaction with a discrete service encounter' (see also Bitner and Hubbert 1994, p. 76). It reflects the customer's feelings about encounters with the service personnel and will result from the evaluation of the events and behaviours that occur during the definable period of time, in this case the tour in question. It is assumed that customers will distinguish their satisfaction with the service encounters (with the tour leader) on the specific tour from their overall satisfaction with the tour operator's services. The overall service satisfaction is defined as: 'The customer's overall dis/satisfaction with the organisation based on all encounters and experiences with that particular organisation' (see also Bitner and Hubbert 1994, p. 77). These multiple service encounters may include several interactions with many persons in the same organisation during one or more tours. Service quality, on the other hand, is seen as a higher order construct than overall service satisfaction and is defined as: 'The customer's overall impression of the relative inferiority/ superiority of the organisation and its services' (see also Bitner and Hubbert 1994, p. 77). The overall service satisfaction is based on experiences of the tour operator in question and of at least one tour, while a person can have perceptions of a tour operator's service quality without taking part in any of their tours. If service quality should be evaluated in connection with tours more variables are influencers such as advertising, service encounters with competing tour operators, word of mouth, and PR (see also Bitner 1990).

In tourism organisations there are certain disadvantages in using prevailing multi-attribute studies, like for example SERVQUAL, although the data can be obtained by studying the tourist's expectations prior to the service and his perceptions after (Larsson Mossberg 1994). In SERVQUAL, and elsewhere, customers' expectations and perceptions are measured at the same time (Parasuraman et al. 1988). However, if the tourist's expectations and perceptions are instead collected and measured separately, changes in opinion at the individual level can be analysed for each of the different attributes. This way of measuring can be difficult to carry out in other service organisations such as bank services, post office services etc. when the time of consumption is short. It is hardly feasible to deliver a questionnaire at the entrance to the bank and another at the exit when the service encounter is over.

In evaluating service satisfaction or service quality in tourism it also has to be recognised that the tourist's expectations are related to his travel motives. These are difficult to measure. As described above, the travel motives are a mixture of conscious and subconscious escape and compensation factors. One must also take into consideration both the individual characteristics of a specific tourist and his cultural background and the attributes of the destination in question such as weather, atmosphere, hotels, activities and attractions. Motives not only change according to, for example, stages in the tourist's life cycle, but might change during the course of one trip. It is essential to understand what the tourist actually occupies himself with when he travels or arrives at the destination, which must not necessarily be the same motive he once had in mind at home. It is interesting to see how, for example, Japanese tourists mention 'nature' as their main travel motive, but how shopping is the most important thing to do—not spending time in a nature environment (Hanefors and Larsson Mossberg 1995).

Conclusion

Figure 5.2 summarises our discussion about the tourism consumer. It shows the tourist's decision making process and its different stages, from a marketing point of view and from the anthropologist's perspective, and it also points out the specific marketing objectives and functions.

The main differences between a tourism consumer and a consumer of other services, such as the bank and post office customer, and the customer at the hairdresser's, are:

- the tourist consumes a total experience, maybe a mental idea, while the tourism product is a package of several products—transport, lodging, food and activities—and is difficult to control;
- production and consumption take place during a longer period of time—motives may alter and change;
- when travelling the tourist executes several parallel motives—in an individual and situational combination;
- the tourist is not always aware of his motives for consumption, maybe the main motive is to take a step out of the ordinary (the

Figure 5.2
Consumers and Tourism

	Ordinary Life	Slowly Letting Go	Animation Phase — Non-ordinary Life	Getting Back	Ordinary Life
Trip and Tourist's Transformation	Corporation Phase — Pre-trip	Emancipation Phase — Gates	Trip	Repatriation Phase — Gates	Reaggregation Phase — Post-trip
Tourist Cultural/Individual Characteristics	Travel Motives Escape/Compensation; Articulating Interest: e.g. ads, videos	Leaving Everyday Life; Information Gathering: e.g. travel agency, brochures	'Touristhood'/'Bubble'; Consumption, Services Encounters	Referring Home; Post-purchase Behaviour; Evaluation	The Trip Matters Little
Marketing Functions Objectives	To Create Interest in the Company and its Services; Traditional Marketing	To Turn General Interest into Sales; Traditional and Interactive Marketing Functions	To Create Enduring Customer Relations, to Prepare for Resales, Cross-sales; Interactive Marketing Functions	The Achieve Loyalty; Traditional and Interactive Marketing Functions	To Turn Specific Interest into Resales

'hidden' motive)—dreams and fantasies, anywhere rather than somewhere;

- when travelling the tourist has left everyday life, for a limited period of time, and is allowed to challenge the norms of the ordinary, he behaves in an extraordinary way, consumes intensively and differently.

REFERENCES

Assael, H. (1992) *Consumer Behaviour and Marketing Action*, 4th ed., (Boston: OWS Publ. Co).

Bitner, M.J. (1990) 'Evaluating Service Encounters: The Effects of Physical Surroundings and Employee Responses', *Journal of Marketing*, 54 (April), pp. 69–82.

Bitner M.J. and Hubbert, A.R. (1994) 'Encounter Satisfaction Versus Overall Satisfaction Versus Quality: The Customer's Voice', in Rust, T. and Oliver, R. (eds) *Service Quality: New Directions in Theory and Practice*, (Thousands Oaks: Sage Publications, Inc.), pp. 72–94.

Boulding, W. et al. (1993) 'A Dynamic Process Model of Service Quality: From Expectations to Behavioural Intentions', *Journal of Marketing Research*, 30 (February), pp. 7–27.

Cohen, E. (1972) 'Towards a Sociology of International Tourism', *Social Research*, 39, 1, pp. 164–182.

Cohen, E. (1974) 'Who is a Tourist? A Conceptual Clarification', *Sociological Review*, 22, 4, pp. 527–555.

Cohen, E. (1979) 'Rethinking the Sociology of Tourism', *Annals of Tourism Research*, 6, 1, pp. 18–35.

Cohen, E. (1988) 'Traditions in the Qualitative Sociology of Tourism', *Annals of Tourism Research*, 15, 1, pp. 29–46.

Cowell, D. (1984) *The Marketing of Services*, (London: Heinemann).

Crick, M. (1985) '"Tracing" the Anthropological Self: Quizzical Reflections on Field Work, Tourism, and the Ludic', *Social Analysis*, 17 (Aug), pp. 307–344.

Crick, M. (1989) 'Representations of International Tourism in the Social Sciences: Sun, Sex, Sights, Savings, and Servility', *Annual Review of Anthropology*, 18, pp. 307–344.

Crompton, J.L. (1979) 'Motivations for Pleasure Vacation', *Annals of Tourism Research*, 6, 4, pp. 408–424.

Crompton, J. and Ankomah, P. (1993) 'Choice Set Propositions in Destination Decisions', *Annals of Tourism Research*, 20, 3, pp. 461–476.

Dann, G.M.S. (1977) 'Anomie, Ego-Enhancement and Tourism', *Annals of Tourism Research*, 4, 4, pp. 184–194.

Dann, G.M.S. (1981) 'Tourist Motivation, An Appraisal', *Annals of Tourism Research*, 8, 2, pp. 187–219.

Dumazedier, J. (1967) *Toward a Society of Leisure*, (New York: The Free Press).

Farrell, B.H. (1979) 'Tourism's Human Conflicts. Cases from the Pacific', *Annals of Tourism Research*, 6, 2, pp. 122–136.

File, K.M., Judd, B. and Prince, R.A. (1992) 'Interacting Marketing: The Influence of Participation on Positive Word-of-Mouth and Referrals', *The Journal of Services Marketing*, 6, 4, pp. 5–14.

Garcia, A. (1988) 'And Why Don't You Go to the Seychelles?', in Rossell, P. (ed.) *Tourism: Manufacturing the Exotic*, IWGIA, Document 61, (Copenhagen), pp. 113ff.

van Gennep, A. (1960) [1908] *The Rites of Passage*, (London: Routledge & Kegan Paul).

Gilbert, D.C. (1991) 'An Examination of the consumer behaviour process related to tourism', in Cooper, C. (ed.) *Progress in Tourism, Recreation and Hospitality Management*, 3, University of Surrey, pp. 78–103.

Goodall, B. (1991) 'Understanding Holiday Choice', in Cooper, C.P. (ed.) *Progress in Tourism, Recreation, and Hospitality Management*, (London: Belhaven Press).

Gorman, B. (1979) 'Seven Days, Five Countries; The Making of a Group', *Urban Life*, 7, 4, pp. 469–491.

Gottlieb, A. (1982) 'Americans's Vacations', *Annals of Tourism Research*, 9, 1, pp. 165–187.

Graburn, N.H.H. (1978) 'Tourism: The Sacred Journey', in Smith, V.L. (ed.) *Hosts and Guests. The Anthropology of Tourism*, (Oxford: Basil Blackwell).

Graburn, N.H.H. (1983) 'The Anthropology of Tourism', *Annals of Tourism Research*, 10, 1, pp. 9–33.

Graburn, N.H.H. (1989) 'Tourism: The Sacred Journey', in Smith, V.L. (ed.) *Hosts and Guests. The Anthropology of Tourism*, 2nd edn, (Philadelphia: University of Philadelphia Press).

Gray, H.P. (1970) *International Travel: International Trade*, (Lexington, MA: Heath Lexington Books).

Grönroos, C. (1979) *Marknadsföring i tjänsteföretag*, (Stockholm: Akademilitteratur).

Grönroos, C. (1990) *Service Management and Marketing: Managing the Moments of Truth in Services*, (Lexington, MA: Lexington Books).

Gummesson, E. (1991) *Kvalitetsstyrning i tjänste- och serviceverksamheter: Tolkning av fenomenet tjänstekvalitet och syntes av internationell forskning*, (Karlstad: Högskolan, Centrum för Tjänsteforskning), Forskningsrapport 91:4.

Hanefors, M. (1979) *Turist i chartergruppen—gäst i overkligheten*, (Göteborgs Universitet: Socialantropologiska institutionen).

Hanefors, M. and Larsson Mossberg, L. (1995) *Den paketresande japanen. En studie av köpbeteende och resmotiv*, (Göteborg: Forskning Turism—Utbildning).

Hubert, H. and Mauss, M. (1898) *Sacrifice: Its Nature and Functions* (transl. by W.D. Halls), (Chicago: University of Chicago Press).

Iso-Ahola, S.E. (1982) 'Toward a Social Psychological Theory of Tourist Motivation', *Annals of Tourism Research*, 9, 2, pp. 256–264.

Iso-Ahola, S.E. (1984) 'Social Psychological Foundations of Leisure and Resultant Implications for Leisure Councelling', in Dowd, E.T. (ed.) *Leisure Counselling: Concept and Applications*, (Illinois: C.C. Thomas).

Jafari, J. (1986) *The Tourist System. Sociocultural Models for Theoretical and Practical Applications*, Paper pres. at 'Tourism in the 1990s' (Nov 27–28, London).

Jafari, J. (1987) 'Tourism Models: The Socio-Cultural Aspects', *Tourism Management*, 8, 2, pp. 151–159.

Krippendorf, J. (1987) *The Holiday Makers*, (London: Heinemann).

Larsson Mossberg, L. (1994) *Servicemöten och deras betydelse vid charterresor*, (Göteborg: BAS).

Leiper, N. (1983) *Why People Travel: A Causal Approach to Tourism*, Working Paper, Sydney Technical College.

Lett, J.W. (1983) 'Ludic and Liminoid Aspects of Charter Yacht Tourism in the British Virgin Islands', *Annals of Tourism Research*, 10, 1, pp. 35–56.

Lundberg, D.E. (1972) *The Tourist Business*, (Boston: Cahners).

Mannell, R.C. and Iso-Ahola, S.E. (1987) 'Psychological Nature of Leisure and Tourism Experience', *Annals of Tourism Research*, 14, 2, pp. 314–331.

Maslow, A. (1954) *Motivation and Personality*, (New York: Harper and Row).

Moore, A. (1980) 'Walt Disney World: Bounded Ritual and Play and the Playful Pilgrimage Center', *Anthropological Quarterly*, 53, 4, pp. 207–218.

Moutinho, L. (1987) 'Consumer Behaviour in Tourism', *European Journal of Marketing*, 11, 4, pp. 5–44.

Murphy, P. (1985) *Tourism, a Community Approach*, (New York: Methuen).

Passariello, P. (1988) 'Never on Sunday? Mexican Tourist at the Beach', *Annals of Tourism Research*, 10, 1, pp. 109–122.

Parasuraman, A., Zeithaml, V. and Berry, L. (1988) 'SERVQUAL: A Multiple-Item Scale for Measuring Consumer Perceptions of Service Quality', *Journal of Retailing*, 64 (Spring), pp. 12–40.

Sampson, A. (1968) *The New Europeans*, (London: Hodder & Stoughton).

Schneider, B. and Bowen, D.E. (1984) 'New Services Design, Development and Implementation and the Employee', in George, W. and Marshall, C. (eds) *Developing New Services*, (Chicago: American Marketing), pp. 82–101.

Shaw, G. and Williams, A.M. (1994) *Critical Issues in Tourism. A Geographical Perspective*, (Oxford, UK & Cambridge, US: Blackwell).

Smith, V.L. (ed.) (1978, 1989) *Hosts and Guests. The Anthropology of Tourism*, (Oxford: Blackwell).

Solomon, M., Surprenant, C., Czepiel, J. and Gutman, E. (1985) 'A Role Theory Perspective on Dyadic Interactions: The Service Encounter', *Journal of Marketing*, 49 (Winter), pp. 99–111.

Surprenant, C. and Solomon, M. (1987) 'Predictability and Personalization in the Service Encounter', *Journal of Marketing*, 86 (April), pp. 86–96.

Thomas, J. (1964) 'What Makes People Travel?', *Asia Travel News*, (Aug), pp. 64–65.

Turner, V.W. (1969) *The Ritual Process*, (London: Routledge & Kegan Paul).

Turner, V.W. (1974a) *Dramas, Fields and Metaphores: Symbolic Action in Human Society*, (New York: Cornell University Press).

Turner, V.W (1974b) *Liminal to Liminoid, in Play, Flow, and Ritual: An Essay in Comparative Symbology*, Rice University Studies, 60.

Um, S. and Crompton, J. (1990) 'Attitude Determinants in Tourism Destination Choice', *Annals of Tourism Research*, 17, 3, pp. 432–448.

UNESCO (1977) 'The Effects of Tourism on Socio-Cultural Values', *Annals of Tourism Research*, 4, 1, pp. 74–105.

Wagner, U. (1977) 'Out of Time and Place—Mass Tourism and Charter Trips', *Ethnos*, 41, 1–2, pp. 38–52.

Webster, C. (1991) 'Influences Upon Consumer Expectations of Services', *The Journal of Services Marketing*, 5, 1, pp. 5–17.

Wilson, D. (1993) 'Time and Tides in the Anthropology of Tourism', in Hitchcock, M. King, V.T. and Parnwell, M. (eds) *Tourism in South-East Asia*, (London: Routledge), pp. 32–47.

CHAPTER 6

THE PROFESSIONAL SERVICES CONSUMER

KITTY KOELEMEIJER AND MARCO VRIENS

INTRODUCTION

The aim of this chaper is to consider the purchase of a particular class of
services characterised as 'professional'. Whilst the precise meaning of
the word has changed in recent years, there are a number of common
characteristics that imply that the purchase of professional services places
different demands on the consumer. Professional services are characterised by special qualifications of the service provider to solve sporadic
or immediate problems, and the presence of a professional organisation,
or governing body, which regulates their conduct through a code of
ethics. In a dynamic, increasingly competitive market the specific
characteristics of professional services have consequences for clients'
selection and evaluation processes and for service providers' marketing
decisions. This chapter highlights a number of important facets of
professional services and discusses their implications for purchasing.
Although consumers as individuals are frequently the customers of these
services, for the purposes of this chapter we consider the purchase of
business services where the consumer is an organisation. The particular

Consumers and Services. Edited by Mark Gabbott and Gillian Hogg.
© 1998 John Wiley & Sons Ltd.

purchasing characteristics of organisations purchasing professional services are discussed and the effect of services on the decision process considered.

Professional service providers are becoming increasingly aware of the need to venture into marketing activities and to gain an understanding of their consumers. There are several trends underlying this development, including legal sanctions on malpractice, overcrowded professions such as law and dentistry, a declining public image (Bloom 1984), rapidly changing technologies (Kotler and Bloom 1984), and increased deregulation and privatisation. Consequently there is an increasing degree of externalisation of activities that have traditionally been managed internally through the use of subcontracting, outsourcing, licensing and franchising (see Whittington, McNulty and Whipp 1994). In addition, competition in the European market is intensifying due to loosening ethical and legal constraints, including restrictions on marketing activities that are enforced by professional societies, certification boards, and government agencies. For example, advertising and price competition are not allowed for legal services in certain European countries. Other marketing challenges that typically affect professional service providers are: client uncertainty; the need to be perceived as having experience, pushing organisations toward specialisation; limited differentiability which creates the need for marketing research; the need for low-cost, carefully targeted advertising; the need to have professionals who can both provide services and sell them; and determining the amount of time each professional should devote to marketing (Bloom 1984; Kotler and Bloom 1984). In sum, professional service organisations are now exposed more directly to market forces.

CHARACTERISTICS OF PROFESSIONAL SERVICES

Professional services are distinguishable from other services through a number of criteria. Firstly, the special qualifications of the service provider to solve problems, for example, lawyers are required to pass the bar exam. Secondly, the fact that such providers belong to a professional organisation or corporation which governs their conduct through a code of ethics (see for example Gummesson 1979; Kotler and Connor 1977;

Nimmo 1995). The 1987 US Standard Industrial Classification (SIC) system includes among professional services accounting, engineering, research, management consulting and public relations services. These services claim 13% of all services establishments, 12% of service employment and 16% of sales, and continue to grow faster than the US national economy (Du, Mergenhagen and Lee 1995).

According to the SIC system, professional services are consultative business-to-business services, but other classifications explicitly allow for consumer services as well. For example, Grönroos (1979) makes a distinction between industrial professional services (i.e. services offered to industry and institutions), and customer professional services (services offered to individuals and households). Like other services, professional services are intangible and heterogeneous, and production and consumption occur, at least partly, simultaneously. In addition, professional services have been reported to share a number of other characteristics. According to Dotchin and Oakland's (1994) classification, professional services are object, rather than people, oriented, high in intangibility, labour intensity, degree of customer interaction (including customer participation and feedback), and the degree of customisation (see also Schmenner 1986). Furthermore, the degree of customer contact with the service system is low for these services. Additional characteristics of the service and the service organisation that were identified from the literature by Lapierre (1993), include presence of a third party, little differentiation between providers, complexity, peak demand periods, an emphasis on future benefits, a shorter, often more direct, distribution network than for goods, and generalisation and decentralisation of the function in the business (see for example Bloom 1984; Crosby and Stephens 1987; Kotler and Bloom 1984). In Table 6.1 the SIC system service categories are classified according to whether the service is a business-to-business (industrial) or a consumer (customer) service, whether the providers of the service belong to a professional organisation which certifies their expertise and governs their conduct through a code of ethics. Additionally services can be categorised by the direct recipient of the service, be they people or things, the latter taken from Lovelock's (1983) classification. Based on our classification we argue that professional services may be people, as well as object, oriented.

Table 6.1
Grouping of Services

Nature of Services:	Industrial Services				Consumer Services	
Expertise and conduct:	Certified		Not Certified		Certified	
Directed Towards:	People	Things	People	Things	People	Things
Service Category:	Professional Services: Training & Motivation	Professional Services: Management Consultancy; Engineering; Accounting; Advertising	Recreation and Amusement Services; Lodging Services	Business Services	Professional Services: Health-care Services	Professional Services: Legal Services

Because of the special expertise necessary to solve the specific problems they encounter, professional service providers need high levels of expertise and specialisation. In addition, most organisations and individual consumers who employ professional services do so because they are unable to solve their particular problem themselves. As as result, for most professional services, consumers may be easily misled or even harmed without being able to assess the significance of the damage done.

Professional services are likely to comprise a series of long-term, individual-to-individual and/or firm-to-firm interactions (Crosby, Evans and Cowles 1990; Iacobucci and Ostrom 1996). The highly credential, process-oriented nature of professional services and the associated high level of perceived risk encourage long-term relationships between clients and service providers. Additional explanations for the existence of long-term relationships for professional services are provided by high perceived switching costs together with a low degree of perceived differentiation among competitors' offerings. In their study among 393 clients of Dutch accountancy firms, Vriens et al. (1992) found that only 5% of respondents considered switching to another accountancy firm. This can be confirmed by other statistics, for example during the period 1971–1986 only 16% of companies that were registered at the Dutch Stock Exchange changed to another accountancy service provider. This suggests that in the first instance, professional service organisations should develop marketing strategies aimed at retaining customers as well as attracting any new players to the market.

The distinctive features of professional services mentioned above are likely to have consequences for the marketing of professional services, in particular customer evaluations of, and choice among, alternative service offerings. In the literature on professional services marketing, topics such as industrial buying behaviour, perceived service quality, new service development, and marketing orientation have begun to attract special attention.

Buying Behaviour

Professional services have been considered occasionally in studies of industrial buying behaviour, however the specific characteristics shared p of services warrant special attention for organisational purchase of professional services. The nature of many professional services suggests a relatively complex and comprehensive purchase process (see Lapierre 1993 for an overview of studies on professional services buying behaviour). It is possible to draw too many general conclusions with respect to professional services buying behaviour.

The term 'professional services' represents a heterogeneous group of services that share certain characteristics, but which differs on a number of other characteristics that may have important consequences for buying behaviour. For example, client-provider service relationships can be characterised on four dimensions (Iacobucci and Ostrom 1996): integration and interdependency, closeness and supportiveness, distance (transactional vs. relational encounters), and power asymmetry. Individual-to-firm relationships, such as a business firm utilising a consultancy agency, tend to be less intense and more short term than individual-level dyads, such as patient-doctor relationships. Marketing tactics that aim to enhance customers' perceptions of their relationships with firms, that is personifying the firm, may therefore be very effective in influencing purchase behaviour.

The Nature of the Purchase Decision

The nature of the purchase decision in professional services is complex and dominated by the perceived risk of the purchase. The concept of perceived risk has been addressed by a number of authors since it was first proposed by Bauer in 1967. Perceived risk in this context is defined as any action that will 'produce consequences which cannot be anticipated with anything approaching certainty, . . . some of which are likely to be unpleasant' (Bauer 1967).

Risk is, therefore, the likelihood of negative consequences of a purchase decision, and is important only to the degree that it is perceived by the purchaser. Perceived risk has two dimensions: uncertainty concerning the outcome of the decision, and the magnitude of the consequences of a wrong choice. In terms of the definitions used, risk in this context could be more accurately described as uncertainty. Cunningham (1967) recognised that purchasers are not able to ascertain the true probabilities of possible outcomes and therefore 'perceived risk' was in fact 'perceived uncertainty'. However, the distinctions between risk and uncertainty have become blurred and the terms are now used interchangeably (Stone and Gronhaug 1993). Seven dimensions of risk have been identified in the literature. These include performance, psychological, social, financial, and time (Jacoby and Kaplan 1972; Roselius 1971; George et al. 1984). These components will be present to a greater or lesser degree according to the particular purchase situation. Overall perceived risk represents the aggregate of these components. It is accepted that in all purchase situations the purchaser is attempting to minimise this degree of perceived risk (see Bauer 1967).

The concept was first applied to the industrial context by Levitt (1969) who suggested that the perception of risk in any purchase situation will be dependent on a number of factors, including the buying situation, the type of product being purchased, organisational-specific factors, and the personality of the purchaser. Much of the research in this field has been carried out on consumers rather than industrial purchasers, with studies concentrating on criteria effecting personal perceptions of risk. These include the degree of anxiety and self confidence (Locander and Hermann 1979), social class (Hisrich 1972) and even the possession of specific religious beliefs (Delener 1990). However, the concept of risk and the need to reduce the uncertainty of purchase decisions is equally applicable to the organisational context. It is likely that in this situation the effect of individual personality will be reduced by the operation of the buying centre which involves a number of people taking responsibility for decision making. Although the theory of 'risky shift', which implies that groups make riskier decisions than individuals, has been discredited (see for instance McGuire et al. 1987), the principle of risk being dissipated throughout a group remains.

Buying Centres

Only a limited amount of research has been published concerning decision-making activities with respect to purchase of industrial services. Johnston and Bonoma (1981b) compared buying centres for capital equipment purchases with those for industrial service purchases. They found that service purchases generally involved fewer levels of corporate hierarchy (vertical involvement), fewer same-level departments (lateral involvement), fewer individuals in the firm overall, and generally more communication than did the purchase of capital equipment items. For most purchase tasks two or less of the firm's functional areas were involved for services, whereas two or more functional areas were involved for capital equipment purchases. In their comparison the authors did not consider the specific purchase situation. Consequently, Dawes, Dowling and Patterson (1992) adopted Johnston and Bonoma's (1981a) approach for exploring the structure of the buying centre for professional advisory services. This takes into account purchase situation variables, such as the relative importance and newness of the purchase task, and the degree of perceived risk and decision complexity, and individual characteristics such as product class knowledge. They found that in general Johnston and Bonoma's results were confirmed for professional services. In addition, the relative importance of the purchase to the organisation and the degree of newness of the purchase had a direct, positive impact on the size of the buying centre. In cases where respondents had greater responsibility in the area in which the consultants were working, buying centres were smaller and fewer management levels were represented. The authors' conclusion is that the factors affecting the size of a buying centre may not be very different for the purchase of a service or capital equipment.

In a study among 162 Dutch firms that hired a human resource management consulting firm at least once during the last two years, van Berkel (1994) found that on average five people made up the buying centre. The relatively high number of people involved in the decision process may be a function of the nature of human resource problems. The results for vertical and lateral involvement matched those of the previous studies: in 57% of the cases two hierarchical levels were involved and 70% of the cases concerned two or three functional areas. Relative newness of the purchase and product class knowledge both related positively to the degree of lateral involvement. Product class knowledge also had a significant positive effect on the degree of vertical involvement.

Purchaser–Provider Relationships

The nature of the relationship between purchaser and provider in services is dependent on the way in which the two parties to the transaction view their relative power within the relationship. The purchasing strength of the buying organisation and the monetary value of the work involved implies that in many cases the organisational purchaser is able to demand a more responsive and flexible service than most individuals could from a similar service. By the very nature of services, the potential for customising the product is a major factor in their delivery; although the outcome may be standard the service provider can customise the process according to specific customer needs. This may result in cleaning or maintenance being carried out at night, for instance, or the service delivery being tailored to the purchaser's requirements. The value to the purchaser of this type of service is such that they are likely to specify a degree of customisation, for example not only the service required but the time and method of delivery. It has been suggested that the flexibility and heterogeneity in the service product is likely to cause problems for purchasers, particularly in pre-purchase information search, discriminating between providers, and evaluating the service post consumption (Gabbott and Hogg 1994).

Information Search

There are two sources of information about any product: internal, that is experience or memory based, and external, that is information that exists about a good or service that can be collected. When faced with a purchase decision purchasers first examine memory for information which may be relevant to the decision. This information may be the result of previous experiences, which constitute a body of knowledge about, or an attitude towards, a product or a product class. If previous service experience is available this is an extremely credible source, even if it is recognised that the experiences which comprise this information are event specific and may not provide any clear indication as to future performance. Cunningham and White (1973) found that the strongest determinant of a buyer's patronage was his past experience, similarly Wilson (1972) describes previous experience as the single most important criteria in the selection process for professional services.

Where information gained from previous experience is not available to purchasers, or the information already held is considered insufficient to discriminate between different offerings, then the purchaser is motivated to search for information externally. The extent of external search is dependent upon a number of factors, such as product category experience, product complexity and the degree of buyer uncertainty. The relevance of information available in purchase decisions is related to the nature of services. In order to discuss the information demands of services, Zeithaml (1981) after Nelson (1974) and Darby and Karni (1973) suggests a framework based on the inherent qualities of products. The framework was first applied in the economic regulation literature and uses three categories of product qualities: *search qualities*, attributes a consumer can determine prior to purchase; *experience qualities*, attributes which can only be determined after purchase or during consumption; and *credence qualities*, characteristics which consumers may find impossible to evaluate even after consumption. All products can be described in terms of proportions of the three qualities. Services are characterised as being low in search qualities, but high in experience and credence qualities.

Zeithaml (1981) suggests that this need for experience information prompts a reliance upon word-of-mouth sources, that is recommendations, as they are perceived to be more credible and less biased. Stock and Zinszer (1987) suggest that in industrial decisions the decision makers rely heavily upon information sources with high expertise and credibility and little or no intention to influence, criteria fulfilled by personal recommendation (Kotler 1977; Lehmann and O'Shaughnessy 1974; Webster 1970). In investigating the sources of business recommendations, Webster (1972) found that informal communication within industrial markets is much less frequent than in consumer markets. Whilst buyers may contact counterparts in other firms to check where to buy certain supplies, they seldom ask what to buy.

Webster's research found that in general, companies felt that the specific nature of their problems precluded the possibility of other organisations' experience being of great assistance. His research also found that buyers avoid giving details of newly purchased goods that gave particular products competitive advantage. The evaluation of advisory services is a very subjective matter (Dornstein 1977; Gummesson 1978), the outcome is dependent upon the skill of the individual advisor and it is not possible to know ahead of time how the result will turn out. For example, the choice of a planning consultant may be between two equally well qualified consultants, neither of whom can predict the outcome with certainty. As a result there is likely to be a high reliance on referral networks (see for instance Greenwood 1957; Dornstein 1977 on referral networks in the professions, or Kotler and Bloom 1984; Rathmell 1974 on the role of referrals in marketing professions).

The experiential nature of the advisory product suggests that the previous experience of individuals in the buying organisation will be of central importance in determining the nature of the information used in making the decision, therefore previous experience is important in understanding both the type of information and the sources of information used. The reliance on this type of information suggests that a number of sources of information within the firm may be consulted, and that particular attention will be paid to information provided by either individuals who have experienced the service or particular service provider in the past or to 'experts' who have experience/training in the service area. For example, an engineer may take on the role of expert prescriber in the purchase of maintenance services. Sheth (1973) and Webster and Wind (1975) suggest that these sources are most effective during the later stages of the adoption process.

Martilla (1971) carried out a similar study to Webster (1972) on intra-firm communication and found that word-of-mouth communication within the firms he studied was significant. Martilla concluded that generalisations regarding the nature of inter-firm cooperation were not possible as they vary between industries, with some industries characterised by friendly collaboration with competitors through both personal contacts and trade federations. The amount of experiential information available will therefore differ between organisations and according to the specific service product purchased, but is likely to be an important source of decision-relevant information.

The final source of information is impersonal from both marketer controlled and non-marketer controlled sources. Due to the characteristics of services, the information available from these sources, such as advertising and trade media editorial comment, does not describe the nature of the service itself, but the potential benefits of the service. They provide data about the range of service attributes available and providers of those services. Such data is useful for providing a set within which to make a choice but does not provide adequate grounds for discrimination within that set. Mitchell (1994) suggests that in general business purchasers do not rely on advertising to locate professional service suppliers, although this may be more appropriate for other business service suppliers.

Choice of Professional

The extensiveness of the choice in this context is a wider concept than simply the 'number of vendors' in a market; it also includes seller concentration, product differentiation and substitutability (Porter 1981; Scherer 1980). Corey (1978) suggests that buyers will seek to expand the choice set when it is perceived to be limited, while conversely Zenz (1981) shows that buyers will seek to narrow the set when presented with too wide a range of alternatives. If we assume that all organisations, regardless of size, may at some time require a specialist advisory service, and in some cases there is a statutory requirement for such a service (for example auditing), then this is an extremely large potential market. If the definition of professional services is extended to include providers who do not belong to recognised professional bodies, then it is theoretically possible for the number of suppliers of 'professional advice' to be equally large. Service providers with a statutory function, such as lawyers or accountants, with legally enforceable barriers to entry are regulated, while there are no such controls over the supply of management consultants or PR consultants, for example. There is, therefore, potentially a very large set of possible service providers. The traditional response from service providers to this situation is to differentiate the product in some way.

Service Differentiation in Professional Services

Differentiation in professional services is a difficult concept as it depends on identifying the core service product, which is itself dependent on an understanding of what the purchaser is buying. If the required outcome is a solution to a problem, there may be a difference in the proposed solution between providers. However, this is a difficult concept on which to base differentiation as it will depend on the particular problem to be addressed and is event specific. Even if there is a clearly defined outcome objective, for example audited accounts, the outcome is difficult to differentiate, the requirements are laid down and there is no scope for altering the core product.

There are two responses to this challenge for service firms. Bloom (1984) suggests that the most effective approach is specialisation in particular market segments leading to differentiation by market sector rather than by product. For example, specialisation in a particular type of industry like the construction sector. Alternatively the service provider can attempt to differentiate the service on the process factors, or how the service is delivered. This separates the outcome and process parts of the service and suggests that if it is not possible to differentiate the outcome then the major competitive variable will be the process.

The final factor that affects the choice of professional is the possibility of geographical restrictions. In most cases the professional service product requires some interaction between advisor and client, a form of personal communication that requires the two parties to meet or 'consult' in order for the problem to be diagnosed. For these reasons the choice set may be limited to a certain geographical area to reduce travel/time costs. The local nature of some issues requiring specialist advice may limit the geographical area of the choice set, or differences in law or government practice may require that the choice set is restricted. Similarly the service product itself may have geographical factors, for example lobbying firms require access to Parliament which may limit the choice of firms. As a result there are likely to be restrictions on the choice set according to the geographical location which have implications for the way that the purchase is approached.

Evaluating Quality

It has been illustrated earlier that professional services are a subset of services that are distinguished with respect to certain characteristics. Due to the particular nature of these services the dimensionality of quality perceptions of clients of professional service providers may refer to other components than those that have been formulated in the 'PZB' (Parasuraman, Zeithaml and Berry 1985; 1988; 1991; 1994) approach to consumer services. Many empirical studies dealing with professional services used the dimensionality suggested by Parasuraman, Zeithaml and Berry, in particular their SERVQUAL scale, (for example Freeman and Dart 1993), whereas other research used dimensions that can be related to Grönroos' (1984; 1988) technical (the outcome-related, or 'what') dimension and functional (the interactive, process-related, or 'how') dimension of perceived service quality (for example Wheatley 1987).

Table 6.2 lists the relevant perceived service quality dimensionalities according to Lapierre, Filiatreault and Koelemeijer (1994). Several findings emerge from their exploratory study among consulting engineers' clients that are in support of Grönroos' (1984, 1988) dimensionalities. First, with respect to professional services the service provider's competence, know-how, or professionalism and skills are of major importance. The firms in the study are evaluated by their customers first and foremost on their performance, on the aspects of technical quality and on schedule and budget constraints. Furthermore, reliability of the outcome (technical quality) and trustworthiness during

Table 6.2
Comparison of Service Quality Dimensions

Grönroos (1984)	Parasuraman et al. (1985)	Parasuraman et al. (1988, 1991)
Technical Quality (what)	Competence Reliability (technical)	Assurance Reliability (technical)
Functional Quality (how)	Reliability (functional)	Reliability (functional)
	Responsiveness Courtesy	Responsiveness Assurance
	Security Tangibles	Assurance Tangibles
	Accessibility Communication Understanding	Empathy
Image	Credibility	Assurance

Source: Lapierre, Filiatreault and Koelemeyer (1994).

the process (functional quality) refer to two aspects of service professionals' performance. Finally, recovery ability seems an especially relevant quality dimension for industrial professional services.

With respect to consumer professional services, the limited number of empirical studies that are available suggest that evaluation is carried out using quality attributes such as competence and professionalism, expertise, specialisation, empathy, and convenience (see for example Brown and Swartz 1989; Darden, Darden and Kisner 1981) and credibility (for example Crosby and Stephens 1987).

Although Grönroos' generic technical, functional and image service quality dimensions seem appropriate within the context of professional services, limited support could be found for his professional services dimensionality. Further research is needed into the dimensionality of perceived quality of professional services. Given the nature of professional services and the fact that many service clients lack experience, traditional service quality models based on disconfirmation, expectation-perceptions (Parasuraman et al. 1988), or perceptions (Cronin and Taylor 1992) are difficult to apply. Because the professional services client-provider relationships are important, the conceptual relationship between perceived quality of professional services and relationship quality (for example Crosby and Stephens 1987) deserves further investigation.

Marketing Orientation

Professional firms, like other business firms, pursue sufficient demand, sustained growth and profitable volume (Kotler and Connor 1977). Due to developments mentioned in the introduction to this chapter, professional service providers have to confront the marketing issues and challenges and adapt their marketing efforts to the dynamics of competitive marketplaces. The market-driven change processes that are required for professional service organisations require changes at each level in the organisational hierarchy (for an overview see Whittington, McNulty and Whipp 1994). Top management should develop from professional administrators into strategic managers, line management is required to change from professional coordinators into business managers, professionals should become part-time marketers, and supportive employees should provide commercial support. These developments entail significant changes in traditional authority structures, especially the inclusion of non-professionals in senior management, decentralisation of responsibility to middle-management, and more effective strategic leadership from the top. In particular, tension may arise between the need for decentralised market control internally and a coherent marketing strategy externally. Both management and researchers will benefit by identifying the factors that determine the success of the complex change towards market-oriented professional service organisations.

CONCLUSION

This chapter considers several themes that emerged in the literature on purchasing professional services, in particular selection and evaluation of professional service firms. We have argued that professional services deserve to be treated as a separate field of interest in marketing due to the specific characteristics these services share. The highly experiental and credential nature of many professional services complicates the processes of supplier selection and evaluation. Customers experience a high degree of uncertainty and risk and consequently seek risk reduction, for example by relying on cues and by developing stable, loyal relationships with service providers.

The market for professional services is changing and is becoming increasingly competitive. Kotler and Connor already argued in 1977:

> Professional service providers have to start to realise themselves that clients will not come to them without organised effort on their part, simply as a result of achieving a good reputation.

Today, many professional service organisations adopt a marketing approach to their service/market opportunities. The relationship-oriented nature of professional services and the market developments that we have described in this chapter suggest development of defensive marketing strategies for professional service organisations. In addition, the relationship-oriented nature of professional service delivery offers many possibilities for future research.

Finally the enormous diversity among professional services caused us to warn against generalisations of the limited amount of research results that have been published. There is a need for development of a professional services classification or typology that can sustain marketing management decisions.

REFERENCES

Bauer, R.A. (1967) 'Consumer behaviour as risk-taking', in Hancock, R. (ed.) *Dynamic Marketing for a Changing World*, (Chicago: American Marketing Association), pp. 389–398.

Berkel, H. van (1994) 'Waarhayn leidt de weg?', unpublished MBA thesis (Tilburg University).

Bloom, P.N. (1984) 'Effective Marketing for Professional Services', *Harvard Business Review* (September–October), pp. 100–110.

Brown, S.W. and Swartz, T.A. (1989) 'A Gap Analysis of Professional Service Quality', *Journal of Marketing*, 53 (April), pp. 92–98.

Cooper, R.G. and de Brentani, U. (1991) 'New Industrial Financial Services: What Distinguishes the Winners', *Journal of Product Innovation Management*, 8, pp. 75–90.

Cooper, R.G. and de Brentani, U. (1992) 'Developing Successful New Financial Services for Businesses', *Industrial Marketing Management*, 21, pp. 231–241.

Corey, R. (1978) 'Procurement Management: Strategy, Organisation and Decision Making', (London: CBI Publishing).

Cronin, J.J. and Taylor, S.A. (1992) 'Measuring Service Quality: A Re-examination and Extension', *Journal of Marketing*, 56 (July), pp. 55–68.

Crosby, L.A., Evans, K.R. and Cowles, D. (1990) 'Relationship Quality in Services Selling', *Journal of Marketing*, 54, pp. 68–81.

Crosby, L.A. and Stephens, N. (1987) 'Effects of relationship in Satisfaction, Retention, and Prices in the Life Insurance Industry', *Journal of Marketing Research*, 24 (November), pp. 404–411.

Cunningham, S. (1967) 'Perceived Risk and Brand Loyalty', in Cox, D. (ed.) *Risk Taking and Information Handling in Consumer Behaviour*, (Boston: Harvard UP), pp. 503–527.

Cunningham, M. and White, J.G. (1973) 'Service industrial. The determinants of choice of Supplier', *European Journal of Marketing*, 7, 3, pp. 189–202.

Dabholkar, P.A. (1996) 'Consumer Evaluations of New Technology-Based Self-Service Options: An Investigation of Alternative Models of Service Quality', *International Journal of Research in Marketing*, 1, pp. 29–51.

Darby, M.R. and Karni, E. (1973) 'Free competition and the optimal amount of fraud', *Journal of Law and Economics*, 16 (April), pp. 67–86.

Darden, D.K., Darden, W.R. and Kisner, G.E. (1981) 'The Marketing of Legal Services', *Journal of Marketing*, 45 (Spring), pp. 123–134.

Dawes, P.L., Dowling, G.R. and Patterson, G.P. (1992) 'Factors Affecting the Structure of Buying Centers for the Purchase of Professional Business Advisory Services', *International Journal of Research in Marketing*, 9, pp. 269–279.

Delener, N. (1990) 'The Effects of Religious Factors on the Perceived Risk in Durable Goods Purchase Decisions', *Journal of Consumer Marketing*, 7, 3 (Summer), pp. 27–38.

Dornstein, M. (1977) 'Some imperfections in the market exchange for professional and executive services', *American Journal of Economics and Sociology*, 36 (April), pp. 113–128.

Dotchin, J.A. and Oakland, J.S. (1994) 'Total Quality Management in Services. Part

1: Understanding and Classifying Services', *International Journal of Quality & Reliability Management*, 11, 3, pp. 9–26.

Du, F., Mergenhagen, P. and Lee, M. (1995) 'The Future of Services', *American Demographics*, 17, 11, pp. 30–47.

Freeman, K.D. and Dart, J. (1993) 'Measuring the Perceived Quality of Professional Business Services', *Journal of Professional Services Marketing*, 9, 1, pp. 27–48.

Gabbott, M. and Hogg, G. (1994) 'Consumer behaviour and services: A review', *Journal of Marketing Management*, 10, pp. 311–324.

George, W.R. et al. (1984) 'Risk Perceptions: A Reexamination of Services Versus Goods', in Kline, D.M. and Smith, A.E. (eds) Proceedings, (Boca Raton, FL: The Southern Marketing Association and Florida Atlantic University).

Greenwood, E. (1957) 'Attributes of a Profession', *Social Work*, 12 (July), pp. 45–55.

Grönroos, C. (1979) *Marknadsföring I tjansteföretag*, (Stockholm: Akademilitteratur).

Grönroos, C. (1984) 'A Service Quality Model and Its Marketing Implications', *European Journal of Marketing*, 18, 4, pp. 36–44.

Grönroos, C. (1988) 'Service Quality: The Six Criteria of Good Perceived Service Quality', *Review of Business*, (St-John's University), 9, 3, pp. 10–13.

Gummesson, E. (1978) 'Toward A Theory of Professional Services Marketing', *Industrial Marketing Management*, (April), pp. 87–94.

Gummesson, E. (1981) 'The Marketing of Professional Services—An Organisational Dilemma', *European Journal of Marketing*, 13, 5, pp. 308–318.

Hisrich, I.J. (1972) 'Perceived Risk in Store Selection', *Journal of Marketing Research*, 9 (November), pp. 435–439.

Iacobucci, D. and Ostrom, A. (1996) 'Commercial and Interpersonal Relationships; Using the Structure of Interpersonal Relationships to Understand Individual-to-Individual, Individual-to-Firm, and Firm-to-Firm Relationships in Commerce', *International Journal of Research in Marketing*, 13, pp. 53–72.

Jacoby, J. and Kaplan, L.B. (1972) 'The Components of Perceived Risk', in Venkaresan, M. (ed.) Proceedings, Third Annual Conference, (Urbana, IL: Association for Consumer Research).

Johnston, W.J. and Bonoma, T.V. (1981a) 'The Buying Center: Structure and Interaction Patterns', *Journal of Marketing*, 45 (Summer), pp. 143–156.

Johnston, W.J. and Bonoma, T.V. (1981b) 'Purchase Processes for Capital Equipment and Services', *Industrial Marketing Management*, 10, pp. 253–264.

Kotler, P. and Bloom, P.N. (1984) *Marketing Professional Services*, (Englewood Cliffs, NJ: Prentice-Hall), p. 296.

Kotler, P. and Connor, R.A. (1977) 'Marketing Professional Services', *Journal of Marketing*, 41 (January), pp. 71–76.

Lapierre, J. (1993) 'The Quality-Value Relationship in the Process for Evaluating Professional Services: The Case of Consulting Engineering', unpublished PhD Thesis (University of Québec at Montréal).

Lapierre, J., Filiatreault, P. and Koelemeijer, K. (1994) 'Industrial Professional Services Quality Evaluation Criteria: A Comparative Analysis Between Consulting Engineers of North America (Québec) and Europe (France)', in Bloemer, J. et al. (eds) *Marketing: Its Dynamics and Challenges*, (Maastricht: European Marketing Academy), pp. 579–598.

Lehmann, D.R. and O'Shaughnessy, J. (1974) 'Difference in Attribute Importance For Different Industrial Products', *Journal of Marketing*, 38 (April), pp. 36–42.

Levitt, T. (1969) 'The New Markets—Think before you Leap', *Harvard Business Review* (July/Aug), pp. 78–90.

Locander, W. and Hermann, P. (1979) 'The effect of self-confidence and anxiety on information seeking in consumer risk reduction', *Journal of Marketing Research*, 19, pp. 268–274.

Lovelock, C.H. (1983) 'Classifying Services to Gain Strategic Marketing Insights', *Journal of Marketing*, 47 (Summer), pp. 9–20.

Lynn, S.A. (1986) 'Segmenting a Business Market for a Professional Service', *Industrial Marketing Management*, 15, pp. 13–21.

Lyons, B.R. (1995) 'Specific Investment, Economies of Scale, and the Make-or-Buy Decision: A Test of Transaction Cost Theory', *Journal of Economic Behavior & Organization*, 26, pp. 431–443.

Martilla, J. (1971) 'Word of Mouth Communication in the Industrial Adoption Process', *Journal of Marketing Research*, 8, 2 (May).

Mitchell, V.W. (1994) 'Problems and Risks in the Purchasing of Consultancy Services', *The Service Industries Journal*, 14, 3, pp. 315–339.

McGuire, T. et al. (1987) 'Group and Computer Mediated Discussion Effects in Risk Decision Making', *Journal of Personality and Social Psychology*, 52, 5, pp. 917–930.

Nelson, P. (1974) 'Advertising as Information', *Journal of Political Economy*, 81 (July/August), pp. 729–754.

Nimmo, M. (1995) 'Matters Affecting Members offering Professional Services (Members in Practice): Changes From 1 January 1995', *Management Accounting*, 73, 1, pp. 51–53.

Parasuraman, A., Zeithaml, V.A. and Berry, L.L. (1985) 'A Conceptual Model of Service Quality and Its Implications for Future Research', *Journal of Marketing*, 49, pp. 41–50.

Parasuraman, A., Zeithaml, V.A. and Berry, L.L. (1988) 'SERVQUAL: A Multiple-Item Scale for Measuring Customer Perceptions of Service Quality', *Journal of Retailing*, 64, pp. 12–40.

Parasuraman, A., Berry, L.L. and Zeithaml, V.A. (1991) 'Refinement and Reassessment of the SERVQUAL Scale', *Journal of Retailing*, 67, 4, pp. 420–450.

Parasuraman, A., Zeithaml, V.A. and Berry, L.L. (1994) 'Alternative Scales for Measuring Service Quality: A Comparative Assessment Based on Psychometric and Diagnostic Criteria', *Journal of Retailing*, 70, 3, pp. 201–230.

Porter, M.E. (1981) 'From competitive advantage to corporate strategy', *Harvard Business Review*, 65 (May/June), pp. 43–59.

Rathmell, J.M. (1974) *Management in the Services Sector*, (Cambridge, MA: Winthrop).

Roselius, T. (1971) 'Consumer rankings of risk reduction methods', *Journal of Marketing*, 35, pp. 32–36.

Scherer, F.M. (1980) 'No Boon in the Merger Boom', *Business and Society Review*, 32 (Winter), pp. 17–23.

Schmenner, R.W. (1986) 'How Can Service Businesses Survive and Prosper', *Sloan Management Review*, 27, 3, pp. 21–32.

Sheth, J.N. (1973) 'A model of industrial buyer behaviour', *Journal of Marketing*, 37, pp. 50–56.

Solomon, M.R. et al. (1985) 'A Role Theory Perspective on Dyadic Interactions: The Service Encounter', *Journal of Marketing*, 49 (Winter), pp. 99–111.

Stephen, F.H. (1994) 'Advertising, Consumer Search Costs and Prices in a Professional Service Market', *Applied Economics*, 26, pp. 1177–1188.

Stock, J.R. and Zinszer, P.H. (1987) 'The intial purchase decision for professional services', *Journal of Business Research*, 15 (Feb), pp. 1–16.

Stone, R.N. and Gronhaug, K. (1993) 'Perceived risk: Further considerations for the marketing discipline', *European Journal of Marketing*, 27, 3, pp. 39–50.

Storey, C. and Easingwood, C. (1993) 'The Impact of the New Product Development Project on the Success of Financial Services', *The Services Industry Journal*, 13, 3, pp. 40–54.

Vriens, M. and Boerkamp, E.J.C. (1993) 'Het Optimaliseren van Dienstverlening', *Maandblad voor Accountancy en Bedrijfseconomie*, 67, 12, pp. 599–612.

Vriens, M., Leeflang, P.S.H., Rosbergen, E. and Wilms, T.J.M. (1992) 'De Markt voor Accountantsdiensten in Nederland (deel 3)', *Maandblad voor Accountancy en Bedrijfseconomie*, (mei), pp. 224–238.

Webster, E. (1972) 'How to attract good staff', *International Management*, 27, 3, pp. 43–45.

Webster, F. (1970) 'Informal Communications in Industrial Markets', *Journal of Marketing Research*, 17, 2 (May).

Webster, F. and Wind, Y. (1975) *Organisational Buying Behaviour*, (New York: Prentice Hall).

Wheatley, E.W. (1987) 'Rainmakers, Mushrooms and Immaculate Conception: Internal Marketing for Professional Firm Associates', *Journal of Professional Services Marketing*, 24, 2, pp. 73–82.

Whittington, R., McNulty, T. and Whipp, R. (1994) 'Market-Driven Change in Professional Services: Problems and Processes', *Journal of Management Studies*, 31, 6, pp. 829–845.

Wilson, A. (1972) *The Marketing of Professional Services*, (London, UK: McGraw-Hill).

Zeithaml, V. (1981) 'How Consumer Evaluation Processes Differ Between Goods and Services', in Donnelly, J.H. and George, W.R. (eds) *Marketing of Services*, (Chicago: AMA).

Zenz, G.J. (1981) 'Material management and purchasing: Projections for the 1980's', *Journal of Purchasing and Materials Management*, 17 (Spring), pp. 15–20.

CHAPTER 7

THE FINANCIAL SERVICES CONSUMER

CHRISTINE ENNEW AND SALLY MCKECHNIE

INTRODUCTION

The relatively slow development of marketing in the financial services sector is often attributed to the idea that financial services are in some sense 'different' and present particular marketing problems. While financial service marketers may experience difficulties in marketing their services, many consumers would suggest that the problems they face as buyers are far greater. The service is often highly complex and may be difficult to evaluate both pre- and post-purchase. As a consequence, consumers typically perceive a high degree of risk in making a purchase decision. Furthermore, the fact that many services (such as pensions and insurance) are tailored to the specific circumstances of the individual means that the extent to which buyers can draw on the experiences of others may be limited. Indeed, any doubts about the problematic nature of financial services buying can easily be resolved by reference to the extensive corpus of rules and regulations which aims to protect the consumer in a buying process in which the potential for mis-selling is not insignificant. Despite these problems, the consumption of financial services has increased considerably over

Consumers and Services. Edited by Mark Gabbott and Gillian Hogg.
© 1998 John Wiley & Sons Ltd.

the past 20 years; around 75% of the population have some form of current account, over 30% have a bank credit card and nearly 60% have some form of life insurance. Not surprisingly, then, the buying process and the relationship between financial institutions and their clients is coming under increased scrutiny (see for example Burton 1994). However, as is the case with services generally, our understanding of this process is still imperfect.

This chapter seeks to enhance our existing understanding of buying behaviour in financial services. Drawing on some of the conceptual discussions earlier in the book, this chapter examines the nature of consumer buying behaviour and the ways in which the industry attempts to address the problems experienced by consumers in making choices. As will be apparent from the discussion, some of these problems are generic to services but others are specific to financial services. We review the specific dimensions of choice which create problems for consumers in the purchase of financial services. The empirical evidence on factors influencing purchase decisions is covered briefly then goes on to discuss industry responses more generally. The final section presents a summary and conclusions.

CONSUMER CHOICE AND FINANCIAL SERVICES

The purchase of financial services, like so many aspects of consumer buying behaviour, is only imperfectly understood. Traditional perspectives on consumer choice have conceptualised buying behaviour as a problem-solving decision process consisting of a number of discrete but interlinked stages. Probably the best example of this is the Engel-Kollat-Blackwell model (Engel et al. 1991) although similar approaches are in evidence in the models developed by Nicosia (1966) and Howard and Sheth (1969). This problem-solving perspective has also been applied in the context of organisational buying behaviour, for example, Robinson, Faris and Wind's (1967) 'Buy Grid' model which analyses buying decisions across a series of sequential 'buy phases' for different types of buying situation and the models proposed by Webster and Wind (1972), Sheth (1973) and Baker (1983).

In essence, the decision process begins when the buyer recognises a 'problem' (that is, a difference between a desired and an actual state) and is motivated to act. To solve the problem the buyer engages in a search for relevant information and on the basis of that information, evaluates the alternative options that are available. Evaluation would usually be followed by purchase and by various post-purchase responses which affect *inter alia* levels of satisfaction, willingness to recommend and willingness to repurchase (Oliver 1997). While the conceptualisation of decision making as a problem-solving process may have a certain intuitive appeal it also has a number of weaknesses. In particular, the concept of the problem-solving decision process is founded on a logical sequence of actions which may assume an unjustifiably high degree of rationality on the part of the consumer. Furthermore, the models as specified typically do not offer any empirically testable hypotheses (Foxall 1991). While recognising the weaknesses inherent in problem-solving decision process models, the basic structure of problem recognition, information search, evaluation of alternatives, purchase and post-purchase behaviour provides a useful framework in which to consider the difficulties that consumers confront when buying financial services.

- *Problem recognition.* Discussion of the problem recognition stage in buying behaviour typically centres around the nature of needs and wants and the extent to which consumers are motivated to satisfy those needs and wants. In principle, there are a range of 'needs' which may be satisfied through the purchase of financial services, including the need to make payments (cheques, debit cards etc.), the need to defer payment (loans, mortgages, credit cards etc.), the need for protection (house insurance, health insurance, life insurance etc.), the need to accumulate wealth (unit trusts, PEPS, life insurance based savings etc.) and the need for advice (tax/financial planning, business start-up advice etc). For many consumers, 'needs' of this nature are intrinsically uninteresting and often there is a preference to ignore certain 'needs' which may be associated with unpleasant events such as burglary, illness or death. As a consequence of the lack of intrinsic appeal and the complexity of the range of financial services available, it is often argued that consumers do not actively recognise that they have 'needs' for various financial products; rather they remain essentially passive participants in a decision process until the point of sale (Knights et al. 1994). At this point, the marketing process then starts to focus on the identification and activation (some would even suggest creation) of those needs.

- *Information search.* To the extent that the nature of financial service induces consumer passivity, the extent of information search is likely to be limited. Even when consumers are willing to be more active in the purchase process, information gathering presents problems. A significant element of information gathering typically relates to search qualities but the intangibility and inseparability mean that financial services are low in search qualities but high in experience and credence qualities (Zeithaml 1981). Unless the consumer can draw on their own prior experience of the product (and this would be rare since most financial services are long term, continuous or both) then there will be a tendency to rely heavily on the experience of others in the form of word-of-mouth recommendations and on the credibility of the organisation as a whole.

Even allowing for the difficulties that consumers face in gathering information, there are further problems in relation to the validity and accessibility of information. First, many financial services are long term in nature; consequently even when consumers gain vicarious experience from word-of-mouth recommendations, that experience may be at best partial since the full benefits of a product (a 10-year savings plan for example) may not have been realised. Second, since many products are effectively customised to individuals (reflecting health status, age, marital status etc.), drawing on the experience of others can be misleading if personal circumstances differ. Third, the complexity of many financial services means that many consumers may collect information, but not actually interpret that information or interpret it incorrectly.

While information search is clearly problematic, it is important to recognise that there has been a considerable increase in consumer understanding and knowledge of financial services and there has been a considerable growth in the various sources of independent information. Most daily papers have sections devoted to personal finance and organisations such as the Consumers' Association do provide regular advice and product comparisons. Thus personal consumers are generally thought to be better informed than they were in the past (Burton 1994). However, as the next paragraph shows, the simple availability of information does not necessarily mean that it can always be used to good effect.

- *Evaluation of alternatives.* If there are difficulties for consumers with respect to the gathering of information, these difficulties are magnified when the consumer attempts to evaluate alternative services. Like many services, financial services are processes rather than physical objects; the predominance of experience qualities makes pre-purchase evaluation difficult and where credence qualities are significant, post-purchase evaluation may also be problematic. Typically, alternatives are evaluated in relation to dimensions specified in the initial problem recognition stage; if consumers are in some sense inert or inactive in relation to problem recognition then the criteria being used for evaluation are likely to be poorly defined. However, even accepting that consumers can make evaluations, the process of so doing will be complicated by a number of features of financial services. There are a variety of different products which may satisfy a particular need; for example, the consumer who wishes to accumulate wealth may consider a range of products, from national savings certificates to guaranteed equity bonds to unit trusts to simple equity investments. The risk-return characteristics of these services vary considerably, as do the prices, and there is rarely any easy way to make direct comparisons across different service types. These problems have been exacerbated by the lack of transparency in the pricing and promotion of many financial services (Diacon and Ennew 1996). Although recent regulatory changes regarding commission disclosure have partly remedied this situation, comparisons across service types remain difficult.

The presence of credence qualities in many financial services also makes evaluation complex. Products which contain a significant element of advice or which require 'managing' over the course of their life may be difficult to evaluate even after purchase. In particular, the performance of many long-term investment products is determined partly by the skill of the relevant fund managers but partly by economic factors which are beyond the control of the supplier. Thus, consumers expose themselves to certain risks (both actual and perceived) in purchasing these products, but will subsequently experience difficulties in determining whether poor performance was due to company-specific factors or to external contingencies. A consequence of this situation is a tendency for customers to evaluate service providers (rather than the services themselves) and to rely heavily on trust and confidence as attributes of those providers.

- *Purchase.* Purchase is normally expected to follow logically as the result of the evaluation of alternatives unless any unexpected problems materialise. However, earlier discussions have suggested that for many financial services customers, needs are only created or activated at the point of purchase. Accordingly, the actual process of purchase will often be the result of an active selling effort by a supplier. Customer interaction with sales staff is then likely to be of particular significance in the purchase process. However, while sympathetic, unpressured selling may be highly effective, the complexity and riskiness of financial services combined with their common status as 'avoidance' products means that many customers may be vulnerable to 'hard' or 'over' selling. There can be little doubt that this has been the case in the past in some parts of the market (OFT 1992, Devlin and Ennew 1993) and that it has resulted in a significant loss of consumer confidence in those parts of the industry where confidence is so important.

Furthermore, the purchase process is influenced by the inseparability of production and consumption in financial services. The front-line service employees play an important 'boundary spanning role' in the production of services, as do the consumers themselves in their capacity as 'partial employees' (Bowen and Schneider 1988). Therefore an important influence on the purchase process will be the interaction between buyer and supplier. Since services depend upon input from both service employees and consumers for their production, the quality of the service output very much depends on the nature of the personal interactions of these parties.

Fiduciary responsibility is often highlighted as an important characteristic which distinguishes financial services from other services and goods (McKechnie 1992); one dimension of fiduciary responsibility is that suppliers need to exercise discretion with respect to the sale of certain products. Thus, for example, it would be inappropriate for a bank to lend money to a business which had few prospects for survival and success. However, until a consumer has signalled an intent to purchase it may not be possible to identify whether or not it is appropriate to provide that product to that customer. Thus, the consumer effectively faces the added problem that even if a conscious decision to purchase has been taken, the financial institution concerned may be unwilling to provide the product.

- *Post-purchase behaviour.* The post-purchase evaluation of financial services is difficult for the reasons mentioned earlier. Indeed it is often suggested that evaluation may place rather more emphasis on functional aspects of the service (how things are done) rather than technical aspects (what is done) because the latter are more difficult to evaluate (Zeithaml 1981). The difficulties of post-purchase evaluation would tend to suggest that the risk of cognitive dissonance among consumers is high and that this may subsequently reduce brand loyalty. Evidence for this is ambiguous; for continuous products such as bank accounts, a high level of cognitive dissonance might be reflected in high levels of switching. In practice, the number of consumers changing bank, although increasing (Burton 1994, Ennew and Binks 1996) is still low. This may reflect a low level of dissonance; alternatively, given switching costs, consumers may be willing to tolerate high levels of dissonance before being motivated to act. In the case of savings and investment products, levels of switching are higher and the relatively low proportion of retained customers may reflect the high level of dissonance experienced.

However, where a high degree of trust is established between buyer and seller, there can be considerable benefits for both parties. The establishment of trust can bring about a degree of inertia in buyer–seller relationships. Since an irreversible amount of time and effort is required by an individual in order to acquire the necessary experience and information on which to assess an institution's reliability, it is usually the case that once satisfied, a consumer is more likely to remain with that institution than incur the costs of searching for and vetting alternative suppliers.

From the discussion above, it should be clear that there are good conceptual reasons for expecting consumers to encounter difficulties with respect to the choice of financial services. The severity of these problems will vary across market segments. Thus, for example, the problem of complexity may be rather less important for a corporate buyer evaluating different leasing companies than it would be for an individual evaluating pension providers. Furthermore, corporate buyers may well be expected to express needs more actively and accurately than personal customers. Nevertheless within the personal market there are clearly some sub-groups of customers (often buying through independent financial agents—IFAs, by phone or by direct mail) who are more actively aware of their need than others. Allowing for this variation in the degree and type of difficulties consumers may experience, there are a number of themes which seem to be of particular relevance to the choice process. These include the importance of trust and confidence in the supplier, the concern about customer passivity, the relative importance of functional aspects of the service product, and the importance of interaction and contact with people.

CONSUMER BUYING BEHAVIOUR IN FINANCIAL SERVICES

The previous section has highlighted some of the difficulties that customers encounter in the purchase of financial services. In this section, we examine briefly some of the existing empirical research relating to buying behaviour and consider the extent to which it corroborates the issues discussed in the previous section. The results of a variety of studies of buying behaviour for both personal and corporate financial services are summarised in Tables 7.1 and 7.2. Most of the work to date has emphasised specific aspects of buying behaviour such as factors affecting the choice of bank, usage of financial services and customer loyalty, rather than attempting to examine the buying process as a whole. This largely reflects the difficulties associated with testing decision process models in their entirety.

Empirical studies relating to the personal market highlight the importance of factors such as confidence, trust and customer loyalty. Some of the common choice criteria in bank selection are dependability and size of the institution, location, convenience and ease of transactions, professionalism of bank personnel and availability of loans. It would appear therefore that the personal consumer is more interested in the functional quality dimension of financial services (i.e. how the service is delivered) rather than the technical quality dimension (i.e. what is actually received as the outcome of the production process) (see Gronroos 1984). This is hardly surprising given the difficulties consumers have in evaluating services which were highlighted in the previous section.

In contrast, work relating to corporate customers places much greater emphasis on the importance of interaction and understanding. This would be consistent with the notion that issues such as passivity, complexity and problems of comparison are perhaps less important to corporate decision makers, but that the intangibility and the lack of search qualities means that personal relationships, trust, confidence and reliability continue to be important influences within the purchase process.

INDUSTRY RESPONSES

The previous two sections have highlighted some of the problems which confront consumers when choosing financial services. These

Table 7.1

Personal Financial Services Buying Behaviour

Author(s)	Field of Study	Geographic Area	Key Finding(s)
Arora, Cavusgil and Nevin (1985)	Choice criteria used in financial institutions	US	Common criteria for bank and savings/loans customers: e.g. dependability of institution, convenience and ease of transactions, variety of services and size of institution
Boyd et al. (1994)	Consumer choice criteria in financial institution selection	US	Reputation and interest rates (loans/savings) more important than friendliness of employees, modern facilities, drive-in service
Burton (1996)	Ethnicity and financial behaviour	UK	Evidence of considerable variety in the take-up of pensions according to ethnic origin; suggests that financial services providers have not yet accommodated the needs/expectations of distinct ethnic groups
Chan (1993)	Banking services for young intellectuals	Hong Kong	Financial sophistication of youth market
Ennew (1992)	Consumer attitudes to independent advice	UK	More importance may be attached to image and reputation of an independent financial adviser than their status
Goode, Moutinho and Chien (1996)	Satisfaction with ATMs	UK	Levels satisfaction and overall usage of services influenced by customer expectations and by perceived risk
Harrison (1994)	Segmentation of market for retail financial services	UK	Distinct segments identified based on financial maturity (based on likely range of product holdings) and perceived knowledge of financial services
Jain, Pinson and Maholtra (1987)	Customer loyalty in retail banking	US	Customer loyalty is a useful construct; bank non-loyal segment swayed by economic rationale, whereas greater emphasis placed on human aspects of banking by bank loyal segment
Joy, Kim and Laroche (1991)	Link between ethnicity and use of financial services	Canada	Ethnicity should be considered as a construct having strong potential impact on consumption

Author	Focus	Country	Findings
Kaynak and Yucelt (1984)	Comparison of attitudinal orientations of US and Canadian credit card users	US/Canada	Similar patterns in attitudes to owning and using a credit card
Kennington, Hill and Rakowska (1996)	Study of banking habits and bank choice in a transitional economy	Poland	Consumers in a transitional economy select banks using the same criteria as consumers in other countries, although pricing concerns do appear to be particularly significant
Laroche, Rosenblatt and Manning (1986)	Factors influencing choice of bank	Canada	Importance of location convenience, speed of service, competence and friendliness of bank personnel
Laroche and Manning (1984)	Information processing activity of consumer bank selection	Canada	Existence of a 'foggy set' of bank brands rather than a 'hold set'
Levesque and McDougall (1996)	Determinants of satisfaction in retail banking	Canada	Satisfaction influenced by service quality, service features, service problems and service quality. These variables also affect intentions to switch bank
Leonard and Spencer (1991)	Importance of bank image as a competitive strategy for increasing customer traffic flow	US	Preference for banks amongst students as providers of financial services; greater confidence in large–medium-sized banks; importance of courtesy of personnel, competitive deposit rates, loan availability
Lewis (1991)	International comparison of bank customers' expectations and perceptions of service quality	UK/US	Very high expectations of service quality and high perceptions of service received, yet gaps did exist
Martenson (1985)	Consumer choice criteria in bank selection	Sweden	Random decisions by a third of respondents; importance of bank location, availability of loans, bank where salary paid through, and parental influences
Meidan & Moutinho (1988)	Bank customer perceptions and loyalty	UK	Banks should develop ATM usage; financial institutions should review basic banking services, e.g. considering a service package; customer loyalty a function of more than one single variable

Table 7.2

Corporate Financial Services Buying Behaviour

Author(s)	Field of Study	Geographic Area	Key Findings
Chan and Ma (1990)	Corporate customer buying behaviour for banking services	Hong Kong	Great importance attached to banks understanding their clients' attitudes in order to serve them better
Edwards (1992)	Current and future use of foreign banks by UK middle corporate market	UK	Very conservative approach to domestic banking with foreign banks used as secondary banks
Ennew and Binks (1996a)	Impact of service quality on customer retention	UK	Both product characteristics and service quality affect potential for small businesses to switch bank
Ennew and Binks (1996b)	Customer involvement in banking relationships	UK	Greater degrees of customer involvement in a banking relationship result in improved service quality
File and Prince (1991)	Purchase dynamics of SME market and financial services	US	Existence of 3 distinctive sociographic segments adopting innovations in bank services: return seekers, relevance seekers and relationship seekers
Teas, Dorsch and Alexander (1988)	Measurement of aspects of the long-term bank and commercial customer relationship: banker's customer knowledge, personal working relationship with bank, banker's reactive and proactive behaviour	US	Banks should take an active interest in the welfare of their commercial customers to be in a better position to develop long-term relationships in them

Reference	Subject	Country	Findings
Turnbull (1983)	Relationship between banks' corporate customers and their sources of financial services	UK	Small-/medium-sized companies do not always consider major UK banks as an appropriate source for all financial services
Turnbull (1982a)	Purchase of international financial services by medium/large sized UK companies with European subsidies	UK	Greater effort required to understand the nature of customer needs and bank/customer relationships through detailed application of the Interaction Theory
Turnbull (1982b)	Role of branch bank manager in bank services marketing	UK	Lack of customer-orientation amongst bank branch managers
Turnbull (1982c)	Use of foreign banks by UK companies	UK	High concentration of decision making and extent of split banking; crucial importance of development and maintenance of a company-bank relationship
Turnbull and Gibbs (1989)	Relationship between large companies and its lead and closest substitute bank	South Africa	Predominant bank selection criteria: importance of quality of service, quality of staff and price of services; split banking common
Yorke (1990)	Interactive perceptions of suppliers and corporate clients in marketing of professional services	UK/Canada/ Sweden	Need to consider atmosphere in which relationship is being conducted to build picture of mutual perceptions of parties into medium- to long-term planning activity
Zineldin (1995)	Bank–company interactions	Sweden	Smaller companies tend to have stable relationships with a single bank but larger organisations operate with a variety of banking relationships. There is evidence of low levels of satisfaction among smaller companies

difficulties are due partly to the generic characteristics of services, partly to the unique features of financial services and partly to the practices employed within the industry itself. Given the existence of these problems, effective marketing must concern itself with reducing or minimising the difficulties which consumers face in the purchase process. In order to examine the current evidence on industry responses, this section considers the nature of strategies and tactics employed in relation to each of the key characteristics of financial services: intangibility, inseparability, heterogeneity, fiduciary responsibility and the long-term nature of many of the products. However, it should be noted that many of these responses can address more than one service characteristic.

- *Intangibility.* Intangibility is probably the dominant characteristic of any service and there are a variety of strategies which can be used to mitigate its effects. The simplest approach is to find some means of 'tangiblising' the service. The provision of some physical evidence (whether essential or peripheral) is probably the most common approach to dealing with intangibility (Shostack 1982). Examples of peripheral physical evidence would include wallets with insurance policies, cheque book covers and even promotional free gifts. Essential physical evidence is typically associated with branch networks or head offices with the appearance and layout being used to give a tangible representation of the organisation. Often physical evidence of this nature is supported by the use of a tangible image or name. Thus, for example, the *Leeds Permanent* or the *Northern Rock* are both organisational names that try to link to an image of stability and security. Equally a tangible image or association such as the *Black Horse* (Lloyds) or Direct Lines 'red telephone on wheels' can serve a similar purpose. Using physical evidence or imagery to make a financial service appear more 'concrete' is a key element of most marketing strategies. Nevertheless, there are pitfalls associated with this approach, particularly with respect to the development of a tangible image. The image developed necessarily creates expectations in the consumer's mind and if the organisation cannot match those expectations then customer satisfaction may decrease.

Tangibilising a service addresses the problem of lack of physical form, but is less effective in relation to product complexity and lack of consumer interest (a form of mental intangibility). Two key strategies are important in this respect. First, to address the complexity issue there is a need to focus on reducing perceived risk through building trust and confidence; if the consumer cannot fully understand the nature of the service then they must be able to trust a supplier and to feel confident that their finances are being safely managed. Attempts to build such trust and confidence often rely on the longevity of the organisations. For example, The Royal Bank of Scotland claims in its literature that: *'You can also be sure that your money is in safe hands. We have been around for more than 260 years which gives us a wealth of banking experience.'*

An alternative approach to dealing with the same underlying issue is that adopted by National Westminster Bank. The bank attempts to address the issue of complexity through a coordinated range of point-of-sale material which demonstrates and reiterates the idea that: *'We're here to make life easier.'* Further copy goes on to state that NatWest aims to: *'take the mystery out of banking and make it as straightforward and friendly as possible . . . you'll discover a wealth of ways NatWest can make life easier for you'*.

These efforts are further reinforced by NatWest's television advertising campaign 'The Bank' which aims to present bank staff as normal, everyday people helping to dispel the aura of complexity and the mystique associated with banking. Despite the best of intentions, this particular campaign proved less than successful as far as audiences were concerned, in part because the message was thought to be unclear and also because of a perceived focus on the internal working of the bank.

The lack of interest in many financial services can often be addressed by focusing on the benefits gained from the purchase of the product. Thus, promotional material for personal loans tends to emphasise the purchases which can be made as a result of the loan (whether cars, hi-fi equipment, holidays or houses). In a similar style, the recent Legal and General TV advertising campaign sought to emphasise the benefits of long-term savings policies by showing the delight experienced by individuals when they received a particular payout. Of course, good marketing would always focus on the benefits of the product rather than the product itself, but while many goods (cars, clothes, house etc.) may be viewed as having some intrinsic value beyond that associated with the benefits they provide, a similar case would be more difficult to argue for financial services. The feeling that financial services are products that generally consumers would prefer to avoid means that emphasising the benefits is crucial in attracting consumer attention.

- *Inseparability.* Inseparability is one obvious consequence of intangibility; the fact that the services are typically produced and consumed simultaneously means that customers have considerable difficulties with respect to pre-purchase evaluation. Although an *ex ante* evaluation of a particular product may be difficult, consumers can evaluate the organisation and can draw on the experience of others. Accordingly a common theme in the marketing of financial services is to emphasise the performance and quality of the organisation and its people in order that there will be a halo effect from organisation to product. Such approaches are often reinforced by active attempts to secure word-of-mouth recommendations. American Express, for example, actively encourages existing customers to recommend new customers and rewards those customers who do introduce new members.

Furthermore, given the importance of the interaction between customers and employees and the potential role of employees in inspiring trust and confidence, many organisations are increasingly looking at human resource policies, training and internal marketing as means of building more effective relationships with customers in order to encourage retention and repurchase. These relationships are seen as being of considerable significance, both in reducing the level of perceived risk pre-purchase and the levels of dissonance post-purchase. First Direct, for example, when recruiting staff for the launch of its telephone banking service, placed much greater emphasis on the interpersonal skills of customer contact staff than it did on their detailed knowledge of banking practice.

- *Heterogeneity.* A logical consequence of inseparability and the important role played by people is that the quality of service delivery has the potential to be highly variable. Clearly the potential for such variability will hinder the process of evaluation by consumers. Mechanisation of service delivery through ATMs, automated phone-based systems and Internet-based systems, for example, or even through the use of expert systems, has the potential to reduce quality variability, although this option may not be available for all services. Where delivery cannot be mechanised, then financial institutions must emphasise internal marketing and training to ensure higher levels of consistency in service delivery.
- *Fiduciary responsibility.* The concept of fiduciary responsibility concerns itself with the implicit and explicit responsibilities of financial institutions with respect to the products they sell. The impact of fiduciary responsibility is arguably at its greatest at the purchase stage when a consumer may find that, despite an active marketing campaign which has stimulated a decision to purchase, the institution indicates that it is unable to provide the product. For example, a common complaint from both personal customers and smaller businesses is that banks will actively promote the fact that they offer a variety of loans but will then turn down applications from some customers. Similar issues arise in relation to insurance where many companies are increasingly looking to sell only to 'good risks'. In part this may simply reflect the overall importance of profit and an unwillingness to supply loans or insurance when the risk is too high (Knights et al. 1994). However, we should perhaps note that such decisions may also reflect an element of fiduciary responsibility in the sense that financial services suppliers are obliged to recognise that many of their 'raw materials' are actually funds provided by other customers. An extension of the idea of responsibility in relation to the management of funds is evidenced in the case of the Co-operative Bank. The bank's positioning and promotional campaign revolves around their ethical stance and their commitment to the responsible sourcing and distribution of funds.

The selling process itself is also an area of concern because of the substantial information asymmetries which exist between supplier and customer. To address these problems is difficult. The simplest route is perhaps to emphasise honesty and prudence as themes in promotional campaigns. Consider, for example, the Prudential campaign built around the character *Prudence* or a recent press campaign for Scottish Widows:

0345 678910
Our advice is just as straightforward

There can't be many adults in the country who haven't experienced financial 'advice' the hard way: unsolicited phone calls at inconvenient times and unwanted pressure.

At Scottish Widows we do things differently

Furthermore there are difficulties for financial service organisations in that fiduciary responsibility means that they may be promoting products to those individuals who are unlikely to be able to purchase because they are considered to be poor risk; while clearly this is something that many suppliers seek to avoid. In practice the identification of exactly who is an appropriate customer is difficult and even with sophisticated marketing information systems, this process will be less than perfect.

Finally, with respect to fiduciary responsibility there is the issue of the purchase (sales) process itself. Given the information asymmetries which exist between supplier and customer, many customers are vulnerable to high pressure selling and bad advice. Indeed this is probably the issue which has done most to undermine the image of the financial services sector in recent years. Nevertheless, there are ways in which these issues can be tackled both internally and externally. One approach which a number of organisations have adopted is to reconsider their reward systems with a view to eliminating or at least reducing the reliance on commission based selling. In a number of cases the nature of the reward structure (i.e. our salesmen aren't paid just on commission) is often used as a component of advertising in order to reassure consumers of the high standards of the supplying organisation.

- *Long-term nature.* Many financial services are either consumed continuously (current accounts, credit cards) and therefore require a long-term relationship or else only yield benefits in the longer term. As indicated earlier, these features of financial services will tend to increase the perceived risk associated with the purchase and decrease the consumer's ability to evaluate the service both *ex ante* and *ex post*. To address this problem, there is again a tendency to rely heavily on marketing activities which emphasise the longevity of the supplier, trust, confidence and reliability. A good illustration of this approach is the TV advertising used by Clerical Medical which emphasises the origins of the company during the middle of the nineteenth century and its success at serving particular customer groups since that time. More recently, Royal Insurance has used a campaign which focuses on the relationship between a particular financial advisor and a client; the advert depicts the two individuals growing older together and seeks to highlight the company's ability to provide a continuous relationship which meets the individual's changing financial needs.

CONCLUSIONS

Although there has been a variety of empirical research examining customer choice, our understanding of the buying process for financial services is still limited. However, what is apparent both conceptually and from existing empirical evidence is that certain characteristics of financial services present a number of problems for consumers when they make choices. Financial services are low in search qualities and high in experience and credence qualities. Information is difficult to collect and interpret and there is a tendency to rely heavily on the experience of others rather than on supplier-provided information. Evaluation is even more complex, partly because of the lack of search qualities but also because of the complexity of many of the products and the reluctance of many suppliers to facilitate comparisons across products. Often consumer needs do not become apparent until the actual point of sale and the problems of information search and evaluation mean that the buyer is always likely to be vulnerable to the 'hard' sell. Having bought a particular financial service, a customer may still find evaluation difficult and many buyers experience high levels of cognitive dissonance post-purchase.

There are a variety of strategies and tactics which marketers can use to address these problematic aspects of consumer choice; these include tangibilising the service, emphasising particular dimensions of image and investing in staff training and internal marketing. However, there are also many aspects of the marketing of financial services which have tended to reinforce some of the problems experienced by consumers. In particular, pricing and product benefits are often not clearly presented and the historic reliance on commission-based selling has resulted in a number of well publicised and damaging cases of over-selling for certain products. Some of these problems are being rectified by a combination of company-specific actions and industry-wide regulation. However, from a marketing perspective it is crucial that financial services organisations recognise that they operate in a high contact business where the nature of buyer-seller interactions and the establishment of long-term relationships based on confidence and trust have real implications for successful retention of customers and recruitment of prospects (Christopher, Payne and Ballantyne 1991).

REFERENCES

Arora, R., Tamer Cavusgil, S. and Nevin, J.R. (1985) 'Evaluation of Financial Institutions by Bank versus Savings & Loan Customers: An Analysis of Factor Congruency', *International Journal of Bank Marketing*, 3, 3, pp. 47–55.

Baker, M.J. (1983) *Market Development*, (Harmondsworth: Penguin).

Boyd, W.L., Leonard, M. and White, C. (1994) 'Customer Preferences for Financial Services: An Analysis', *International Journal of Bank Marketing*, 12, 1, pp. 9–15.

Bowen, D.E. and Schneider, B. (1988) 'Services Marketing & Management:

Implications for Organizational Behaviour', *Research in Organizational Behaviour*, 10, pp. 43–80.

Burton, D. (1994) *Financial Services and the Consumer*, (London: Routledge).

Burton, D. (1996) 'Ethnicity and Consumer Financial Behaviour: a Case Study of British Asians in the Pensions Market', *International Journal of Bank Marketing*, 14, 7, pp. 21–31.

Chan, R.Y-K. (1993) 'Banking Services for Young Intellectuals', *International Journal of Bank Marketing*, 11, 5, pp. 33–40.

Chan, A.K.K and Ma, V.S.M. (1990) 'Corporate Banking Behaviour: A Survey in Hong Kong', *International Journal of Bank Marketing*, 8, 2, pp. 25–31.

Christopher, M., Payne, Adrian F.T. and Ballantyne, D. (1991) *Relationship Marketing: Bring Quality, Customer Service and Marketing Together*, (Oxford: Butterworth Heinemann).

Devlin, J.F. and Ennew, C.T. (1993) 'Regulating the Distribution of Savings and Investment Products: Retrospect and Prospect', *International Journal of Bank Marketing*, 11, 7, pp. 3–10.

Diacon, S.R. and Ennew, C.T. (1996) 'Ethical Issues in Insurance Marketing in the UK', *European Journal of Marketing*, 30, 5, pp. 67–80.

Engel, J.F., Blackwell, R.D. and Miniard, P.W. (1991) *Consumer Behavior*, 6th edn, (US: The Dryden Press).

Ennew, C.T. (1992) 'Consumer Attitudes to Independent Financial Advice', *International Journal of Bank Marketing*, 10, 5, pp. 13–18.

Ennew, C.T. and Binks, M.R. (1996a) 'Good and Bad Customers: The Benefits of Participating in the Banking Relationship', *International Journal of Bank Marketing*, 14, 2, pp. 5–13.

Ennew, C.T. and Binks, M. (1996b) 'The Impact of Service Quality and Service Characteristics on Customer Retention: Small Businesses and their Banks in the UK', *British Journal of Management*, 7, 3, pp. 219–230.

Foxall, G.R. (1991) 'Consumer Behaviour', in Baker, M.J. (ed.), *The Marketing Book*, 2nd ed., (Oxford: Butterworth-Heinemann).

Gabbott, M. and Hogg, G. (1994) 'Consumer Behaviour and Services: A Review', *Journal of Marketing Management*, 10, pp. 311–324.

Goode, M., Moutinho, L.A. and Chien, C. (1996) 'Structural Equation Modelling of Overall Satisfaction and Full Use of Services for ATMs', *International Journal of Bank Marketing*, 14, 7, pp. 4–12.

Gronroos, C. (1984) 'A Service Quality Model and its Marketing Implications', *European Journal of Marketing*, 18, 4, pp. 36–44.

Howard, J.A. and Sheth, J.N. (1969) *The Theory of Buying Behavior*, (New York: John Wiley).

Jain, A.K., Pinson, C. and Malhotra, N.K. (1987) 'Customer Loyalty as a Construct in the Marketing of Bank Services', *International Journal of Bank Marketing*, 5, 3, pp. 49–72.

Joy, A., Kim, C. and Laroche, M. (1991) 'Ethnicity as a Factor Influencing Use of Financial Services', *International Journal of Bank Marketing*, 9, 4, pp. 10–16.

Harrison, T.S. (1994) 'Mapping Customer Segments for Personal Financial Services', *International Journal of Bank Marketing*, 12, 8, pp. 17–25.

Kaynak, E. and Yucelt, U. (1984) 'A Cross-Cultural Study of Credit Card Usage Behaviours: Canadian and American Credit Card Users Contrasted', *International Journal of Bank Marketing*, 2, 2, pp. 45–57.

Kennington, C., Hill, J. and Rakowska (1996) 'Consumer Selection Criteria for Banks in Poland', *International Journal of Bank Marketing*, 14, 4, pp. 12–21.

Knights, D., Sturdy, A. and Morgan, G. (1994) 'The Consumer Rules: An Examination of Rhetoric and "Reality" of Marketing in Financial Services', *European Journal of Marketing*, 28, 3, pp. 42–54.

Laroche, M. and Manning, T. (1984) 'Consumer Brand Selection & Categorisation Processes: A Study of Bank Choice', *International Journal of Bank Marketing*, 2, 3, pp. 3–21.

Laroche, M., Rosenblatt, J.A. and Manning, T. (1986) 'Services Used and Factors Considered Important in Selecting a Bank: An Investigation across Diverse Demographic Segments', *International Journal of Bank Marketing*, 4, 1, pp. 35–55.

Leonard, M. and Spencer, A. (1991) 'The Importance of Image as a Competitive Strategy: An Exploratory Study in Commercial Banks', *International Journal of Bank Marketing*, 9, 4, pp. 25–29.

Levesque, T. and McDougall, G. (1996) 'Determinants of Customer Satisfaction in Retail Banking', *International Journal of Bank Marketing*, 14, 7, pp. 12–20.

Lewis, B.R. (1991) 'Service Quality: an International Comparison of Bank Customers' Expectations and Perceptions', *Journal of Marketing Management*, 7, 1, pp. 47–62.

Martenson, R. (1985) 'Consumer Choice Selection in Retail Bank Selection', *International Journal of Bank Marketing*, 3, 2, pp. 64–74.

McKechnie, S. (1992) 'Consumer Buying Behaviour in Financial Services: An Overview', *International Journal of Bank Marketing*, 10, 5, pp. 4–12.

Meidan, A. and Moutinho, L. (1988) 'Bank Customers' Perceptions & Loyalty: An Attitudinal Research', in *European Marketing Academy Proceedings*, pp. 472–493.

Murray, K.B. (1991) 'A Test of Services Marketing Theory: Consumer Information Acquisition Activities', *Journal of Marketing*, 55 (January), pp. 10–25.

Nicosia, F.N. (1966) *Consumer Decision Processes*, (Englewood Cliffs, New Jersey: Prentice Hall).

OFT 'Savings and Investments: Consumer Issues', Occasional Paper to the OFT based on reports by two consultants—Jeremy Mitchell and Helena Wiesner, OFT (June), 1992.

Oliver, R.L. (1997) *Satisfaction: A Behavioural Perspective on the Consumer*, (New York: McGraw Hill).

Parasuraman, A., Berry, L.L. and Zeithaml, V.A. (1991) 'Understanding Customer Expectations of Service', *Sloan Management Review*, 32, 3, pp. 39–48.

Robinson, P.J., Faris, C.W. and Wind (1967) *Industrial Buying, Creative Marketing*, (Boston: Allyn & Bacon).

Sheth, J.N. (1973) 'A Model of Industrial Buyer Behaviour', *Journal of Marketing*, 37, 4 (October), pp. 50–56.

Shostack, G.L. (1982) 'How to Design a Service', *European Journal of Marketing*, 16, 1, pp. 49–63.

Teas, R.K., Dorsch, M.J. and McAlexander, J.H. (1988) 'Measuring Commercial Bank Customers Attitudes towards the Quality of the Bank Services Marketing Relationship', *Journal of Professional Services Marketing*, 4, 1, pp. 75–95.

Turnbull, P.W. (1982a) 'The Purchasing of International Financial Services by Medium- and Large-sized UK companies with European Subsidiaries', *European Journal of Marketing*, 16, 3, pp. 111–121.

Turnbull, P.W. (1982b) 'The Role of the Branch Bank Manager in the Marketing of Bank Services', *European Journal of Marketing*, 16, 3, pp. 31–36.

Turnbull, P.W. (1982c) 'The Use of Foreign Banks by British Companies', *European Journal of Marketing*, 16, 3, pp. 133–145.

Turnbull, P.W. (1983) 'Corporate Attitudes towards Bank Services', *International Journal of Bank Marketing*, 1, 1, pp. 53–66.

Turnbull, P.W. and Gibbs, M.L. (1989) 'The Selection of Banks & Banking Services among Corporate Customers in South Africa', *International Journal of Bank Marketing*, 7, 5, pp. 36–39.

Webster Jr., F.E. and Wind, Y. (1972) 'A General Model of Understanding Organizational Buying Behaviour', *Journal of Marketing*, 36 (April), pp. 12–19.

Zeithaml, V. (1981) 'How Consumer Evaluation Processes differ between Goods and Services' in Donnelly, J.H. and George, W.R. (eds), *The Marketing of Services*, Proceedings, (Chicago: AMA), pp. 186–190.

Zineldin, M. (1995) 'Bank–Company Interactions and Relationships: Some empirical Evidence', *International Journal of Bank Marketing*, 13, 2, pp. 30–40.

CHAPTER 8

THE HEALTHCARE CONSUMER

JOBY JOHN, MARK GABBOTT AND GILLIAN HOGG

INTRODUCTION

The provision of efficient, effective healthcare for their citizens is a
challenge for all Western democracies. Despite a wide variety of
funding and delivery mechanisms there appears to be a constant
striving for a 'better' system, more able to reconcile the demands of
consumers, the medical profession, politicians and economists.
Although the structural and cultural bases of the systems may vary,
the fundamental purpose of healthcare for the consumer remains the
same—the delivery of health, characterised as 'well being'. The
purpose of this chapter is to examine the role of the consumer in two
very different healthcare systems, the state controlled and highly
regulated National Health Service (NHS) in the UK and the market-
driven, insurance-based system in the US. Although the systems may
be ideologically different, they face similar problems of containing
costs, whilst at the same time delivering effective services in an area of
ever-increasing consumer demand. In this chapter we first describe the
choices available to consumers within the system and then examine an
issue common to all healthcare consumers regardless of the structure of
provision: how consumers evaluate the service they receive.

Consumers and Services. Edited by Mark Gabbott and Gillian Hogg.
© 1998 John Wiley & Sons Ltd.

As Ham et al. (1990) point out, there appears to be a recent convergence in the culture of healthcare, with market-oriented systems like that in the US making greater use of regulation and planning, while countries where healthcare has been traditionally based upon planning and regulation such as the UK, are moving towards a more competitive model. In both cases reform requires changes in attitude, not only amongst the healthcare providers, but in consumer behaviour, which may challenge deep-rooted beliefs about the nature and provision of social welfare. These fundamental consumer beliefs constitute constraints in the healthcare delivery system which can only be addressed by understanding the consumer's role in the system. As a precursor to discussing consumer behaviour in this context it is first necessary to describe the basis on which the two systems operate.

THE UK NATIONAL HEALTH SERVICE

When the UK government set up the NHS in 1948, the advantages to patients of a centrally funded service, available to all regardless of status and free at the point of delivery, were obvious. However, they did not receive the wholehearted support of the medical profession who had traditionally enjoyed considerable autonomy. In order to win the support of the main doctors' union two major concessions were made. First, doctors were to have managerial independence within hospital services and were not included within the management hierarchy; and secondly General Practitioners (GPs), who previously had been in effect independent businessmen, retained their separate status. GPs are in fact contractors who are paid by the NHS to provide services for their patients; as all UK citizens are required by law to register with a GP and the number of GPs in any one area is controlled, they have traditionally been guaranteed their income.

The role of the GP is crucial to the operation of the NHS. By acting as gatekeepers to the hospital services they control consumer access to specialist services; it is not possible for a consumer to be treated in a hospital, other than in an emergency, without first being referred by a GP. Neither is it possible to bypass the system by going to an emergency department for non-urgent treatment—the patient would simply be referred back to their GP. The GP is, therefore, the first point of access to healthcare and plays a vital part in patient care. Prior to the 1990 reforms it was the norm for patients to register with a GP as a child and only to change doctors if they moved house. Indeed there were significant barriers to changing doctor without specific reasons and as a result less than 6% of the population changed their doctors in any year. The culture of the NHS was of a benevolent doctor dispensing care to a grateful patient, with neither party expected to assess the relationship in any meaningful manner.

1990 and Beyond

Whether or not the government intended to implement a radical reform of the NHS is debatable. Butler (1993) suggests that the policy reforms proposed in 1989 were brought about as a response to a funding crisis rather than a commitment to restructuring the NHS. By considering ways in which the output of services could be improved and concentrating on making services more efficient and responsive, attention could be deflected from a severe resourcing problem. The policies introduced were in line with the government's policy of controlling public spending and the privatisation of state-owned industries which it had pursued throughout the 1980s. The political philosophy behind these policies was based on a belief that social policy should be subservient to economic policy; that individuals are the best judges of their own welfare and should therefore be given the maximum opportunity to exercise choice. This belief in the market mechanism as a way of ensuring consumer choice implied that providers should have real incentives to maximise quality in order to attract customers and supply the services that consumers want, rather than those which others believe should be provided, if they had the stimulus of competition.

However, simply breaking up or selling off the NHS, which had happened to other state-owned industries, was not a politically acceptable option. Consumers are fiercely protective of their health service and whilst willing to acknowledge that there are inefficiencies and problems in the delivery of the service, the principles on which it is based are sacrosanct. The challenge for Margaret Thatcher's government was to introduce a market culture with its inherent benefits, whilst at the same time preserving the core values of the welfare state. Their response was to create an internal market: health services that could be bought and sold, but within the umbrella of the NHS. This type of internal market had already been tried in other countries, most notably The Netherlands and New Zealand, and in its simplest form involves the separation of the responsibilities for providing and purchasing services. On the provider side there are independent (Trust) hospitals and directly managed hospitals still wholly controlled by the NHS delivering hospital services, as well as a vast number of GPs, usually operating within group practices, responsible for primary care. On the purchaser side are the health authorities, responsible for ensuring that services are available for residents in their area and in addition GPs can choose to operate as purchasers. By allocating budgets for GPs to purchase services on behalf of their patients the government created a specialist buying group able to purchase hospital care according to the needs of individual patients. In this way consumers are assumed to gain the benefits of the choice of where and when to be treated, whilst at the same time preserving the central tenet of the NHS, that care is provided free of charge to the individual.

In effect this structure created two distinct markets, between purchasers (GPs or health authorities) and hospitals; and within the primary healthcare sector, with individual GPs encouraged to compete for patients who are now regarded as consumers. Attention was given to giving consumers more information about the availability of GP services, removing the barriers to changing GPs thus allowing much easier transfer of patients between practices, and introducing a performance-related remuneration system allowing GPs who attract more patients to be better paid. These objectives are summed up in the 1990 GP Contract which states:

> Central to the Government's plans . . . is giving patients better choice by providing them with more information . . . there will be more competition and it will be easier to change doctors.

This policy makes two major assumptions. First, that patients have the motivation to make a choice and second, that doctors are prepared to differentiate their offering in such a way that patients are able to discriminate between practices. Evidence suggests that consumers in the UK are not exercising their right to choice in this market, the implications of which are far reaching. Without patients moving between practices as a result of competition between GPs, then the benefits of competition which were the rationale for reforms will not be realised. GPs will have little incentive to change their activities, hospitals will have no pressure from GPs to offer services tailored to consumer needs and the market collapses. The consumer is, therefore, paramount to the success of this system.

One of the problems with consumer choice in this context is the lack of knowledge to be able to make this type of decision. GP services, like certain other membership services, are continuous, i.e. rather than a decision to return to the same practice on the basis of satisfaction, the decision to change GP must be framed in terms of dissatisfaction: in this market the motivation is required to change, not to return. The nature of the relationship between doctor and patient and the psychological effect of that relationship in treating patients makes this dimension particularly important. Patients have an investment in the doctor/patient relationship, which militates against arbitrarily changing doctor unless there has been significant breakdown in the relationship. In addition Leavey et al. (1989) point out the circumstances in which most patients require GP services do not motivate them to embark upon a search for a better doctor, since their need for these services is spasmodic and minimal. The average GP patient in the UK consults their doctor 4.4 times per year (see Gann 1991). If an urgent need does arise, the very fact that it requires immediate treatment precludes the likelihood of the patient searching for a different GP.

The final issue regarding choice in UK healthcare is the lack of experience of alternatives. Brucks (1985) identifies a relationship between prior knowledge and the characteristics of information search, specifically what kind of information will be sought by consumers in order to make consumption decisions. Expectations about service provision are formed as a result of experiences with both specific service providers and experiences with the service category in general. Since every person in the UK will have been registered with a GP since birth, generally they will have experience with a small number of specific providers. As a consequence, while there will be very few novice consumers in this market there will also be very few knowledgeable consumers. This restricted experience has a dual effect; first, patients are likely to remain satisfied with their current provider as long as service provision is constant. Second, if a choice is prompted it is likely to be based upon expectations derived entirely from current consumption. In the UK no advertising is allowed, direct marketing is very limited, and there is no overt recruitment of patients already registered with other practices. There is a commonly held view, supported by the medical establishment, that all doctors are equally good and all offer access to similar, equal quality secondary services. In these circumstances choice is likely to be made on convenience factors such as proximity to home or work, surgery hours or accessibility (Gabbott and Hogg 1996). Whilst these searchable aspects of the service do not necessarily predict the outcome they provide one of the few bases for choice.

THE US HEALTHCARE SYSTEM

The structure of the US healthcare system is vast and very complex in terms of the financing, reimbursement, and delivery of healthcare. For a population of approximately a quarter of a billion people, there are about 650 000 physicians, 180 000 dentists, 1.9 million nurses, 7000 hospitals and 33 000 nursing homes. In 1993, the total of 6467 hospitals had just over 1.1 million beds for over 33.2 million admissions. Health expenditures accounted for 14.9% of the GDP in 1993, up from 5.9% in 1965 and amounted to an estimated trillion dollars, spending more in total and in proportion to GDP than any other OECD country. From 1982 to 1991 there was a 4.8% increase per year in real per capita costs, which includes hospitals, physicians and prescription drugs.

Some argue that the multifaceted nature of the US healthcare system in its pluralistic structure accounts for the relatively high expenditures devoted to medical care. A multitude of government agencies are involved in healthcare issues, and various types of health-care insurance arrangements complicate the organisation, delivery and financing of healthcare. There are government-funded agencies covering healthcare costs for the poor and elderly through Medicaid and Medicare. In addition, there are over 1000 managed care plans, over 1000 commercial health insurance companies, over 70 other different private not-for-profit healthcare insurance plans. Other reasons attributed to the increasing costs of healthcare are the ageing population, the growth in incomes and the reduction in cost sharing by consumers, slow productivity growth in most healthcare services, and technological change.

In the United States, there is no single nationwide system of health insurance. About 86% of the population is covered by healthcare insurance. In 1991, private insurance paid 32%, federal programs 31%, out-of-pocket consumers 22% and state/local funding 12% of the total healthcare costs. Approximately 81% of the private health insurance coverage is purchased through the employer and individual insurance policies are purchased by the other 19%. Nearly 62% of the working population is covered by the conventional health insurance plan which allows unrestricted choice of healthcare provider and reimburses on a fee-for-service basis. These plans monitor and control healthcare utilisation through such requirements as pre-admission certification, concurrent review of length of stay and mandatory second opinions for surgery. These plans differ in the medical services that are covered and the co-payment and deductible amounts. The non-conventional health plans are called managed health insurance plans of which there are two major types—health maintenance organisations (HMOs) and preferred provider organisations (PPOs). The Health Insurance Association of America define managed care plans as:

> systems that integrate the financing and delivery of appropriate healthcare services to covered individuals by means of: arrangements with selected providers to furnish a comprehensive set of healthcare services to members;

explicit criteria for the selection of healthcare providers; formal programs for ongoing quality assurance and utilisation review; and significant financial incentives for members to use providers and procedures associated with the plan.

The difference between the HMO and the PPO is becoming obscure. HMOs are prepaid plans employing physicians on a salary where consumers receive a comprehensive medical service for a fixed annual capitation fee and a small co-payment for each visit. A version of the HMO contracts with an independent group of physicians on a fee-for-service or capitation basis. Both versions either own or contract with a community hospital, restricting choice of provider to those physicians in the network, except where otherwise authorised by the HMO. In PPOs, a group of providers—physicians and hospitals—are bound together by contract under fees negotiated with the PPO and are subject to utilisation review protocols. Unlike the HMO, PPOs reimburse for medical care services received from healthcare providers outside the network, although the consumer typically must pay a higher co-payment which acts as a disincentive to go outside the network.

The nearly 23% of the US population covered by public health insurance (Medicare and Medicaid) have the same kind of choice in provider and medical care as the managed care consumers, except in this case the costs are reimbursed by the federal and state governments. At any given time, about 14% of the population is uninsured and receive medical care through public clinics and hospitals, financed by state and local programs, through charity organisations and by shifting costs on to other payers.

It becomes clear from the above discussion that, unlike the UK single-payer system, in the US multipayer-system healthcare providers are reimbursed on a fee-for-service or on pre-payments by a variety of different third-party payers, including federal and state governments and commercial insurance companies. The rising costs have forced all entities in the US healthcare system to institute cost-containment measures. Recognising the imperative, President Clinton promised healthcare reform before his election, but no dramatic healthcare reform has been approved by Congress. What has happened is that the healthcare industry, in general, has attempted to reduce costs through streamlining operations. However, with the increasing attention paid to cost of care, there is fear of a resulting decline in overall quality of care.

Unlike the UK system US consumers make three key choices: choice of insurance plan, choice of doctor and choice of hospital.

Choice of Insurance Plan

There is fierce competition in the healthcare industry as healthcare costs continue to rise and the variety of choices continues to grow. In choosing a healthcare insurance plan, consumers make trade-offs among various criteria as they decide on the insurance provider. Employees share the insurance premiums with the employer and most employers offer more than one plan for their employees. A recent study found that consumers use about 19 attributes in making a choice of healthcare insurance plan. The most important attribute was hospitalisation coverage, followed by choice of doctors, policy premium, dental coverage, and choice of hospitals. Thus, the ability to choose (among doctors and hospitals) is an important criterion in the choice of insurance plans.

Choice of Doctor

The level of choice activity has changed considerably in the last couple of decades, before which studies showed that patients did not really exercise their choice of physicians. When choosing family physicians patients use such characteristics as responsiveness, immediacy of care, personal rapport with the physician, as well as experience attributes such as competence, courtesy, interpersonal skills, friendliness, and other personality characteristics. Credence variables such as credibility and reputation are also important characteristics that patients consider in the choice of healthcare provider. Being nice and being trusted were found to be important characteristics for personal physicians. The problem for consumers, as with all experiential information, is that this type of information is the most difficult to obtain in the pre-purchase phase. As a result recent findings reveal that most consumers rely on the advice of friends, relatives, and other non-medical personnel in choosing a doctor.

Choice of Hospital

The decision to purchase the healthcare service is generally made by a third party and not just the consumer. Until most recently this decision was made by the physician, but now the insurance companies, managed care programs, government agencies and even employers influence the healthcare consumption process. However, studies show that the patient's role in healthcare decision making has increased. This is also evidenced by the emergence of advertising directed at the healthcare consumer, rather than just the physician. When patients need the use of specialised healthcare from another physician or a hospital, as in the UK, the primary physician acts as the gatekeeper and the insurance plan requires a referral from him or her. One study found that physicians receive almost 45% of their new patients from referrals, with the figure being much higher for certain specialities. Word of mouth therefore plays a vital part in this market.

Whilst the choices available to the patient differ between the two systems, the criteria used to discriminate between the alternatives are fundamentally the same. Essentially the consumer will return to the same healthcare provider as long as they are satisfied with the treatment they receive. The key consideration in understanding consumer behaviour in this market, therefore, is how consumers evaluate satisfaction.

CONSUMER SATISFACTION WITH HEALTHCARE

Whether the consumer is operating within a regulated or deregulated system the basis of choice is the same; what the consumer is choosing is not healthcare *per se*, but health or the doctor's ability to deliver 'cure'. Rather than a repeat purchase being made on the basis of satisfaction, change is prompted by dissatisfaction. This link between satisfaction and choice is inextricable in the healthcare context. The measurement and promotion of patient satisfaction has been a central concern of medical sociologists for some time, not only because it reflects quality of care from the patient's view, but also because patient satisfaction assures patient loyalty. Numerous studies have shown a strong link between quality, satisfaction and return behaviour. In most published surveys one might find that a larger proportion of people are loyal to a healthcare provider than those who shop for care. In order to understand consumer choice in this context we must therefore understand evaluation and the criteria by which patients, as consumers, assess the healthcare they receive.

Care and Cure

The fundamental expectation of healthcare services is associated with a response to the illness, often referred to as 'well-being' or con- ceptualised as 'cure'. By contrast, the process of achieving that end is characterised by the delivery of the service experience, conceptualised as 'care'. This simplistic framework has been used to describe the basis of healthcare evaluation, where the technically complex 'cure' dimen- sion is assessed on the basis of the more familiar 'care' experience. In other service contexts models have been presented which have similar bases, despite different terminology. For instance, Gronroos (1991) refers to technical v functional aspects, Zeithaml (1988) uses an intrinsic v extrinsic distinction, Lawson (1986) a motivation v hygiene model and Iacobucci et al. (1994) describe 'core' and 'peripheral' aspects of the service. Although the word pairs may not be entirely interchangeable there are strong conceptual parallels. The issue in healthcare is that the individual consumer (the patient) does not have the technical knowledge to assess the 'cure' dimension, even after service delivery. The patient may know that his/her symptoms have been relieved, but not that he/she has been cured, or that the treatment was the most effective available. A patient has an investment in believing in the ability of the medical practitioner to deliver health, the psychological effects of which have been explored by Frank (1968) and Shapiro (1959). Faced with this impossibility of evaluating outcome patients will use other criteria to assess the cure dimension. In these circumstances *how* the service is delivered is used to evaluate *what* was delivered, i.e. clinical competence is inferred from the process of care.

The 'care' dimension of medical treatment relates closely to Zeithaml, Parasuraman and Berry's (1990) process dimensions of responsiveness, assurance, empathy and tangibles. These care expectations are particularly important in building the relationship of trust between patient and doctor. A number of authors, including Bitner (1992) have identified situational factors as an important aspect of service satisfaction. The implication is that patients will regard the surgery premises and even the way that the staff are dressed as an indication of the standard of care provided. Convenience can be broken down into physical accessibility, i.e. car parking, public transport etc., and treatment accessibility, i.e. the availability of appointment times, the range of specialist clinics provided. To these aspects of the service are added the responsiveness of the staff (willingness to help), assurance (knowledge and courtesy of the providers), empathy (caring individualised attention, 'bedside manner') and the tangible aspects relating to the signs, symbols and artefacts of delivery. These concepts are important contributions to our understanding of patient evaluation of the healthcare experience, where the outcome of the service is so difficult for consumers to evaluate and delay between treatment and cure may make the relationship difficult to assess.

However, the relationship between cure and care is not as simplistic as might be suggested. In the context of healthcare it could be argued that the core part of the service product is the clinical response to illness (cure), whilst the peripheral parts are associated with the process of care (see Brown and Swartz 1989, Ware et al. 1977, John 1992). As we have discussed, evaluation of the clinical aspect of the service is particularly complex for individual patients, but the impact of it upon overall satisfaction is beyond question, i.e. if the patient considers the medical response to have been inadequate, aspects of care cannot compensate sufficiently to result in satisfaction overall. Since core and peripheral aspects of a service are not normative but subjective, Gabbott and Hogg (1996) suggest that the notion of patients making trade-offs has some appeal, i.e. that evaluation is likely to be multi-attribute and multi-dimensional. In this context, satisfaction with healthcare could be a function of either good organisation in the doctor's practice or good personal relations with the physician or other members of the practice staff, i.e. good administration could negate the impact of a less than satisfactory personal relationship with staff or vice-versa.

The challenge for the consumer in this scenario is to identify which aspects of the service are most likely to be a reliable indicator of the doctor's ability to deliver health. The use of cues in service markets has been explored by a number of authors (see for instance Bitner 1992). However this research has concentrated on identifying what these cues are, rather than any detailed consideration of how consumers use these cues. As services are a performance over time the use and effectiveness of the cues will change not only with successive service encounters, but within the same service encounter. Thus a cue such as the decoration of the surgery will be of use only until the consultation with the doctor when other cues are available, such as manner, dress or level of diagnostic equipment. Whilst researching tangible goods has identified a number of cues that consumers use to reduce the risk associated with consumption decisions, this is still a relatively under-researched area in services marketing. The importance of these cues in healthcare suggests that this research is urgently needed.

CONCLUSION

This chapter attempts to examine some of the decisions available to consumers in two culturally dissimilar healthcare markets. Whilst the structure of the two systems results in consumers having different decisions to make regarding supplier, and therefore acquiring different skills, the evaluation of the service is similar. For the consumer the purpose of healthcare is to deliver health and well being and the problems associated with the evaluation of this remain the same whichever delivery system the patient operates within.

The response of the consumer to these evaluative problems in either healthcare system is loyalty, remaining with the same doctor unless forced to move. This has been shown to be true in both systems. Despite the reforms to the health service in the UK, less than 6% of the population change doctors in any year and most are still motivated to do so by circumstances such as moving house, GP retiring etc. (see Leavey et al. 1989). However the baby-boomer generation typifies modern healthcare consumers who do not have the same confidence in the healthcare system as their forefathers did. The modern healthcare consumer takes a more prevention-oriented approach to consuming healthcare services. The consumerism movement in health care which took place in the 1980s saw patients taking a more active role in all aspects of the consumption decision. In the US newer versions of healthcare insurance are being forced to accommodate the desire of the healthcare consumer for more freedom of choice. In the UK this consumerist movement is still in its infancy, however it is clearly the way of the future.

REFERENCES

Bitner, Mary Jo (1992) 'Servicescapes: The Impact of Physical Surroundings on Customers and Employees', *Journal of Marketing*, 56, pp. 57–71.

Brown, S. and Swartz, T. (1989) 'A Gap Analysis of Professional Service Quality', *Journal of Marketing*, 53 (April), pp. 92–98.

Brucks, M. (1985) 'The Effects of Product Class Knowledge on Information Search Behaviour', *Journal of Consumer Research*, 12 (March), pp. 1–16.

Butler, J. (1993) 'A Case Study in the National Health Service: Working For Patients', in Taylor-Gooby, P. and Lawson, R. (eds) *Markets and Managers*, (Buckingham: OUP), pp. 55–68.

Dant, R., Lumpkin, J.R. and Bush, R. (1990) 'Private Physicians or Walk-in Clinics: Do the Patients Differ?', *Journal of Health Care Marketing*, 10 (June), pp. 25–35.

Fisk, R. (1981) 'Toward a Consumption/Evaluation Process Model for Services', in

Donnelly, J. and George, W. (eds) *Marketing of Services*, (Chicago: American Marketing Association), pp. 191–195.

Frank, J. (1968) 'The Influence of Patients and Therapists' Expectations on the Outcome of Psychotherapy', *British Journal of Medical Psychology*, 41, pp. 349–356.

Gabbott, M. and Hogg, G. (1996) 'Information for Choice: An Investigation of Evaluative Criteria in UK Primary Health Care', *Journal of Health Care Marketing*, 14, 3, pp. 28–34.

Gann, R. (1991) *The Health Consumer Guide*, (London: Faber).

Gronroos, C. (1991) 'Strategic Management and Marketing in the Services Sector', (Lund, Sweden: Studentlitteratur).

Ham, C., Robinson, R. and Benzeval, M. (1990) *Health Check: Healthcare Reforms in an International Context*, (London: Kings Institute).

Health Departments of Great Britain (1989) General Practice in the National Health Service—The 1990 Contract.

HMSO (1989) Working For Patients, Cmnd 555, Pub. HMSO.

Iacobucci, D., Grayson, K. and Ostrom, A. (1994) 'The Calculus of Service Quality and Customer Satisfaction', in Swartz, T. and Brown, S. (eds) *Advances in Services Marketing and Management Vol 3*, (Connecticut: JAI Press).

John, Joby (1992) 'Patient Satisfaction: The Impact of Past Experience', *Journal of Health Care Marketing*, 3 (September), pp. 56–64.

Lawson, R. (1986) 'Consumer Satisfaction: Motivation Factors and Hygiene Factors', Marketing Discussion Paper, (NZ: University of Otago), referenced in Iacobucci et al. (1994), op. cit.

Leavey, R., Wilkin, D. and Metcalfe, D. (1989) 'Consumerism and General Practice', *British Medical Journal*, 298, pp. 737–739.

Lovelock, C. (1991) *Services Marketing*, 2nd edn, (New York: Prentice Hall).

Rust, R., Zahorik, A. and Keiningham, T. (1993) 'A Decision Support System for Service Quality Improvement', paper presented to AMA Frontiers in Service Marketing Conference, Vanderbilt University, Nashville, TN.

Schleglmilch, B., Carman, J. and Moore, S.A. (1992) 'Choice and Perceived Quality of Family Practitioners in the United States and the United Kingdom', *The Service Industries Journal*, 12 (April), pp. 263–284.

Shapiro, A. (1959) 'The Placebo Effect in the History of Medical Treatment: Implications for Psychiatry', *American Journal of Psychiatry*, 116 (October), pp. 298–304.

Ware, J., Davies-Avery, A. and Stewart, A. (1977) *The Measurement and Meaning of Patient Satisfaction: A Review of the Literature*, (Santa Monica, CA: Rand).

Ziethaml, V. (1988) 'Consumer Perceptions of Price, Quality and Value: A Means-End Model and Synthesis', *Journal of Marketing*, 52 (July), pp. 2–22.

Zeithaml, V., Parasuraman, A. and Berry, L. (1990) *Delivering Quality Service*, (New York: Collier Macmillan).

CHAPTER 9

THE CHARITY CONSUMER

SUZANNE HORNE AND SALLY HIBBERT

INTRODUCTION

Since the article by Kotler and Levy (1969), there has been much debate about the relevance of the marketing concept to non-profit organis-ations. The debate has continued, but a general consensus has emerged that the marketing concept is applicable in a broad range of contexts including non-profit (see Shapiro 1973; Kotler 1986; Arndt 1978; Yorke 1984). Increasingly, the marketing paradigm has been adopted by many non-profit organisations as they have faced new and complex marketplace problems (Kotler 1979). In the UK charity sector, these problems can be summed up as waning governmental and public support which has diminished their financial resources. As a result, charitable organisations have had to look toward marketing as a way of competing for 'market share' and as a means of increasing income from existing donors. Moreover, the charity sector in the UK has burgeoned in recent years, which has led to a rapid rise in competition making marketing a crucial fundraising function for organisations as donor pounds become scarce. Increasingly, charities are having to spend a large part of their marketing budgets on fundraising from donor groups, the most important of which are: (1) the general public, (2) the commercial

Consumers and Services. Edited by Mark Gabbott and Gillian Hogg.
© 1998 John Wiley & Sons Ltd.

sector, (3) the statutory sector and (4) trust funds. In Britain, however, about 80% of the total amount donated to charities is given by the general public and about 80% of adults make some kind of donation in the course of the year. This is broadly comparable with countries such as the United States, Canada and Australia (Burnett 1993). However, because such a large proportion of the income for charities is provided by individual donations, it is important that the design of fundraising campaigns maximises response amongst these individual contributors.

Since the basis of charitable giving is the consumption of value through the donation itself, this particular aspect of service consumption behaviour presents a number of interesting issues. First, what is being received by the consumer is intangible, although it may result in tangible outcomes to recipients. Second, because the charities' work is delivered (in the main) to those other than the donor, there is likely to be a physical distance between the 'input' and 'output', suggesting difficulty for the donor in assessing at least one form of service outcome. Finally, the success of the charity relies to a great extent upon the perceptions of consumers since outcomes are unverifiable in most instances. As a consequence, charity services rely almost entirely upon credence factors. The purpose of this chapter is to enhance the understanding of individual donor behaviour using existing consumer buyer behaviour principles. To this end it is divided into three sections. In the first section the nature of the donor exchange is outlined; secondly there is a brief review of the role of marketing in the charity sector; thirdly, a three-stage model of services consumer behaviour (see Bateson 1995; Zeithaml and Bitner 1996) is used as a framework within which to view donor behaviour. It should be noted that the focus here is on monetary donations to charity, although voluntary work and donations in kind are also important forms of giving that enable charities to carry out their work. However, they require separate consideration and consequently are not covered here.

THE NATURE OF DONOR EXCHANGE

Donating money to charity tends to be considered as a form of helping behaviour. However, because this form of helping involves giving resources that have an economic value (by contrast to other types of helping, such as intervening in a crisis) it is brought into the realms of consumer behaviour (Burnett and Wood 1988). It seems appropriate, therefore, to take the view that donors are involved in a marketing exchange with the charity and therefore it is feasible to analyse donors' perceptions of the costs and rewards of entering into that relationship. Analysing the perceived costs and rewards of engaging in helping behaviour by giving to charity is complex. Although the costs of giving can be relatively easily evaluated because of the external, economic value of the monetary gift, the benefits of giving, as for any other form of helping, tend to be highly intangible. Radley and Kennedy (1995) asserted that perceived benefits of giving depend on three factors: beliefs about altruism, beliefs about social norms and expectations, and situational characteristics of the giving occasion. With respect to altruism, there appears to be a general consensus that there is a need for charity in society and that, as members of society, we have an obligation to contribute (although there is significant variation in the levels of obligation felt). In this regard, therefore, the rewards of giving relate to an individual's satisfaction at having fulfilled the role of *good citizen*.

This type of reward may be enhanced if a donation is made to a cause towards which an individual feels particularly empathetic or responsible. As far as social norms are concerned people differ in the extent to which they feel that giving is *expected* of them under certain circumstances and this influences their perceptions of the social rewards of giving (or the punishment for not giving). Finally, situational factors at the time of giving, such as a person's mood (see Isen 1987), also effect potential donors' perceptions of the rewards of giving. The highly abstract nature of the rewards associated with making a donation present difficulties for a charity attempting to manage relationships with its donors. Insights can be developed, however, by considering the body of service marketing literature. Because services are characterised as providing largely intangible rewards to consumers (see Shostack 1977), charities should be considered as complex services involving multiple intangible rewards and therefore much of the services literature is applicable to this product class.

Fundraising Marketing in the Charity Sector

Fundraising initiatives aimed at raising money from individual donors are many and varied. The Charities Aid Foundation (CAF) funds research on an annual basis one of the aims of which is to identify the methods of fundraising that are most popular and/or raise the most money. Within the range of alternative fundraising methods the distinction is made between those that involve *planned* and *ad hoc* giving, where planned giving involves a commitment to give on a repeated basis and *ad hoc* giving is a one-off donation often made in response to some form of marketing communication. *Ad hoc* giving has formerly been labelled as prompted giving, however this is potentially misleading as people may be prompted to partake in planned giving schemes (Love et al. 1993). Examples of planned giving include the use of covenants, payroll deduction schemes (PAYE), Gift Aid, membership fees and subscriptions. *Ad hoc* giving includes the more popular fundraising methods including door-to-door, street and church collections, as well as collections in the pub and the workplace. It also includes telephone and television appeals, letter and advertisement appeals, and the purchase of raffle tickets and tickets for charity events (Halfpenny and Lowe 1994).

The fundraising methods that charities use are formulated and implemented according to the particular segment of the potential donor market that the fundraiser is targeting. One basis for segmentation of potential donors relates to their geo- and sociodemographic characteristics. However, charities increasingly segment their target donor groups in relation to their level of commitment to the charity in the past, which can be described in terms of the recency of donation, the frequency of donation and the amount given on previous occasions (Ryan and Murdoch 1986). On the basis of these criteria the market is conventionally divided into *core donors, medium donors, light donors* and *non-donors*.

Empirical studies have shown that people have favourite charities which are likely to be those that they feel some kind of sympathy towards (Batson 1990; Fultz et al. 1986). In particular, if a person has experienced a need for services provided by a charity it is more likely that donations will be directed towards that cause. For example, many people who support cancer charities do so because a close relative has suffered from, or died of, cancer. First-hand experience of distressful circumstances, illness or other needs is also a key determinant of strong support for particular charitable causes, as is vicarious experience. Individuals who favour a charity for such reasons are likely to be among its core donors, who give on a repeat basis, probably by means of one of the planned giving methods. At the other end of the scale are the non-donors, that is, those people who have never given to a particular charity. These individuals are also a potential target market for fundraisers. Most people are susceptible to *ad hoc* appeals from charities, although their responsiveness to *ad hoc* fundraising efforts varies. Some people give almost whenever they are asked and are virtually uncritical in their giving decision, feeling that unless there is a reason *not* to give, it is an expected and normal reaction (Radley and Kennedy 1995). Others are more selective in their response to *ad hoc* solicitations but can, nevertheless, be targeted by fundraisers.

Whatever the target market, fundraising strategies must be carefully managed. The methods used have changed over the years. Traditionally charities relied heavily on *ad hoc* fundraising methods; they later adopted marketing techniques such as direct mailing, which had proved to be successful for providers of consumer goods and services in commercial contexts. Although many traditional fundraising methods remain part of the overall strategy, more recently charities have realised that in order to ensure their long-term survival, they need to recruit donors onto schemes in which they are committed to making regular donations over extended periods of time. In other words, they realised that the secret to efficient and effective fundraising was to increase the number of core donors as a proportion of their total donor market and that the way to effectively manage these core donors was to develop schemes for planned giving by means of which they could nurture their relationships with these donors. However, a balance is required in the combination of fundraising methods employed. A portfolio of fundraising methods is necessary in order to appeal to different target markets; some methods satisfy donors' needs to be spontaneously generous, which is an intrinsic feature of altruism, while others enable people to fulfil their practical obligations to make regular donations.

In order to maximise the financial return from each of these fundraising methods it is necessary to develop an understanding of why people give and how people make donation decisions. Guy and Patton (1989) proposed a model of donor decision making on the basis of social-psychology theories of 'why people help' but, beyond this, the issue has received scant attention in the marketing sphere. Yet, scrutiny of the different aspects of donor decision making is required by fundraisers as examination of the decision processes that donors go through when giving to charity in each of these situations provides information vital to the implementation of the various methods. Such insights into decision processes can be achieved by using and adapting models of consumer decision processes and buyer behaviour.

Donor Decision Making: The Three-stage Model

The donor decision-making process is discussed within a three-stage model which splits the process into pre-donation stage, donation stage and post-donation stage. It should be emphasised at this point that the distinction between these three stages is not always clear cut. In particular, because many donations are the result of a person's response to some kind of marketing activity the pre-donation stage and the actual donation can, and often do, occur virtually simultaneously. By dividing the donor decision process in this way, however, it can be viewed from a consumer behaviour perspective and these principles applied to the charity context.

Stage 1: The Pre-donation Stage

Need Activation and Recognition

The pre-donation stage involves all those processes that occur before making the donation. This stage begins with the recognition of a need or problem. Need recognition is defined as a perception of a difference between an actual and a desired state that is sufficient to arouse and activate a decision process (Engel et al. 1990). Factors identified in consumer behaviour texts to activate needs include a change in a person's circumstances, the acquisition of product, consumption of a product and marketing activities. When a need is activated and recognised there is a reasonable possibility that a person will make a purchase in order to satisfy them. However, it is not entirely clear whether donation behaviour is prompted by focused processing upon the individual's need for altruistic reward or whether it is focused upon recognition of need in other consumers (i.e. the recipients).

People's motivations for giving to charity (altruism, social norms and situational factors) have already been noted, but motivation needs translation into action. In some cases, as is characteristic of altruism, people make spontaneous donations which may be activated, for example, by a relative's death or illness. However, in most instances a person's need or obligation to give is felt only in response to a request of some kind. As a consequence marketing communications are of the utmost importance for the charity sector because of their salience as a source of need activation. In addition, charity marketing activities must appeal effectively and immediately to potential donors because consumers' motivation to satisfy a need to give is likely to be less urgent than their motivation to satisfy other needs and wants. If they are not immediately 'turned on' (or, worse, are 'turned off') by the communications, they are likely to pass up the opportunity to donate. For example, literature on charitable giving reports that people are more likely to give if an appeal makes them *feel good* rather than *feel guilty* (Benson and Catt 1978) and if the appearance and manner of the collector is deemed suitable (Bull and Gibson-Robinson 1981).

Information Search and the Evaluation of Alternatives

This pre-donation (pre-consumption) stage may also include a donor's search for information and evaluation of alternative offerings. This stage presupposes that a motivation to give has sufficient saliency for the consumer to search for alternative donation routes. This is particularly associated with long-term donor behaviour rather than the impulse donation referred to above. For these long-term donors, the sources of information consulted pre-purchase can be categorised as internal and external. The internal sources relate to information source in memory (Bettman 1979; Leigh and Rethans 1984, Lynch and Srull 1982), and external sources are discriminative environmental stimuli that people use to predict the outcome of their actions (Cox 1967). The extent to which internal sources of information are used by donors will depend upon their existing levels of knowledge and experience with the sector. Literature on consumer decision making suggests that when an individual has strong existing attitudes towards the object of their decision, or where there are low levels of involvement and perceived risk, a person is less likely to invest much time and energy in searching for external information and comparing alternatives. Rather, the decision will rely on internal sources of information and external sources easily derived from the immediate purchase environment. When a person's existing attitudes are weak, or where there is high involvement with the object of the decision or with the decision process and high perceived risk, it becomes increasingly likely that the search for and evaluation of external information will increase in order to enable the person to arrive at a satisfactory decision (Howard and Sheth 1969). Consumer behaviour researchers have found, however, that the majority of decisions involve only a limited amount of information search and processing, even when the purchases of expensive consumer durables are concerned (Olshavsky and Granbois 1979; Robertson 1976). When considering long-term donation to charities, because of the underlying motivations we could expect the donation behaviour to be relatively static and the initial choice of charity to take place within fairly well defined evoked set. There is very little empirical research as yet which discusses the expiry of information held about charities and the role which outcome information in the form of media coverage and direct communication has upon maintaining the currency of perceptions about the charity.

External Information Search. External sources of information may also be consulted, especially if the donor does not have the knowledge and/or experience to make a satisfactory donation decision or if there remains some ambiguity about the donation. For example, when an individual is confronted by a door-to-door collection he or she might be confident that the charity in question works for a genuine cause, but may doubt the credibility of the person collecting. In this case the donor is likely to seek and consider at least some external information to reduce the perceived risk.

With regard to the types of external information used by donors, services consumer behaviour literature offers some insight into those that are likely to be used in making donation decisions. Distinction is drawn among external sources between intrinsic and extrinsic cues. Intrinsic cues are the objective, physical characteristics inherent to the good or service whereas extrinsic cues bear no actual relation to the physical features of the offering but influence the consumer's overall subjective evaluation. The service literature suggests that where an offering is largely intangible, there is a lack of objective intrinsic cues and people are more likely to draw on extrinsic cues to predict the outcome of their behaviour (Carmen and Uhl 1973, Gabbott and Hogg 1994). In giving money to charity the rewards for the donor tend to be highly intangible. It could be argued that in this context the donor might make reference to the nature of the goods and service provided by the charity to the beneficiary and use intrinsic and extrinsic cues inherent to that exchange as sources of information for decision making. However, this information tends not to be readily available to the donor, therefore there is heavy reliance on extrinsic cues which are features of the situation in which the donation is made. Examples include the stickers that a street collector hands out when people put money into the collecting box, the dress and manner of the collector, the label on a collecting box in a pub, the literature provided and demeanour of the representative when an organisation receives a charity attempting to engage people on a payroll deduction scheme (PAYE) scheme. Charity marketers need to pay close attention to the extrinsic cues that influence donor decision making in situations typical of each separate method of fundraising.

Given the position of charity in society, the general belief that everyone has an obligation to contribute, and the virtual impossibility that any adult living in Britain or any other Western society will have avoided fundraising efforts, pretty much everybody has experience of and attitudes towards giving to charity. In the majority of situations, potential donors rely heavily on such attitudes. Rados (1981) observes that donors are often unable to say why they made a donation to charity, which implies that conscious information processing does not play a prominent part in many donation decisions. This is particularly true when individuals are giving in response to a form of fundraising which does not allow them much time to make a decision, such as a street collection. It is also the case when the donation is a small one, for example putting 20 pence in a collecting box has limited consequences for most people and therefore does not merit any great investment of time and effort in making the donation decision (see Hibbert and Horne 1996).

Attitudes Towards Charitable Services. People's attitudes towards charities, which influence their decision to give or not to give to a particular appeal, relate to perceptions of three aspects of a charity's operations:

1. the work that it carries out
2. its efficient and effective use of funds
3. the methods of fundraising that it employs.

As emphasised earlier, some people have favourite charities and, by definition, have strong attitudes towards those causes which justify their support. Strong attitudes are also held about the use of funds by charities, Hibbert and Horne (1997) reveal that some potential donors withhold their support for charities which they believe to be spending an unacceptable proportion of funds raised on activities which do not directly benefit the beneficiaries (including marketing). For example, charities whose administrative costs are believed to be high because they spend money on expensive office space and recruit administrative staff at high cost are discriminated against by some potential donors. Similarly, some discriminate against those charities whose communications and fundraising methods they believe to be expensive because they use channels such as television or put large advertisements in the press. In the same study, cases where charities use commercial organisations to carry out door-to-door collections were cited as unacceptable. Such opposition is partly because of the prevailing attitudes of the donors, that when people give to charity it is because they want to help the beneficiary, not to contribute to the economic success of a commercial enterprise or an individual. Unfortunately media information, which is sometimes unfair or un-informed, is all that the 'thinking donor' has to use to form opinions about the justification of fundraising costs (Quint 1996). A recent suggestion of independent accreditation of charities is a possible method by which interested donors might be able to assess whether the charity to which they wish to make a donation has sufficient safeguards to prevent abuse.

In some cases, people's beliefs about charity *per se* are contravened when a charity's operations are seen to have a commercial character. The nature of charity implies that organisations set up to do good works for various causes exist because those people working within the organisation have the cause at heart and, by gaining the support of the wider community through contributions, are able to shape events in a way that would not otherwise be possible. Some potential donors, therefore, are affronted when it appears that people work to raise money for charity, whether they have been contracted or subcon-tracted for the job, for financial gain. Although people may agree that those working full time for charity need to earn a living, they do not agree with the payment of wages equivalent to those paid in commercial contexts. Moreover, people who are of this attitude tend to sponsor the notion that much of a charity's fundraising work should be carried out by volunteers.

Attitudes about fundraising may also affect where, when and how a potential donor is approached. In the same way that beliefs about the nature of charitable organisations influence attitudes towards the use of funds, beliefs about altruism influence attitudes towards methods of fundraising. One of the primary features of altruism is that it is voluntary, that is to say, making a donation should be a spontaneous act of generosity. Both Hibbert and Horne (1997) and Radley and Kennedy (1995) found that people were opposed to certain methods of fundraising that exerted excessive pressure on potential donors or that intruded on their privacy. These factors were seen to rob people of their control over the giving process and to deprive them of the feeling that they are giving of their own free will. Guilt is the enemy of generosity in the sense that people do not want to feel that they have been shamed into making a donation, either by the use of forceful fundraising methods or exposure to communications which aim to raise social conscience. Radley and Kennedy illustrate this with the following quote from one respondent in their study:

> I think if a charity starts to make me feel guilty then really I'm not too interested in that charity. That's not what its about. What they should want to make me feel is that I would like to give, and if I don't give then all right . . .
> Radley and Kennedy (1995) p. 690

Attitudes about the right to personal privacy are exhibited when people decline to donate through such methods as telephone appeals and direct mail. Whereas people might feel that they are breaching social norms when they do not give in some situations such as in response to public demands when surrounded by other 'consumers', in others the consumer may feel that the charity has, in effect, invaded their personal space and that they have every right to withhold their support. The heavy reliance on existing attitudes to arrive at donation decisions means that charities need to take a long-term view, developing aspects of their marketing strategy whose attributes form the basis of donors' attitudes.

Stage 2: Donation

In commercial contexts one outcome of the pre-purchase stage is the decision to buy a certain good or service. The purchase decision is accompanied by a set of expectations about the performance of the good or service. The consumption of goods, simply speaking, involves the use of the material object and disposal of any waste. Consumption of services is more complex as it consists of the experience that is delivered through interaction with the service environment and personnel (Bateson 1995).

Turning the focus back to donors, an important outcome of the pre-donation stage is the decision to give or not to give, and following this a decision about whether to donate to a particular charity on a particular occasion. It is arguable that, as is true of consumer purchase decisions, the decision to give is accompanied by expectations about performance—but the performance of what? This question reflects the problem of analysing the exchange relationship between the charity and the donor. One aspect of donors' expectations about performance refers to the goods and services that a charity is able to provide to its beneficiaries by using funds that have been collectively contributed by donors. However, as suggested above, in most cases a donor does not get feedback on how the money donated has been used. A second aspect of expectations about performance, which is specific to the charity-donor exchange, relates to a donor's experience of giving which is a product of the individual's interface with the inanimate and/or human features of the fundraising environment. In this respect making a donation bears a similarity to services marketing. A donor's consumption experience varies depending on the fundraising method and the situational factors that typically surround it. Performance of fundraising activities, to the extent that they provide a donor with a positive experience, can be enhanced by considering how the various features of the donation environment contribute to the production of a positive experience for donors.

Some charities have responded to this challenge. In many instances the interface between the donor and the fundraising environment is very brief, for example giving money in a street collection. Because the interactive process is so short certain charities have tried to extend the donor experience by providing some tangible good such as flowers, stickers, balloons and other tokens at the point of donation. This is also intended to add a tangible element to the largely intangible rewards of giving and to encourage repeat giving and loyalty to the charity. It may also have the effect of signalling to other consumers that they have engaged in charitable giving, adding pressure to those without the token to conform. Methods of fundraising such as direct mail appeals completely exclude personal interface between the charity and the donor. In these cases consumption bears some resemblance to the consumption of advertising and communications. The consumption experience consists of the thoughts and feelings experienced while reading the letter or seeing the advertisement and while going through the motions of writing a cheque and sending it off. One important advance for charities raising funds through this method was the move to include *suggested donations of,* for example, £10, £20, £50 or other, on letters, advertisement appeals and other similar forms. These suggestions, which are often accompanied by a description of what can be achieved for that amount, are meant to guide the donor's giving and reduce any dissonance experienced when going through the motions of making the donation. An additional issue related to donating through such methods is raised by Hibbert and Horne (1997) who reveal that when people give through this type of channel they tend not to see the communication as anonymous, but look to its origin and develop some kind of image of the responsible party. Some individuals did not give through these channels because they believed the responsible party to be 'some well-paid person in London . . . and it will probably only go to pay their wages'. This type of statement links back to the attitude discussed earlier in this chapter that people who work for charities should do so because they have the cause at heart, not because they are being highly paid for it. Evidently, there are other charities of which the image is very different. The point is that, although the donor's direct interaction is with the communication materials, for some donors the invisible communicator also influences their experience of that interaction. Compared to other service organisations, which strive to enhance the consumer's experience through providing pleasant premises, trained staff and all the cues associated with service quality, the charity sector may have to 'dress down' in front of consumers to achieve the desired appeal.

Stage 3: Post-donation Evaluation

Although the post-donation evaluation is covered here under a separate section, service marketing literature emphasises that where services are concerned, post-choice evaluation goes on both during and after the consumption of a service. That is to say, evaluative processes are set in motion as a consumer interacts with the service, environment and personnel. Similar timing is also characteristic of post-donation evaluation, especially that aspect of evaluation relating to the direct experience of giving.

With regard to the evaluation of the charity's use of the donated funds the process of post-choice evaluation might extend over long periods of time or be extremely short. Feedback of relevant information may be provided either directly by the charity, through the press or other sources, enabling the donors to evaluate their decision to give after the event. In some cases streams of information enable repeated review of the decision, for example, people who have contributed money for a local hospice to be built are likely to hear various reports over many years about its progress and may re-evaluate their own donation in light of this information. By contrast, donors often do not find out how a charity uses funds raised, or whether the service provided to beneficiaries satisfied their needs, indeed many do not care what the outcome is. In this event they may simply put it out of their minds in the hope that good works will be done. However, such instances when an individual does not have the knowledge or experience to assess what has been delivered can be problematic for marketers because of the implications for satisfaction, future behaviour and loyalty. The dominance of credence factors in the charities context suggests a heavy reliance by consumers upon cues to reliability and trust. This problem is raised as an issue for the marketing of consumer goods, but is particularly pertinent in this service context. These aspects that are difficult to assess are usually referred to as *credence qualities* (see Darby and Karni 1973). Fundraisers must note the impact of these credence qualities and formulate communications strategies to confront the problems that lack of feedback raises for donors.

CONCLUSIONS

To summarise briefly, this chapter has considered people's motivations for giving money to charity. It has noted a variety of fundraising methods that charities employ, suggesting that various methods are used to appeal to potential donors across a range of market segments. The main body of the chapter focuses on the donor decision process, making use of existing consumer behaviour principles and insights from services marketing literature.

The rising number of charities, waning government funding and the increasing need for the services offered by charities means that the level of individual giving has to be increased. It is of vital importance to fund-raisers to know who gives and what it is that stimulates or inhibits giving. The use of buyer behaviour literature takes the search for why a person donates beyond motivational issues, which have been well researched in sociology and social psychology, into the realms of what actually activates that giving motivation and effects the action which leads to money changing hands. As knowledge of consumer behaviour has brought financial reward in the commercial world, so with individual giving will the understanding of donor behaviour enable charities to raise money in a more effective and efficient manner.

REFERENCES

Arndt, J. (1978) 'How Broad Should The Marketing Concept Be?', *Journal of Marketing*, (January), pp. 101–103.

Bateson, J.E.G. (1995) *Managing Service Marketing*, 3rd edn, (London: The Dryden Press).

Batson, C.D. (1990) 'How social an animal? The human capacity for caring', *American Psychologist*, 45, pp. 336–346.

Benson, P.L. and Catt, V.L. (1978) 'Soliciting charity contributions: The parlance of asking for money', *Journal of Applied Social Psychology*, 8, pp. 84–95.

Bettman, J.R. (1979a) *An Information Processing Theory of Consumer Choice*, (Reading, Mass: Addison-Wesley).

Bruce, I. (1994) *Meeting Need: Successful Charity Marketing*, (Hemel Hempstead: ICSA Publishing).

Bull, R. and Gibson-Robinson, E. (1981) 'The influence of eye-gaze, style of dress and locality on the amounts of money donated to a charity', *Human Relations*, 34, pp. 895–905.

Burnett, K. (1993) *Relationship Fund-raising*, (London: The White Lion Press).

Burnett, J. and Wood, V.R. (1988) 'A Proposed Model of the Donation Process', *Research in Consumer Behaviour*, 3, pp. 1–47.

Carmen, J. and Uhl, K. (1973) *Marketing: Principles and Methods*, (Homewood, Ill., Irwin).

Cox, D. (1967) 'The Sorting Rule in the Consumer Product Evaluation Process', in Cox, D. (ed.) *Risk Taking and Information Handling in Consumer Behaviour*, (Boston: Harvard University Press).

Darby, M.R. and Karni, E. (1973) 'Free Competition and the Optimal amount of Fraud', *Journal of Law and Economics*, 16 (April), pp. 67–86.

Engel, J.F., Blackwell, R.D. and Miniard, P.W. (1990) *Consumer Behavior*, 6th edn, (Orlando, FL: Dryden Press).

Fultz, J. et al. (1986) 'Social evaluation and the empathy-altruism hypothesis', *Journal of Personality and Social Psychology*, 50, pp. 761–769 (from Radley and Kennedy article).

Gabbott, M. and Hogg, G. (1994) 'Competing For Patients: Understanding Consumer Evaluation Of Primary Care', *Journal of Management In Medicine*, 8, 1, pp. 12–18.

Guy, B.S. and Patton, W.E. (1989) 'The Marketing of Altruistic Causes: Understanding Why People Help', *The Journal of Consumer Marketing*, 6, 1, pp. 19–30.

Halfpenny, P. and Lowe, D. (1994) *Individual Giving and Volunteering in Britain: Who Gives and Why*, 7th edn, (Kent: Charities Aid Foundation).

Hibbert, S.A. and Horne, S. (1996) 'Giving to charity: questioning the donor decision', *Journal of Consumer Marketing*, 13, 2, pp. 4–13.

Hibbert, S.A. and Horne, S. (1997) 'Donation Dilemmas: A Consumer Behaviour Perspective', *Journal of Nonprofit and Voluntary Marketing*, 2, 3, pp. 261–274.

Howard, J.A. and Sheth, J.N. (1969) *The Theory of Buyer Behavior*, (NY: John Wiley).

Isen, A. (1987) 'Positive Affect, Cognitive Processes and Social Behaviour', in Berkowitz, L. (ed.) *Advances in Experimental Social-Psychology*, 20, pp. 203–253.

Kassarjian, H.H. (1981) 'Low Involvement—A Second Look', *Advances in Consumer Research*, 8, (Chicago: American Marketing Association), pp. 31–34.

Kotler, P. (1979) 'Strategies For Introducing Marketing Into Non-Profit Organisations', *Journal of Marketing*, 43 (January), pp. 37–44.

Kotler, P. (1986) 'Marketing for Non-Profit Organisations', 2nd edn, (NJ: Prentice Hall).

Kotler, P. and Levy, S.J. (1969) 'Broadening the Concept of Marketing', *Journal of Marketing*, 33 (January), pp. 10–15.

Leigh, T.W. and Rethans, A.J. (1984) 'A Script Theoretical Analysis of Industrial Purchasing Behaviour', *Journal of Marketing*, 48 (Fall), pp. 22–32.

Love, A., Diamantopolous, A., Schlegelmilch, B. (1993) 'Response to Different Charity Appeals: The Impact of Donor Characteristics on the Level of Donations', *Proceedings of the 1993 Annual MEG Conference*, 2, pp. 602–613.

Lynch Jr, J.G. and Srull, T.K. (1982) 'Memory and Attentional Factors in Consumer Choice: Concepts and Research Methods', *Journal of Consumer Research*, 9 (June), pp. 18–37.

Mindak, W.A. and Bybee, H.M. (1971) 'Marketing Applications to Fund-raising', *Journal of Marketing*, 35 (July), pp. 13–18.

Olshavsky, R.W. and Granbois, D.H. (1979) 'Consumer Decision Making: Fact or Fiction?', *Journal of Consumer Research*, 6, pp. 93–100.

Quint, F. (1996) 'Help for the Thinking Donor', *The Henderson Guide to UK Charities*, (London: Hemmington Scott), pp. 27–30.

Radley and Kennedy (1995) 'Charitable Giving by Individuals: A Study of Attitude and Practice', *Human Relations*, 48, 6 (June), pp. 685–709.

Rados, D.L. (1981) *Marketing for Non-Profit Organisations*, (Dover, MA: Auburn House).

Robertson, T.S. (1976) 'Low Commitment Consumer Behaviour', *Journal of Advertising Research*, 16, pp. 19–24.

Ryan, D. and Murdoch, R. (1986) 'Identifying and Nurturing Core Donors', *Fund Raising Management*, 16 (February), pp. 20–32.

Shapiro, B. (1973) 'Marketing for Non-profit Organisations', *Harvard Business Review*, 51, pp. 123–132.

Shostack, G.L. (1977) 'Breaking Free from Product Marketing', *Journal of Marketing*, 41, 2 (April), pp. 73–80.

Yorke, D.A. (1984) 'Marketing and Non-Profit-Making Organisations', *European Journal of Marketing*, 18, 2, pp. 17–22.

Zeithaml, V. and Bitner, M.J. (1996) *Services Marketing*, (NY: McGraw Hill).

PART III

CONCLUSION

CHAPTER 10

CONCLUSION

At the beginning of this book we sought to outline the rationale for service marketers and consumer behaviourists to consider the impact of service product characteristics upon consumers. Having reviewed the case and examined some of the evidence we would like to think that this book goes some way toward turning the attention of service marketers towards a fundamental area of study which has been neglected for far too long. It is the first time in which consumer behaviour in services has been presented explicitly and we hope that the material will go some way toward encouraging greater academic enquiry into accepted representations about how consumers behave. The task has not been without problems, primarily the difficulties in integrating two areas of research which view consumption through different lenses. Equally we have tried to avoid the problems of multi-dimensional product attributes by concentrating the discussion on pure service product forms. We hope that you will recognise the benefits in limiting the discussion in this way but will also see the approach as one which is a first step along the road.

The task of this book was not to provide a complete and exhaustive summary of consumer behaviour literature, nor to rework services marketing literature with a consumer behaviour flavour, but to raise issues and questions at both a general level and across specific contexts which we, among others, will attempt to answer in our academic work. We accept that there are those on both sides of the academic community who will question the rationale for this book, but we hope that by now there is sufficient evidence for a reappraisal of that position which is characterised by statements such as 'goods have always been assumed to be goods and services, so what's the problem?' Implicitly in this book we have taken an inductive approach to the material with a heavy emphasis upon context to inform our evaluation of theory and in order to present a general approach to the topic. In this conclusion we would like to quickly summarise the case for the book and then to synthesise some of the material presented. Finally we consider the managerial implications of this work and suggest to other academics some of the research imperatives we have identified.

RESTATEMENT AND ARGUMENT

The early consumer behaviourists were concerned with broad behavioural and cognitive constructs and, perforce, their concentration was upon the consumer. However, as researchers moved to consider the impact of environment and situation on individuals, as well as mood and attitude structures, the basic foundation constructs of the discipline remained unmoved; the treatment of product form was as an exogenous variable. It is clear that physical based products lent themselves very well to this form of enquiry and served to provide a quasi-controllable product or stimulus variable in the early studies of behaviour, used mainly to verify model forms. Constructs such as direct emotional and physical involvement in the product were too complex to incorporate, as was the sequencing of a product or experience delivered over time. Recently, consumer behaviour research has started to break out from the traditions of the past to recognise other studies of consumption, so prolific in the sociological and psychological literature. We believe that this is a step forward in the integration of product form variants. Over the last 15 years, since the paper by Zeithaml in 1981, consideration of services as a distinctive product form demanding different reaction and behaviour from consumers has been stated, but apart from some notable exceptions has not been developed. When services researchers emerged from the 'primordial swamp' (Fisk, Brown and Bitner 1994) in the late 1960s and 70s with a direct focus upon a specific type of product, their attention was focused upon how product form altered the marketing considerations of organisations, and latterly, how quality, satisfaction and loyalty are interrelated. In effect, a consideration of how service products impact upon some of the basic tenets of buyer behaviour had fallen between two paths. It was assumed that consumer behaviour theory was constructed upon a non-product differentiated basis. The appearance of terms like 'goods and services' in the consumer behaviour literature was considered sufficiently encompassing to avoid any detailed consideration of product-specific and contextualised behaviour. Services researchers in contrast, have used their own approach to understanding consumers, borrowing concepts and variables from the product-based literature when and where convenient but without the necessary validation or theoretical rigour to be wholly convincing outside the context of their application.

We are now at a point in time where the divergence needs to be resolved, physical goods marketers have to accept that products embody inseparable physical and non-physical components and that elements of the non-physical are being used increasingly to establish competitive advantage. However, in the design and implementation of service-based product development, there is a tendency to switch into 'services consumption mode' dealing with performance, environment design and human delivery considerations in isolation from some of the physical product modes of thinking and vice versa. For instance, service researchers talk of product perceptions and even satisfaction without considering these to be related to motivation, involvement or some process mediated by cognition. Equally consumer behaviour talks of product choice but not how a product is perceived and consumed over time, or indeed the response to different delivery formats or the extent of physical activity involved. What we are faced with is a confusion, not just in research and management practice, but also in teaching. Buyer behaviour courses are taught using a physical goods orientation and then the students are normally introduced to services marketing as if this sequence is progressive rather than discontinuous. Services hardly appear in consumer behaviour texts even at the 'purchase' stage in the underlying models. In most degree courses services marketing is pursued as a context for marketing rather than a core. Despite some innovative teaching designs such as that pursued at the Owen Graduate School which integrates buyer behaviour, services marketing, relationship marketing and satisfaction into a single course, we instill the same silo structure upon our students and upon our environment. From our review of the material in this book, we can identify four key themes which serve to epitomise the relationship between consumer behaviour and services marketing.

CONCEPTUALISING SERVICE

The first fundamental issue is in conceptualising the service product which is not necessarily transaction bound. It comprises multiple episodes, often with many people, to form an experience. As such it is a dynamic real-time product, rather than static. In essence the service product is a chameleon, changing its complexion for every consumer on a continuous basis. A consideration of Chapters 3 and 4, as well as the chapters on tourism services (Chapter 5) and charities (Chapter 9) suggests the variable nature of reaction by consumers to essentially the same set of product attributes. For service marketers, this chameleon-like quality has meant a concentration upon the components of the service product, a desire to create an arsenal of manipulable characteristics to control as best as possible the service delivery environment. This approach, however, has to be in recognition of the fact that once these manageable parts of the service process are placed before the market, they move outside their control. If we accept that service products are actually a number of small events, strung together in a sequence, the challenge is to identify how these small events affect the consumer's overall perception and their subsequent impact on micro behaviour, i.e. from episode to episode.

What is often ignored in the literature is that consumers do not necessarily make rational evaluations of a service based on the sum of the parts, but respond unexpectedly to individual events; this has asymmetric evaluative impact. Thus, while the service may deliver what was promised, meeting or exceeding expectations, the consumer may respond not to the overall process, but to a small feature within the sequence of events that will have a disproportionate effect on their perceptions of the rest of the service. It is only by fully appreciating the complexities of aggregate service perceptions over time that the service manager can respond appropriately to maintain loyalty and attract new customers. The problem is how to gain that understanding of the consumer. Services marketing research has been dominated, for whatever reason, by quantitative, normative research, a concentration on measuring aspects of consumer reaction to the service and comparing attributes on the basis of these 'scores'. However, as Iaccobucci et al. (1994) point out, the criteria for satisfaction are not necessarily subject to such a positivistic comparison. For example, in a quantitative questionnaire about airlines no one would rate safety as unimportant, yet it is not a criteria for satisfaction. There is a need, therefore, for research that enables managers to establish how consumers view their services and which parts are likely to impact on satisfaction in a less rigid manner than the traditional satisfaction/ quality questionnaire.

MAKING THE SELECTION

The second issue is associated with early procedural components associated with choice of provider, explicitly the inability to sufficiently discriminate between offerings on the basis of the core product or outcome. This would include the problems associated with gaining or approximating experiential information, predicting outcome benefits and coping with the uncertainty associated with reliance upon peripheral cues. This part of the service consumption experience includes the use of physical and temporal cues and the relationships between intrinsic and extrinsic information as formative stages in the development of expectations. This in turn impacts upon communication and presentation of the service product and the emphasis upon meta-constructs such as security, reliability and the quality of experience. Whilst most service marketing literature concentrates on the service provider, the consumer motivation for purchase is frequently ignored. This 'whether vs which' debate has received some attention in consumer behaviour, especially in the behaviourist and experiential consumption literature, yet has largely been disregarded in services research. As most of our responses to service situations are in some way governed by the reasons why we entered into them, this appears to be a gap in the literature, indicative of the marketing rather than the consumer focus of much of the research.

TEMPORAL CONSUMPTION

The third key theme is the extended 'purchase' component. Increasingly sectors and organisations which only relatively recently identified their core activity as a service are entering the 'services fold'. Government institutions (such as local councils and police forces) privatised utilities and the non-profit sector, to name but a few who inhabit a world of continuous service. For these providers the relationship with customers over time is a given factor of their market, rather than one which is pursued. If we take a very simple decision process model, consumer behaviour theorists have always characterised consumption as an event dominated by the physical acquisition of an already defined product, the physical selection, the visual comparison and so on. The perusal of published research associated with 'purchase' rather than pre-purchase 'choice' is testament to this emphasis. However, for many services the period traditionally defined as the purchase phase, in which consumers and service products interact most fundamentally, may not punctuate a beginning or an end to delivery. As a consequence, purchase or payment or financial maintenance of the service is incidental, more like a measure of continued commitment and satisfaction, re-emphasising the relationship focus. Further we can extract and rearrange many of the attributes ascribed to a physical transaction (or purchase) when considering services. We can remove the handling, manipulation and physical selection of things, we can remove the 'choice-selection-payment sequence', and we can remove physical comparison of alternatives. We can also remove availability as a dichotomous variable except within circumstances associated with time such as queuing. To this depleted set of 'purchase' considerations, a service consumer perspective would add social interaction, extended delivery sequences, evaluation (pre-termination of delivery) customisation options, other consumers' consumption and sequential emotional responses. By any assessment the 'purchase' phase is dominant for a services consumer yet is relatively undervalued by current literature.

Within this phase we cannot underestimate the effect of the individual; services are provided *by* people *to* people (within the caveats outlined in Chapter 1). As individuals we make frequent judgements about the people with whom we come into contact based on an assessment of their personality, similarity or fit with our perceptions of how they do, or should, behave. Services marketing, with its emphasis on dramaturgy, role theory and scripts, demonstrates that as social beings many of our interactions follow patterns within which we display learned behaviours. These judgements are inherently personal and difficult to generalise as they are a feature of individual personality and difficult to comprehend but research has shown that by adhering to roles expected of service providers managers can map the service delivery. However, considerable research in psychology and psychotherapy indicates that many of our perceptions of interpersonal interactions are based on non-verbal behaviour, the interpretation of body language and other cues in human social behaviour that have yet to be studied in service encounters. Within the rubric of non-verbal behaviour is facial expression, eye contact, posture, gesture and interpersonal distance, all of which convey meaning and affect the consumer's perceptions of the service. The problem for service managers is that these non-verbal cues are both difficult to identify and to teach to employees yet ultimately they may be the key to consumer satisfaction.

MAKING AN EVALUATION

A related issue in considering the consumers' evaluation of the service delivery is the possibility of 'no dissatisfaction'. Most research in the services field assumes that consumers are either satisfied or dissatisfied. In reality consumers are frequently neutral towards a service or part of a service. Satisfaction or dissatisfaction is, in effect, activated by asking the consumer to examine how they feel about a service or a specific event. For example, most consumers of public utilities are not dissatisfied with the service they receive, unless they are specifically asked whether or not they are satisfied. If service managers then break down the service into its constituent parts and ask consumers how they feel about the different aspects, they will produce results showing that certain parts are more satisfactory than others. This does not necessarily mean that the consumer will be more satisfied if these aspects are improved, or that these aspects will alter their overall consumption behaviour. Indeed, 'no dissatisfaction' may be an aim for certain service businesses as it implies the consumer has no motivation to change. The concentration of services marketing literature on quality and satisfaction, places an emphasis on a positive or negative 'result' when actually one is not always necessary.

RELATING TO SERVICES

The final issue highlighted by this book relates to the prospects for the building and maintenance of relationships. This is not the place to engage in a long and circuitous argument about relationship marketing or the management of an extended consumption process. Suffice it to say that the role of the personal provider in services, the nature of some service products, such as utilities, and the degree of personalisation would suggest a greater emphasis upon longitudinal and sequenced consumption activity, characterised as a 'relationship'. It is clear that in the final analysis the consumer is looking for 'value' (Holbrook 1995, Ruyter et al. 1997); it is the *definition* of value in the services context that causes problems. Whilst the traditional, cognitive, economic conceptualisation of value as 'what is received for what is given up' has relevance, in reality value is a more subjective judgement. The cost of service failure extends past the monetary price to include temporal, emotional and physical elements that make the relationship between process and outcome, purchaser and provider, price and quality, complex. Within the relationship marketing literature, as Tzokas and Saren (1997) point out, although exhortations abound calling for suppliers to acquaint themselves with customers to build and consolidate lasting bonds, there is still uncertainty about just how such relationships are created and maintained. A number of authors have commented that much of the current writing on relationships in general, and relationship marketing in particular, has been concerned with the point of view of the supplier (Blois 1996; Tzokas and Saren 1997). As relationships are by their very nature dyadic the need to understand the consumer is a vital part of the future development of relationship marketing, the first stage of which is to address the issue of customer value in the exchange. Services provide the ideal platform from which to examine these issues because of the role of both consumer and supplier in the creation of the product.

If we consider these four issues individually, and together in comparison, with the accepted (and admittedly simplistic), decision process model, we can detect immediately where the approaches differ in terms of focus. The traditional model concentrates upon the antecedents of consumption where the purchase is the culmination and which marks the beginning of the consumption phase of activity. The services approach is much more focused upon consumption after the choice of 'product' in what could loosely be termed post-choice engagement. This difference in emphasis is represented in diagrammatic form in Figure 10.1 to highlight the arrangement of the material. At the centre of the model is the core conceptual sequence that we adopted at the beginning of this book: the construction of a pre-consumption, consumption and post-consumption sequence adopted in reaction to the inadequacy of the five-stage decision process conceptualisation. At the right-hand side of the diagram we have included issues which have been raised in relation to the three stages through the context chapters (and by implication the five-stage approach), but which have not been explicitly considered in established presentations of consumer behaviour theory. In this part of the diagram we highlight the central issues identified as impacting upon both our three-stage sequence and the traditional five-stage sequence.

Within the first stage of the consumption model we can see that the two approaches are parallel in that issues associated with problem recognition, search and evaluation are assumed to be similar. We have made explicit the need for a distinction between core and other

Figure 10.1
Synthesis of the Approach

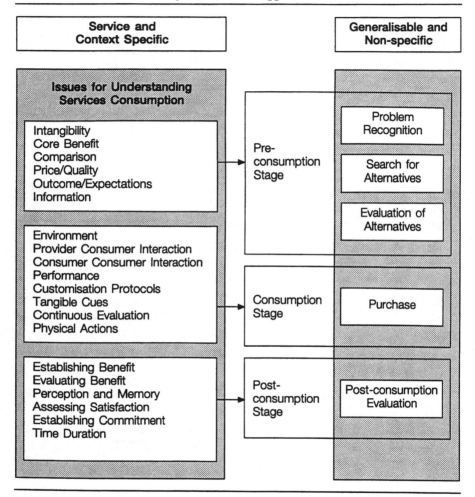

benefits in the early stages of the sequence which for some services may be especially difficult to conceptualise. Charity donation and the feelings of altruism are different kinds of behaviour motivation to the normally proffered needs and motivations associated with physical products.

There is also unlikely to be much distinction between problem recognition associated with services or physical goods except an increased emphasis upon time as a factor in defining need. Similarly the issues associated with search criteria, source credibility and the mechanisms of comparison (above content) between offerings are likely to be similar. However, we identify intangibility as a key variable in terms of the association between needs/wants and actual consumption, as well as in evaluating alternatives. While the mechanisms of comparison may be similar, clearly the detail of attribute formation and the ways in which incomparability are coped with, will differ across product forms. The option of self production (not usually associated with physical goods), the basis of comparison and the problematic considerations of a price quality relationship are also identified as areas in which our understanding is limited.

At the second stage we have already made clear the relative paucity of material associated with purchase when considering physical goods transactions, and list those items which we believe represent significant omissions from physical goods treatments of consumer behaviour when applied to services. This set of factors has been relatively well covered in terms of research by services researchers and may provide valuable insights for physical goods marketers in their consideration of purchase environments. Finally, in the last stage we identify those elements relevant to evaluation of the service performance, including the identification of benefits beyond consumption and those related to the credence qualities that many services possess. This set of factors also makes reference to the extended time horizon of service products and issues associated with satisfaction.

It is important to note here that the inclusion of the services issues are not meant to be exhaustive nor meant to imply that they have been totally ignored by consumer behaviour researchers. However, they do give a flavour of the issues which are being grappled with daily by services marketers in trying to understand consumption and in trying to pursue a means of communicating benefit to their customer groups. This summary can be considered as an indication of research priorities. From a research perspective many of the most recent consumer behaviour texts have started to move away from pure cognitive approaches to behaviour (see especially Hirschman and Holbrook 1992; Holbrook 1995 and Gabriel and Laing 1996). We would suggest that this 'leakage at the seams' is a positive move and that services as a specific product form will reap the benefits of this expansive and eclectic approach to consumption.

IMPLICATIONS FOR SERVICE MANAGERS

Pick up any book on services marketing and it will inevitably describe the transition from industrial to service-based economies which has overtaken the Western world. Reasons for this change are well documented, as are the economic implications and effect of services on GDP. Managers are coming to terms with the fact that not only are services becoming increasingly important, but that customer service is frequently the differentiating factor in a number of industries. Although we can point to a number of so-called defining characteristics of services, Levitt's 1972 comment appears increasingly relevant—'we are all in service'. Managers in all sectors are becoming aware of the demands of the service management part of their role, the need to understand the way in which consumers respond to services and the effect of the actual service delivered on the consumer's subsequent behaviour. It is apparent that the service component of many physical products lends itself well to extended marketing activity. Indeed Rust and Oliver's (1994) argument that all products are purchased for the service they provide is an interesting idea. We do not, after all, buy a washing machine because it has any intrinsic value as an object, we buy it for the service of washing clothes, and with it come the product augmentations of servicing maintenance, insurance etc. It is no longer appropriate for managers to categorise their industry as manufacturing or service-based, the two are inseparable and indelibly bound.

One of the key issues for managers is how to get the service message across to consumers, which in turn is dependent on the conveyance of relevant information from credible sources. The nature of pre-purchase information in services (described in Chapter 2), and the high reliance on word-of-mouth sources as being most credible and least biased, places particular demands on managers. The creation of satisfied customers is not only important for the sake of customer retention, but also for the dissemination of positive word-of-mouth recommendation. There is a surprising paucity of research into the advertising of services, perhaps explained by the same stance as consumer behaviourists would adopt, that there is little reason to discriminate. In fact, they take the view that most published advertising research is based on models of decision making which are based upon linear, hierarchy of effects models which are themselves increasingly questioned. However, service managers must address the issue of communicating with consumers, developing brand awareness, encouraging customisation or standardisation, and promotional activity by looking at how to achieve these goals for a service product and how the mechanisms can be best communicated. This may be via the effective use of word of mouth, by manipulating the tangible cues, or by more direct communication messages.

One of the most important challenges for service managers in the next 10 years will be to come to terms with the introduction of technology and its subsequent effect on consumer behaviour. We are already seeing the introduction of technology into service delivery as technological innovations allow for the increased control, reduced cost and greater efficiency in service delivery. However, whilst technologies such as ATMs in banking, scanning in retailing or automated reservation systems in the hotel industry have gained wide-ranging consumer acceptance, there is still a lack of understanding of the impact of technology on service delivery (see Gabbott 1996). Managers must face the fact that increased technology frequently has the effect of reducing personal service, which may alienate some consumers whilst attracting others. The elderly, for example, are likely to be less technologically aware than younger consumers and more concerned with receiving personal service. The introduction of many technologies requires a change to the consumer's role in service delivery, consumers become more integrated into the production process by the need to push buttons, enter information or swipe cards. The implications of this go beyond the simple convenience of the parties. As Kelley et al. (1990) point out, the consumer becomes partially employed by the firm, but in a relationship without sanction or control which can create problems for the provider. Similarly this participation may alter the consumers' attribution of blame when things go wrong, or satisfaction when they go right.

In addition certain services are more suited to the introduction of technology and more likely to gain high acceptance from consumers. Innovations building on technologies that consumers are already familiar with, such as telephone ordering, have different diffusion rates than entirely new or unfamiliar technologies. As we move from the 'remote control generation'—consumers who are familiar with simple technologies such as the TV remote control panel, to the 'mouse generation'—consumers who are comfortable with computers and more complex technologies, service managers must be cognisant of the laggards. There are sections of the market which are, in effect, disenfranchised by their lack of technological awareness or their reluctance to give up the interpersonal aspects of the service exchange. A second important group to be considered in the rush for technologically-based service innovations, is the employees. If service employees are not comfortable with the introduction of technology or fail to understand the problems of consumers in extracting benefit, then the investment will be lost.

A final point to make about technologies in services is the one Lovelock (1996) makes: in focusing on new and emerging technologies, it is vital not to lose sight of the 'old' technologies. If the infrastructure or the tangible parts of the service delivery are not in place, then technology will not improve the service. A sophisticated telephone ordering system is of little use to the consumer if the items ordered are not in stock; an ATM is of no benefit to the consumer if it is constantly needing to be refilled. There is a danger that service managers adopt 'technology myopia', a belief in the benefits of technology to the exclusion of the basics of service delivery that ultimately determine the success or failure of the service to the consumer.

FUTURE RESEARCH DIRECTION

Although it is not the aim of this book to be predictive, we believe that the future for services marketing research lies with the consumer.

As the academic community moves away from the need to justify the study of services as a separate discipline, and service characteristics and classifications assume their own validity, we can look beyond the current metaphors for services research to a new paradigm. Services marketing, in an attempt to 'crawl out of' the evolutionary process, has acquired its own articles of faith, received wisdom upon which most of our current thinking about services is based. The problem is that this has resulted in a concentration upon narrow research agenda dominated by an implicitly managerial approach to the definition and measurement of quality and satisfaction in service delivery. Whilst it could be argued that satisfaction and quality are subjective and, therefore, consumer focused, current services research has largely 'dipped' into consumer behaviour literature without ever coming to terms with some of the underlying concepts. Recent published material which proposes that service quality and satisfaction are mirrors of attitudinal constructs have opened up another bridge between the disciplines.

Similarly research into consumer involvement—a social psychological construct described by Koziey and Anderson (1989) as part of a person's individual cognitive map which affects their model of reality and gives form to their behaviour in everyday situations (Sherif and Cantril 1947; Krugman 1965 and 1967; Rothschild 1979; Mitchell 1981; Greenwald and Levitt 1984; Batra and Ray 1985; Kassarjian 1981; Zaichowsky 1985; Mittal 1989). If a service-orientated involvement construct can be refined, which avoids the instability of goods-based measures in service environments and encompasses the highly differentiated nature of the service experience, it is evident that other services concepts may also need re-examination. Perceptions of service quality, for instance, may be dependent upon the degree of involvement with the product, or indeed the nature of interaction with service providers. The implication of this argument is wide reaching and has both retrospective and prospective dimensions. It would require a reassessment of currently accepted service consumption concepts such as service expectations, gap analysis and service quality perceptions. It may also affect emerging research areas such as service recovery, technology in service delivery and enduring relationships.

The point was made above that the introduction of new technology presents a number of challenges to service managers. In the same way it offers a number of opportunities to service researchers. Technologies alter the nature of the service delivery and the nature of the interaction between purchaser and provider (see Chapter 3). This area of innovation in service delivery has still to be fully addressed in the context of service consumers. Wiefels (1997) suggests an adaptation of the traditional adoption life cycle model for technologies. He draws a distinction between enthusiasts, who are relatively risk immune and embrace new offerings; visionaries who see the advantages of technologies early in their lifecycle; pragmatists who, once there is enough evidence of benefits, move in unison to adopt its use, through to conservatives and laggards who are resistant to technological change. In order for a new technology to gain widescale acceptance it is necessary to identify the visionaries. However, a number of studies have suggested that in the adoption of technology, traditional consumer demographic variables are insufficient to identify market segments (see for example Gabbott 1996). An alternative approach, taken by Ellen et al. (1991), Gatignon and Robertson (1989) and Hiltz and Johnson (1990), is to consider individual consumer factors such as tolerance for risk, environmental reaction, autonomy/control and perceived ability to use the technology or 'self efficacy'. Gabbott (1996) suggests that where the nature of the service interaction is fundamentally altered by the introduction of technology, i.e. the personal element of the encounter is replaced or substantially diminished, personality factors such as interpersonal orientation provide a better basis for identifying customer segments.

However, what is not clear is how service consumers react to new technologies in services. By changing, the very nature of service consumption technology removes a number of the interpersonal cues that we are accustomed to use in service encounters. Whilst we have suggested that managers need to consider the interpretation of non-verbal cues by consumers during the encounter, there is a similar need to identify the effect of the removal of these cues in technology-mediated encounters. A recent survey by a high street bank identified what they termed 'telephone rage', akin to road rage, where consumers become frustrated attempting to resolve problems over the telephone without the aid of the non-verbal cues used in face-to-face encounters, and lose their tempers. With the increased use of technology researchers need to understand what replaces these verbal cues and how consumers react to the technology. In addition, as technology moves increasingly to providing a closer or virtual version of reality, research is required to assist in the construction of that reality by identifying what consumers look for in service encounters that can be replicated by technology.

A third area for research that has—as yet—received little consideration in the literature is the trend toward the internationalisation of services and the cultural impact of delivering services across national boundaries. Consumer behaviour has addressed the issue of culture and sub-culture at length in terms of the shared beliefs, values and expectations held by consumers as members of a group. Services literature has only recently considered the impact of culture, yet a causal examination of any of the text book definitions of cultural similarities or differences indicates that this is an important research area for services. If consumers have different expectations, values, use different communication techniques and cues, then their perception of the service delivery will be affected. At a very basic level, for example, Japanese consumers view social hierarchy as vertical and can arrange individuals into a detailed rank order within their immediate social groups. After education people fit into different groups depending on sex, age, occupation, income, living area, housing type and so on, and it is not just market researchers who make these distinctions—Japanese themselves are well aware of the differences (see Woronoff 1981). This hierarchy can affect the nature of the service delivered especially in service situations where the participation of the customer is required. If the customer deems the service provider as inferior the degree of interaction and involvement will be low. Similarly, where the service provider considers themselves superior to the customer the level of service is also likely to be low. This imposition of hierarchy considerations upon the encounter will also affect perceptions of the quality of service received. There are innumerable similar examples that suggest that if services are to be 'international', service providers have to understand the characteristics of the consumer in their culture.

In conclusion we return to the theme of this book, consumer behaviour in the services context. As consumer behaviour theorists address the implication of the rise in spending power across the social strata, increased leisure time and the nature of consumption in a post-Fordist and post-modern society, services provide the ideal format to question some traditional assumptions. Whilst the current trend in consumer behaviour research is to examine consumption as a result of, and manifestation of, cultural and societal change, there is an assumption that this is commodity based. In fact if consumption is socially constructed, based on ritual and interpretation of belief, then services provide the context in which to consider the experience of consumers, without the complication of objects, and to bridge the gap between what the commodity actually is and how it is perceived. Consumers, as Gabriel and Lang (1995) point out, can not be detached from their experiences as social, political and moral agents, with a 'vital unpredictability' (p. 4) which characterises their actions. It is by understanding the consumer that marketers will shape the future of the discipline. Focusing on services as a product class may assist in that understanding.

REFERENCES

Batra, R. and Ray, M.L. (1985) 'How Advertising Works at Contact', in Alwitt, L. and Mitchell, A. (eds) *Psychological Processes and Advertising Effects: Theory, Research and Applications*, (New Jersey: Erlbaum), pp. 13–39.

Blois, K. (1996) 'Relationship Marketing in Organisational Markets: when is it appropriate?', *Journal of Marketing Management*, 12, pp. 161–173.

Ellen, P.S. et al. (1991) 'Resistance to Technological Innovations: An Examination of the Role of Self Efficacy and Performance Satisfaction', *Journal of the Academy of Marketing Science*, 19, 4, pp. 297–307.

Fisk, R., Brown, S. and Bitner, M.J. (1993) 'Tracking the Evolution of Services Marketing Literature', *Journal of Retailing*, 69, 1, pp. 61–103.

Gabbott, M. (1996) 'Don't just sit there—Stand up and talk to me! Interpersonal orientation and service technology', *1996 Winter Educators Conference: Marketing Theory and Applications*, (Chicago: AMA).

Gabbott, M. and Hogg, G. (1996) 'The Glory of Stories: Using Critical Incidents to

CONCLUSION

Understand Service Evaluation in the Primary Healthcare Context', *Journal of Marketing Management,* 12, pp. 493–503.

Gabriel, Y. and Lang, T. (1996) *The Unmanageable Consumer,* (London: Sage).

Gatignon, H. and Robertson, T.S. (1989) 'Technology diffusion: An empirical test of competitive effects', *Journal of Marketing,* 53, 1, pp. 35–49.

Greenwold, A.G. and Leavitt, C. (1984) 'Audience Involvement in Advertising: Four Levels', *Journal of Consumer Research,* 11, 1, pp. 581–592.

Hiltz, S. and Johnson, K. (1990) 'User Satisfaction with Computer Mediated Communications Systems', *Management Science,* 36, 6, pp. 739–764.

Hirschman, E. and Holbrook, M. (1992) *Postmodern Consumer Research,* (London: Sage).

Holbrook, M. (1995) *Consumer Research: Introspective Essays on the Study of Consumption,* (London: Sage).

Iacobucci, D., Grayson, K. and Ostrom, A. (1994) 'The Calculus of Service Quality and Customer Satisfaction: Theoretical and Empirical Differentiation and Integration', in *Advances in Services Marketing and Management,* 3, pp. 1–67.

Kassarjian, H. (1981) 'Low Involvement—A Second Look', in Monroe, K.B. (ed.) *Advances in Consumer Research,* VIII, (MI: Ann Arbor), pp. 31–34.

Kelley, S., Donnelly, J. and Skinner, S. (1990) 'Customer Participation in Service Production and Delivery', *Journal of Retailing,* 66, 3, pp. 315–335.

Koziey, P. and Anderson, T. (1989) 'Patterning Interpersonal Involvement', *The Journal of Psychology,* 123, 3, pp. 217–235.

Krugman, H.E. (1965) 'The Impact of Television Advertising: Learning Without Involvement', *Public Opinion Quarterly,* 29 (Fall), pp. 349–356.

Krugman, H.E. (1967) 'The Measuring of Advertising Involvement', *Public Opinion Quarterly,* 30 (Winter), pp. 583–596.

Lovelock, C. (1996) *Services Marketing,* 3rd edn, (NJ: Prentice Hall).

Mitchell, S. (1981) 'Appealing to shoppers through a CRT terminal—seeing isn't necessarily buying', *Data Management,* 9, 4, pp. 32–33, 37.

Mittal, B. (1989) 'Measuring Purchase-Decision Involvement', *Psychology & Marketing,* 6, pp. 147–162.

Rothschild, M.L. (1979) 'Advertising Strategies for High and Low Involvement Situations', in *Attitude Research Plays for High Stakes,* Maloney, J.C. and Silverman, B. (eds) (Chicago: AMA), pp. 74–93.

Rust, R.T. and Oliver, R.L. (1994) *Service Quality: New Directions in Theory and Practice,* (London: Sage), pp. 1–21.

Ruyter K. et al. (1997) 'The dynamics of the service delivery process: A value-based approach', *International Journal of Research in Marketing,* 14, pp. 231–243.

Sherif, M. and Cantril, H. (1947) 'The Psychology of Ego-Involvement', in Maloney, J.C. and Silverman, B. (eds) *Attitude Research Plays for High Stakes,* (Chicago: AMA), pp. 74–93.

Tzokas, N. and Saren, M. (1997) 'Building relationship platforms in consumer markets: A Value Chain approach', *Journal of Strategic Marketing*, 5, pp. 1–16.

Woronoff, Jon (1981) *Japan: the Coming Social Crisis*, (Tokyo: Lotus Press).

Zaichowsky, J.L. (1985) 'Measuring the Involvement Construct', *Journal of Consumer Research*, 12, pp. 341–352.

Zeithaml, V. (1981) 'How Consumer Evaluation Processes differ between Goods and Services', in Donnelly, J.H. and George, W.R. (eds) *The Marketing of Services*, Proceedings, (Chicago: AMA), pp. 186–190.

INDEX

Index compiled by Annette Musker